Richard Wevill turned to the study of history after a successful career in investment banking. Richard gained an MA in War and Society and his PhD from the University of Exeter where he was recently appointed a Research Fellow. Richard is currently working on the authorised biography of Roger Makins who was the British Ambassador in Washington from 1952 to 1956.

BRITAIN AND AMERICA AFTER WORLD WAR II

Bilateral Relations and the Beginnings of the Cold War

RICHARD WEVILL

I.B. TAURIS

LONDON · NEW YORK

Published in 2012 by I.B.Tauris & Co Ltd
6 Salem Road, London W2 4BU
175 Fifth Avenue, New York NY 10010
www.ibtauris.com

Distributed in the United States and Canada
Exclusively by Palgrave Macmillan
175 Fifth Avenue, New York NY 10010

International Library of Twentieth Century History, Vol. 46

ISBN 978 1 84885 980 7

A full CIP record for this book is available from the British Library
A full CIP record for this book is available from the Library of Congress

Library of Congress catalog card: available

Typeset by Newgen Publishers, Chennai
Printed and bound by CPI Group (UK) Ltd, Croydon, CR0 4YY

For Lin, Emma, Carla, Amy and Freddie

CONTENTS

ACKNOWLEDGEMENTS

In writing this book I have acquired debts to many people. Their mention here is only a small part of my gratitude. My primary debt is to Professor Andrew Thorpe. The quality of his advice and the counsel he offered can only come from years of experience of teaching, combined with a mastery of his subject. I am also grateful to Dr Richard Toye whose advice 'do not be afraid to write about the apparently trivial' proved invaluable. I also owe a debt to other members of the Department of History at the University of Exeter. These include Dr Joseph Smith, who inspired my interest in Anglo-American diplomacy, and Professor Jeremy Black, who was encouraging and helpful whilst I was a student at Exeter.

Almost without exception the staff at the various archives I have visited have proved to be both professional and helpful. Their assistance has made the task considerably easier than it might otherwise have been. I am particularly indebted to the George C. Marshall Foundation not only for awarding me a Marshall Fellowship but also because of the welcome and assistance they offered me whilst I was in Virginia. The enthusiasm and kindness of Paul Barron and Joanne Hartog was exceptional.

I am also grateful to Lin who patiently and diligently read several early drafts. There is no question that as a result of her efforts this book reads better than it otherwise would have. Finally, I would like to thank Freddie who has been a constant companion throughout the writing of this book.

INTRODUCTION

The call for diplomacy in the aftermath of World War II was considerable. The world had been broken, and putting it back together again was a difficult task. The relationships between nations were in a state of flux, and politicians and diplomats laboured to impose an order upon them whilst at the same time seeking to preserve national advantage. The conduct of international relations was an essential part of the post-war agenda for nearly all governments. Of particular importance for Britain were its relations with America. These relations fell into three categories. First, there were those which were related to the United Nations and other multinational agencies. These included, for example, the international control of atomic energy, multilateral trade talks and the international aspect of civil aviation. Second, there were relations of a quadrilateral or trilateral character concerned in the main with occupation matters and the peace treaties. These included discussions regarding the occupation of Germany and Japan and the meetings of the Council of Foreign Ministers. Finally, there were relations of a bilateral character.[1] This book is concerned with this last category.

The period 1945 to 1948 was a crucial one in post-war history. It was the period which formed the link between World War II and the Cold War. As World War II ended, there was still an element of cordiality between the Allies who had fought the war together. By 1948, with the implementation of the Marshall Plan, there was, however, a clear division between the Western powers and the Soviets. It was a short step from the Marshall Plan to signing the North Atlantic Treaty in April 1949 and the subsequent establishment of North Atlantic Treaty Organisation (NATO). At the same time, as this broad movement was

taking place, there was also a reassessment of Anglo-American relations. Britain had been remarkably close to America during World War
II. There had been a complete unification of military effort, a sharing
of intelligence and weaponry, all underpinned by the vast transfer of
resources from America to Britain in the form of Lend Lease and the presence in Washington of over 9,000 British officials.[2] Notwithstanding
this, Britain was deeply disappointed by the American response to a
number of issues in the immediate post-war period; these included the
terms of the Financial Agreement signed in December 1945 whereby
the United States extended a line of credit of $3.75 billion to the United
Kingdom, the failure to continue collaboration in the atomic energy
field and the American response to Britain's problems in Palestine. By
early 1947, however, there was a perceptible change in the American
approach. America, more aware of Britain and Europe's weaknesses and
galvanised by the truculent behaviour of the Soviets, became more supportive of Anglo-American relations. This change led to the 'Modus
Vivendi' and Pentagon talks, which, in turn, cleared the way for the
legislature to approve the Marshall Plan. This book considers these
bilateral events and pays particular attention to the role, and therefore
the influence, that the British ambassadors and other members of the
British embassy in Washington had upon them.

The activities of Britain's Washington embassy are considered in
the context of a number of significant events. The first challenge
the embassy faced in the post-war period was the negotiation of the
Financial Agreement. The book begins with a consideration of the
embassy's role in the pre-negotiation period; that is from early 1945
onwards. It ends with a consideration of the part the embassy played
in the Marshall Plan proposals. By the time the US Congress approved
the Marshall Plan and passed the Economic Cooperation Act in April
1948, there had been a fundamental shift in international relations.

The period saw one of the most important changes in international
politics that took place during the twentieth century – America's
clear confirmation in the post-war period of its earlier shift away from
isolationism. It is interesting to consider the voting in Congress on
some of the key foreign policy issues during this period. The Financial
Agreement (1946) passed through the House of Representatives by

219 votes to 155. Aid to Greece and Turkey after the British withdrawal (1947) passed by 287 votes to 107. The Marshall Plan (1947) passed by 318 votes to 75. The trend in the Senate was no less clear. The Financial Agreement passed by 46 votes to 34, aid to Greece and Turkey by 67 votes to 23 and the Marshall Plan was passed with general acclamation without the need for a vote.[3]

The period 1945 to 1948 includes the last year of Lord Halifax's ambassadorship and the whole of Lord Inverchapel's service as British ambassador to Washington. Halifax was appointed ambassador in January 1941 following the death of Lord Lothian. Initially reluctant to go to Washington, Halifax came to enjoy the role and even to excel at it. He remained in Washington until May 1946. Halifax was one of the twentieth century's longest-serving British ambassadors in America. He was replaced by Inverchapel, who had served as the ambassador in Moscow. At the time of his appointment to the post in Washington, Inverchapel was regarded as a brilliant diplomat. He met with mixed success in America, however, and Bevin replaced him with Sir Oliver Franks in May 1948. It may seem curious to review a period in the embassy's history, which includes the end of one ambassadorship and the entirety of another. But as well as the reason mentioned above regarding the choice of period, i.e. that it coincided with a post-war shift in America's international outlook, there is another reason. The end of the war brought with it a change in government in Britain and this change affected the character of the Washington embassy's activities. Halifax's ambassadorship is usually treated as a whole but it might more properly be considered in two parts: the first part when Churchill was in office and the second after Attlee took over in 1945. As is well documented, these two prime ministers adopted different styles, and these two styles resulted in very different roles for Halifax. It seems at least as appropriate to consider Halifax's post-war ambassadorship alongside Inverchapel's as it does to consider it alongside the period he spent serving under Churchill.

The archival sources used for this book are listed in the bibliography. The starting point, of course, is the National Archives at Kew. The most frequently consulted sources are the Political Departments General Correspondence, FO 371, and the Private Office papers, FO 800.

There are numerous other sources at Kew and many of these have been used. Three record groups, which are not encountered very frequently in the literature, however, deserve special mention. The records of the Diplomatic Administrative Offices, FO 366, proved invaluable in piecing together the structure of the embassy in chapter 1. The Washington embassy papers, FO 115, although not voluminous and often repetitive with FO 371, contain some interesting material, including some documents on the aftermath of the Pentagon talks, which are discussed in chapter 5. Finally, the Ministry of Supply papers, AB16, contained some interesting references to the embassy's work in the atomic energy field and these are used primarily in chapter 5.

The private papers of the ambassadors are something of a contrast. The excellent source of the Halifax diaries and the other Halifax papers provide a clear account of Halifax's thinking during the period under review. Unfortunately the section of the Inverchapel papers which covers his period at the Washington embassy is rather limited and, apart from containing over 40 of his speeches, this source is something of a disappointment. However, while writing Inverchapel's biography, Donald Gillies contacted several of Inverchapel's contemporaries and has lodged his correspondence and notes of his conversations with them at the Bodleian. This affords some compensation for the lack of papers on Inverchapel.

The principal American source is the comprehensive and reliable series *Foreign Relations of the United States*. This source has been supplemented by a review of a range of private papers. These include those of the two most important secretaries of state during Truman's first Administration, that is James Byrnes (papers at Clemson University, South Carolina) and George Marshall (papers at the Marshall Foundation, Lexington, Virginia). Other members of the Administration have been considered and visits were made to the Library of Congress to review the Clifford and Harriman papers (among others), the University of Kentucky to review Fred Vinson's papers and the Truman Library to consider not only some of the President's files but also certain State Department papers and those of other important members of the Administration.

The period between 1945 and 1948 has been the subject of considerable historical discussion. This body of work covers a variety of topics including, for example, the origins of the Cold War and British foreign policy. It is therefore legitimate to ask whether we need further work on a period of history that has already received a great deal of attention. Despite this, there is no specific or systematic account of the part the British embassy in Washington played in the events or its influence upon them. Not only is there no systematic account: there are only scant references to the embassy in the body of work, which does exist on the period.[4] An area where one would have expected the role of the embassy to be discussed in more depth is in the work on Anglo-American relations. Here too, however, there is no great detail on either the ambassadors or the work of the embassy.[5]

There are two works which stand alone in terms of addressing the role of the British embassy in Washington. The first is Michael Hopkins' *Oliver Franks and the Truman Administration: Anglo American Relations 1948–1952* (2003). This work explores Oliver Franks' ambassadorship and in particular his relationship with Dean Acheson and the consequences that had for the Anglo-American relationship. The other is *The Washington Embassy: British Ambassadors to the United States, 1939–77* (2009) edited by Michael Hopkins, Saul Kelly and John Young. As the editors themselves suggest, the work 'fills something of a lacuna in the existing literature'.[6] The content of the book reflects the title. It offers a commentary on 11 ambassadors who served in Washington from World War II until 1977. The nature of the book dictates that it is only able to offer a summary account of each period and it cannot therefore offer any detailed discussion on what the embassy was doing in relation to many of the events that occurred within those periods. It does, however, provide, for both Halifax and Inverchapel, an account which offers interesting insights into their ambassadorships and some detail on the embassy set-up.

It is clear, then, that there is something of a void in the literature when it comes to discussing the role of the British embassy in Washington between 1945 and 1948. But this, of itself, does not mean that the void should be filled. If, for example, the embassy contributed very little in the way of policy formation, did nothing to inform the agenda in London or provided little in the way of insight into American affairs then there would be good reasons for the topic's neglect. This book, however, refutes any suggestion that this may have been the case, and offers a sustained and coherent account of the embassy's contribution and why it was important.

The book begins with a consideration of structure. What do we mean by 'the embassy'? What did the embassy consist of? What were its functions and who worked there? These are all issues which can impact an embassy's effectiveness and, therefore, its contribution to Anglo-American relations. Of special consideration when discussing the embassy is the ambassador. It was he who was responsible for every aspect of the embassy's work and was at the centre of the British establishment in Washington. He was, as Lord Strang put it, 'the sun in his own planetary system'.[7] The character and suitability of both Halifax and Inverchapel to the tasks in hand were therefore a significant influence on the effectiveness of the embassy. Both the embassy and the ambassador operated in America within a particular political environment. This environment was influenced by a multitude of factors, all of which could have an effect upon diplomatic activity. Chapter 1, then, addresses the structure of the embassy, the background to the ambassadors and the political environment in which they operated.

Chapter 2 considers one of the first challenges the embassy faced in the post-war period, i.e. the negotiation of the Financial Agreement. The part the embassy played in these negotiations was significant, but so too was its role in advising London on the tactics to be employed in any negotiation and, indeed, on the credentials of the team with which the British would be negotiating. As mentioned above, Congress's endorsement of the Financial Agreement was not overwhelming and the closeness of the embassy to the Legislature is also explored when discussing the agreement. The negotiation was not only about what was gained or lost but also about the process itself and how the embassy conducted itself and responded to pressures from both London and the Americans.

Although the dollar was a crucial component in the Anglo-American relationship in the post-war world, it was not the only source of friction between the two countries. The loss of Anglo-American collaboration in the atomic energy field is discussed in chapter 3. The end of collaboration was a blow for Britain, not simply because of the loss of 'know-how' but because of the loss of status it implied. The embassy was perceptive in understanding the change in American attitudes to atomic energy collaboration but less effective in seeking to head off the threat. The consideration of the atomic energy issue highlights the way the embassy could, on occasions, set the agenda for London. It also serves to demonstrate, as indeed the book as a whole does, the variety of roles the embassy played and the range of its influence and the limitations to it.

The limitations upon the effectiveness of the embassy are one of the interesting themes which come out of a consideration of the Palestinian issue, which is discussed in chapter 4. Channels of communication matter in diplomacy and the extent to which the embassy's effectiveness was impaired by the fact that Truman pursued policy initiatives independent of the Department of State is instructive. It was also an issue which highlighted the part an embassy can play in policy formation. Had the embassy been listened to more carefully, perhaps some of the friction which developed between America and Britain over the Palestinian issue might have been avoided.

The final chapter of this book offers a review of the embassy's contribution to the progress of the Marshall Plan proposals. It looks at the part the embassy played in reporting to London on the background and imminence of Marshall's proposals and their consequences, as well as the embassy's role in building a coalition of support for the proposals across the American political system. Chapter 5 also considers the embassy's role in explaining one of the principal drivers behind the Marshall Plan proposals, that is, Britain's financial weakness. This weakness was most vividly demonstrated by Britain's withdrawal of aid to Greece and Turkey and by its failure to honour its convertibility obligations under the Financial Agreement. Finally, it is acknowledged that diplomats and politicians are only human and suffer from the same frailties and emotions that the rest of us do. The relationship between the diplomats at the embassy and their home government is important and when this relationship is strained there are consequences for the diplomatic process.

Within the limited literature which is available on the subject of diplomacy, there is a tendency to seek to isolate the influence of an individual. This approach is not unreasonable; much historical writing is about an individual and his or her influence. This book, however, takes a different approach. It has widened the playing field, looking beyond one individual and seeking to consider the embassy as a whole. Not only does it consider the part played by Halifax and Inverchapel but also the parts played by a range of other diplomats including John Balfour, Robert Brand, William Edwards, Alan Judson, Roger Makins and Robert Munro. The consequence of this approach is to emphasise the importance of the embassy as an institution during the period 1945 to 1948 and to underline its permanence and, indeed, its reach across the American political system.

Similarly the literature also tends to focus on occasions where the embassy, whether through an individual or collectively, was able to influence events decisively. Decisive influence is important and it is discussed in this book. The problem with this type of approach, however, is that it runs the risk of underestimating the importance of other aspects of the embassy's work. Yet it was the regular reporting and the conducting of negotiations which made up the daily and systematic part of the embassy's activities that underlined its strength. This book argues that the importance of the embassy in the period under review resides not only in the contribution of any one individual or in decisive influence, but also in the embassy's permanence as an institution, or rather the knowledge and contact base that arose from that permanence.

CHAPTER 1

THE EMBASSY, THE AMBASSADOR AND THE POLITICAL ENVIRONMENT

It must be accepted that policy will be increasingly decided in Washington. To proceed as if it can be made in London and 'put over' in Washington, or as if British policy can in the main develop independently and can be only 'coordinated' with American, is merely to kick against the pricks. Policy will thus be increasingly Washington made policy. But it need not therefore be American. It may be Anglo-American.[1]

One of the outcomes of World War II was an irrevocable shift in power to Washington. This shift in the making of policy towards Washington, together with Britain's post-war aspirations in the field of Anglo-American relations, inevitably escalated the importance of the British embassy. This chapter considers the structure of the embassy, the ambassadors who led the embassy during the period under review and the political environment in which they operated. Before considering these issues, however, it is appropriate to consider briefly where the embassy fitted into the machinery of the Foreign Office and therefore of the British government, and the role diplomacy played in the making of foreign policy.

The Foreign Service came into being in 1943 and was the result of the amalgamation of the Foreign Office and Diplomatic Service with the Commercial Diplomatic and the Consular Services.[2] This new Crown service was the means by which official relations between Britain and other sovereign states were conducted.[3] The minister responsible to Parliament for the Foreign Service and the conduct of foreign affairs was the Secretary of State for Foreign Affairs, a position held by Ernest Bevin from 1945 to 1951. The headquarters of this new service was the Foreign Office. The head of the Foreign Office and the Foreign Service was the Permanent Under-Secretary. This position was held by Sir Alexander Cadogan from 1938 to 1946 and by Sir Orme Sargent from 1946 to 1949.[4]

The Foreign Office was divided into 35 departments.[5] The most important of these, from the Washington embassy's point of view, were the North American Department and the newly formed Economic Relations Department. The Superintending Under-Secretary of the North American Department from 1945 to 1947 was Sir Neville Butler; he was replaced by Sir Michael Wright in 1948.[6] Both had spent time at the embassy in Washington; Butler served from 1939 to 1941 and Wright served with Lord Halifax until 1946. The Superintending Under-Secretary of the Economic Relations Department until 1947 was Sir Edmond Hall-Patch, who had moved from the Treasury in 1944 and had laid the foundations for the Foreign Office's growing economic work. He was one of the principal economic advisers to Ernest Bevin and played a significant role in both the Financial Agreement negotiations, being one of the team sent to Washington in September 1945, and in the British response to the Marshall Plan. He was succeeded as Superintending Under-Secretary by Roger Makins (discussed more fully below) who returned from Washington in 1947.

The role of these departments was twofold: firstly to collect and analyse information received from the overseas missions, e.g. the Washington embassy, with a view to assisting the Foreign Secretary in the formulation of policy proposals, and secondly to assist in the execution of policy by drafting instructions for use by the overseas representatives.[7] The purported function of the embassy, then, in relation to the Foreign Office was (and still is) to collect information and pass it on, and to receive instructions and act upon them. This two-way flow formed the basis of the essential relationship between the Foreign

Office and the embassy.[8] The detailed structure of the embassy is considered below.

During the war, a 'mini Whitehall' was established in Washington with virtually every government department having an establishment in the city. In addition to this mini Whitehall, a variety of new missions and other British agencies were established. These included the Supply Mission, the Shipping Mission and the embassy Relief and War Supplies Department. Combined Boards with the Americans and later the Canadians were also formed; these included the Combined Production and Resources Board (CPRB), the Combined Raw Materials Board (CRMB) and the Combined Food Board (CFB), The result of this was that 'the official British presence in Washington swelled to a peak of 9000'.[9] These various bodies were, however, formed mainly for the purpose of waging war. The majority of them were closed down shortly after the war ended, some became dormant and yet others metamorphosed into international bodies. The CPRB and the CRMB, both formed in 1942, were, in accordance with America's aspirations for free trade, closed down in December 1945.[10] The CFB, after consultation with 19 other countries, turned itself into the International Emergency Food Council in recognition of the world's continuing food shortages.[11] The missions were also largely dissipated; some were shut down while others had their functions or a part of them transferred to the embassy. One of the largest missions, the Supply Council, was closed down in March 1946.

Although the British presence in Washington during the war was exceptional, the benefit of close collaboration with the Americans during the war had not been overlooked. As Hall Patch noted in 1945:

> Through our war time machinery we receive from Washington a mass of most valuable material of high quality covering a very wide field, and we are able to make our views known ... among the innumerable US agencies.[12]

Britain wanted to retain access to this high-quality material and to continue making its views known across the US Administration. One method of achieving this, at least in part, was to retain the establishment that the embassy had developed into during the war and indeed expand it. In 1938, the total staff at the embassy in Washington amounted to 52 people; by August 1946, shortly after Inverchapel took over, the figure had grown to over 400.[13] The embassy was to continue growing. This change in numbers from the pre-war level to the post-war level is a vivid demonstration of the change in Britain's policy towards America over that period.

Chart I is a reconstruction of what the Washington embassy looked like in mid-1946.[14] Attempting to draw a picture of the embassy is rather like drawing a landscape; one is faced with an ever-changing scene. This is particularly so in the period 1945 to 1948 when the embassy was adjusting to the post-war world. Nevertheless it is believed that the image presented as at mid-1946 is representative of what the embassy looked like in the period. It also has the merit of coinciding with the time Lord Inverchapel took over from Lord Halifax and it contains most of the key players in the period under review. The work of the embassy might perhaps be divided into five parts: Chancery, including administration, registry and reports; Economic and Commercial, including the relevant attachés; British Information Service (BIS) covering publicity and communications; the Consular section and finally the Defence attachés.

In considering Chart I, it is worth noting the titles for respective persons. Although it may be obvious, the seniority ranged downwards from ambassador, through to Minister, Counsellor, First Secretary, Second Secretary and finally to Third Secretary. An indication of the relative status of these positions might be gleaned from their remuneration. Inverchapel received a salary of £3,500 with a *frais de représentation* (the term given to allowances received by the heads of missions) of £16,000. Sir John Balfour (minister) received £2,500 plus a *frais de représentation* of £2,500, and Roger Makins (minister) received a salary of £2,000 and an allowance of £2,000. The following salaries were received by certain Counsellors: William Edwards £1,700, Michael Wright £1,300, H.A. Greaves £1,200. The First Secretaries might receive between £600 and £900 and Second Secretaries around £450. The Counsellors and Secretaries would also have received allowances commensurate with their status and duties.[15]

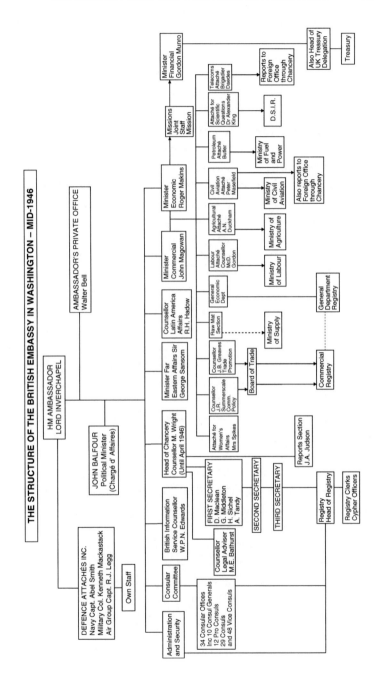

THE STRUCTURE OF THE BRITISH EMBASSY IN WASHINGTON – MID-1946

HM AMBASSADOR
LORD INVERCHAPEL

AMBASSADOR'S PRIVATE OFFICE
Walter Bell

JOHN BALFOUR
Political Minister
(Chargé d' Affaires)

DEFENCE ATTACHÉS INC.
Navy Capt. Abel Smith
Military Col. Kenneth Mackastack
Air Group Capt. R.J. Legg

Own Staff

Administration
and Security

Consular
Committee

British Information
Service Counsellor
W.P.N. Edwards

Counsellor
Legal Adviser
M.E. Bathurst

34 Consular Offices
Inc 10 Consul Generals
12 Pro Consuls
29 Consuls
and 48 Vice Consuls

FIRST SECRETARY
D. Maclean
G. Middleton
H. Sichel
A. Tandy

SECOND SECRETARY

THIRD SECRETARY

Registry
Head of Registry

Registry Clerks
Cypher Officers

Head of Chancery
Counsellor M. Wright
(Until April 1946)

Attaché for
Women's
Affairs
Mrs Spikes

Reports Section
J.A. Judson

Minister Far
Eastern Affairs Sir
George Sansom

Counsellor
J.R.
Summerscale
Comm.
Policy

Counsellor
J.B. Greaves
Trade
Promotion

Board of Trade

Commercial
Registry

Counsellor
Latin America
Affairs
R.H. Hadow

Raw Mat
Section

General
Economic
Dept

Ministry
of Supply

General
Department
Registry

Minister
Commercial
John Magowan

Labour
Attaché
Counsellor
McD.
Gordon

Agricultural
Attaché
A.N.
Duckham

Ministry
of Labour

Ministry of
Agriculture

Minister
Economic
Roger Makins

Civil
Aviation
Attaché
Peter
Masefield

Petroleum
Attaché
Butler

Ministry
of Civil
Aviation

Ministry
of Fuel
and
Power

Also reports to
Foreign Office
through
Chancery

Missions
Joint
Staff
Mission

Attaché for
Scientific
Questions
Dr Alexander
King

Telecoms
Attaché
Brigadier
Daledies

Reports to
Foreign
Office
through
Chancery

D.S.I.R.

Minister
Financial
Gordon Munro

Also Head of
UK Treasury
Delegation

Treasury

Aside from the ambassadors, who are discussed below, the most senior person serving at the embassy between 1945 and 1948 was Sir John Balfour. After Eton, Oxford and internment during World War I, Balfour joined the Foreign and Diplomatic Service in 1919. Between 1924 and 1928 he served with the embassy in Washington, initially as a Second Secretary and then as a First Secretary. It was to be the first of three postings to America. In 1940, after postings in Sofia, Budapest and Belgrade, he returned to the Foreign Office to head the American Department. It was a posting where he learnt something, in part from Lord Lothian, of the American mood and of its propensity to veer towards isolationism. In 1943, after a spell in Lisbon, he moved to the British embassy in Moscow where he worked for, and developed a close relationship with Inverchapel, or Sir Archibald Clark Kerr, as he was then known. Along with Averell Harriman, the American ambassador in Moscow, Balfour was one of the early converts to the view that the Soviets would be a source of agitation and conflict in the post-war world. In April 1945 Balfour moved to the Washington embassy as the number two under Lord Halifax. In Washington, he frequently had occasion to act as the Chargé d'Affaires, a role he had sometimes fulfilled in Moscow.[16] Balfour remained in Washington until the summer of 1948. It will be seen in subsequent chapters that Balfour's ability, evidenced in his political reports, to combine his perception of the American mood with his views of Soviet behaviour in the post-war world was both perceptive and accurate. After the stint at Washington, Balfour became the ambassador to Argentina. He remained there for three years before ending his mainstream diplomatic career as the ambassador to Spain. In 1955 Balfour had one final stint in America when he became a UK delegate to the United Nations.[17] It can be difficult to discern why a diplomat is moved from one posting to another. It is possible that Balfour was moved to Washington in 1945 because of his knowledge of Russia and his experience in Eastern Europe. This was, perhaps, an early indication that the Foreign Office understood the importance of the Russian card in Anglo-American relations. By the time Bevin was established in the Foreign Office this thinking was certainly influential. Writing to Halifax regarding Inverchapel's appointment Bevin wrote: 'I felt it was important for the future to have someone in Washington who had a good knowledge of Russia and the East as well as Europe.'[18]

The ambassadors' private office was headed by their respective private secretaries, who included Jack Lockhart for Halifax and Walter Bell for Inverchapel. The private office was important not just for the smooth running of social events and the organisation of the ambassadors' entertaining, but also because it was an 'efficient unit for seeing that he [the ambassador] is equipped...to put over his own personality and the British case to the "great American public"'. The private secretary played a significant role in the preparation of the ambassadors' speeches.[19]

The core of the Washington embassy's work was the consideration of political questions and this work was centred in Chancery. Chancery consisted of unspecialised members of staff who dealt with political issues and '[were] thus in a sense the backbone of the mission'.[20] Although members of Chancery were not specialists in the sense that, for example, Commercial Counsellors were, they did tend to have their own areas of specialisation within the political work. A.H. Tandy, for example, covered the Near and Middle East, Jewish and Zionist affairs; D. Maclean looked after Civil Affairs, Reparations and Western Europe; and G.H. Middleton specialised in Soviet and Eastern bloc affairs, among other things.[21] Chancery was also responsible for advising the ambassador on any legal matters that arose out of negotiations between America and Britain.[22]

Paul Gore-Booth, who worked in Chancery in 1945 and was its acting head for a period of time, described the head of Chancery in an embassy like Washington as a 'kind of universal joint between all sections of embassy activity and to a considerable extent between those sections and the head of the Mission...the good functioning of the embassy machine depends greatly on the performance of this universal joint'.[23] The head of Chancery in 1946 was Michael Wright who, as previously mentioned, went on to become the head of the North American Department at the Foreign Office and later was to hold the ambassadorships of both Norway and Iraq. Gore-Booth, too, was destined for high office. He was the ambassador to Burma and High Commissioner in India prior to becoming the Permanent Under-Secretary at the Foreign Office. The specialisation within Chancery enabled the diplomats to establish relations with their counterparts in the State Department, thus cementing a closer relationship between the embassy and the American Administration.

The Reports Division of the embassy was responsible for the Weekly, Quarterly and Annual Political reports produced primarily for the benefit of the Foreign Office, although they were also circulated to certain ministers. Their objective was to report trends in public opinion and changes in the opinion of the establishment, particularly when these changes might affect Anglo-American relations. During most of the war, the division was headed by Isaiah Berlin.[24] Although these reports usually went out in the name of the ambassador or the Chargé d'Affaires, they were usually written by members of this department and were edited, where necessary, by the head of Chancery. In addition to the regular political reports, the division was also responsible for more ad hoc reports, such as one entitled 'American comment on the British loan and the course of the Congressional hearings and debates on the subject'.[25] These particular reports on the loan were, in fact, drafted by a less famous member of this division, J.A. Judson.

Judson was also the embassy's liaison officer with Congress. Michael Wright had the idea in 1946 for the embassy to have a full-time Congressional specialist. The objective was to strengthen the relationship between Congress and the embassy by increasing and focusing upon Congressional liaison. An example of this was a series of 'stag parties' organised by the embassy with the ambassador and/or John Balfour attending together with any visiting Members of Parliament or other British notables and half a dozen or so Congressmen. The result of this increased liaison was that 'the stage now seems to have been reached when we can . . . put our hand on any group of Congressmen and either find out the broad outlines of what they are thinking on particular subjects or tell them something of our own views'. Judson further reported that 'we were on terms of some sort . . . with about 165 members of the House and some 35 in the Senate'.[26]

The economic and commercial aspects of the embassy's work took on a particular importance after the war and it is interesting to note that both Halifax and Inverchapel felt the need to form committees to keep themselves abreast of economic and financial issues. Halifax refers in his diary to 'a meeting of our Economics embassy Group which we are by way of having once a fortnight, to keep ourselves straight and, perhaps more important, to keep me informed of what is going on'.[27] Inverchapel remarks in a memorandum to Bevin that 'I have also constituted a small committee with a secretariat to advise me on general questions which come up in the economic and financial side'.[28] Perhaps this need was a reflection both of their insecurities when it came to financial matters and the fact that they were operating in a period where economic issues were becoming increasingly important.

In the period under review, the commercial side of the embassy was headed up by John Magowan and it was primarily concerned with the protection and promotion of trade. Magowan, who was a minister, was assisted by Counsellors J. Summerscale and J. Greaves. The former was responsible for Board of Trade work on current export policy, liaison with Supply Council Missions and the Treasury Delegation on matters concerned with Britain's commercial interest, and for the production of reports including the preparation of the embassy, Economic Summary. Greaves was responsible for Board of Trade work in respect of direct British–American trade including diplomatic and informal representations on specific matters to the State Department and the supervision of the trade work of the British consuls.[29] Prior to the Foreign Service Reforms of 1943, this type of work was undertaken by the Commercial Diplomatic Officers reporting to the Department of Overseas Trade, which in turn was under the control of the Foreign Office and the Board of Trade. The Department of Overseas Trade was absorbed by the Foreign Office after the war and, as can be seen from Chart I, the commercial section reported to the Board of Trade as well as upwards to the ambassador.

Working closely with the commercial section was Roger Makins. Makins was educated at Winchester and Oxford, where he was elected a Fellow of All Souls. His first Foreign Office overseas posting was as a Third Secretary in the Washington embassy in 1931 when he married the daughter of Senator Dwight Davis. 'Thereafter...he travelled frequently to the United States establishing an invaluable network of American diplomatic, political and family friends.'[30] After several other postings, Makins took up his second Washington appointment; this time as minister for Economic Affairs in March 1945. In July the same year, he also became the Joint Secretary of the Combined Policy Committee, the body set up during the war to coordinate Anglo-American collaboration on atomic energy issues. Although Makins was described as the Economics minister and did a certain amount of economic work it transpired that his 'main task was to deal ... with the problems in the atomic energy field between the two countries, with particular reference to the development of nuclear weapons'.[31] This atomic energy facet of Makins' work is discussed more fully in chapter 3.

The original role envisaged for Makins, and one on which he spent less than half his time, was to consider the wartime machinery which existed in Washington outside of the embassy and to 'make proposals as to staffing and mechanism which would ensure a smooth transition from the war organisation to the peace time embassy'.[32] Makins was also responsible for other short-term economic issues such as work on the United Nations Relief and Rehabilitation Administration (UNRRA). By January 1946, however, it seems that this economic work was progressing rapidly and Halifax suggested that 'in six or seven months time there will not be sufficient work for two ministers in the economic field [i.e. both a commercial and economic minister] and both the organisation and the nature of the work will call for a single supervisory head'.[33]

The consequence of Halifax's correspondence was that Inverchapel was confronted with a 'request' for Makins to return to the Foreign Office almost as soon as he, i.e. Inverchapel, had arrived.[34] Makins was to take Hall Patch's place as Superintending Under-Secretary upon Hall Patch's promotion to Deputy Under-Secretary for the Functional Departments. Inverchapel protested at this and Makins did not, in fact, return to the Foreign Office until February 1947.[35] The commercial and economic affairs side of the embassy were eventually merged, initially under the leadership of John Magowan. Makins was to return to Washington embassy for a third time in 1952 when he replaced Sir Oliver Franks as the ambassador.

The ending of wartime conditions in Washington and the transfer of certain members of the various supply missions to the embassy resulted in a proliferation in the number of attachés at the embassy.[36] A number of these attachés, including those for labour, agriculture, civil aviation, petroleum, scientific issues and telecom, worked along-side the Commercial Counsellors. The attachés tended not to have dip-lomatic rank and as representatives of other government departments were not members of the Foreign Service. (There were exceptions to this; for example the Labour attaché, Archie Gordon, also carried the rank of Counsellor.) In general terms, they were designated as Civil attachés and ranked below the longer-serving Military attachés. The attachés were, of course, specialists in their chosen field and would offer advice to both the ambassador and, where relevant, their own particular Whitehall departments. A classic example of this special-ised reporting was a memorandum prepared by Archie Gordon on 'The Attitude of Labour Organisations in the United States towards the Anglo-American Loan Agreement'.[37]

A surprising civil attaché given the period, although not directly connected with the commercial side, was Mrs Spikes. Mrs Spikes joined the embassy in October 1945 as the attaché for Women's Affairs. Her work entailed maintaining contact with the various women's groups headquartered in Washington and touring the country speaking to various women's groups throughout America. These included the Federation of Women's Clubs, the Business and Professional Women's Organisation and the League of Women Voters.[38] This latter group played a significant role in the promotion of the Anglo-American Loan Agreement when it was before Congress.

Connected to the commercial and economic side of the embassy, but also distinct from it, was the Treasury Delegation which, as the name implies, consisted of the UK Treasury's representatives in Washington. Gordon Munro, who was appointed in May 1946, was both the head of the Treasury Delegation in Washington and the minister at the embassy responsible for Financial Affairs. Before May 1946, however, the head of the Treasury Delegation was not a minister at the embassy and did not hold diplomatic rank. Before Munro, the position was held by Robert Brand. Brand was an important part of the British estab-lishment in Washington in the immediate post-war period.

After Marlborough and Oxford, where he was elected a fellow of All Souls, Brand worked in the Colonial Service in South Africa (1902–1909). Brand, who discovered a talent for administration, spent some time working as the personal assistant to J.C. Smuts. Brand joined Lazard Brothers, one of Britain's leading merchant banks in 1913 and became Managing Director in 1919. During World War I, however, he moved into government service to assist in the funding of munitions. This included being sent to Washington, where he was Deputy Chairman of the British War Mission from 1917 to 1918. After the war, Brand attended the Paris Peace Conference where he met Maynard Keynes. In 1919, he returned to Lazards and remained there until 1941 when he moved to Washington. Initially he served as head of the Food Mission but in 1944 he became the head of the Treasury Delegation, where he remained until he was succeeded by Munro. Brand also chaired the British Supply Council in North America in 1942 and again in 1945– 1946. After the war, Brand received a peerage and returned to Lazard Brothers where he remained a Director until his retirement in 1960.[39]

Brand was 'one of the first class brains whom Britain threw into the financial struggle with the USA'. He played a crucial role in the negotiations of the Anglo-American Loan Agreement and the fact that he was 'dazzled but not overwhelmed by [Keynes'] brilliance was an asset to the pre negotiations'.[40] Brand was also very familiar with the American way, having married Phyllis Langhorne, Nancy Astor's sister, on his earlier trip to America in 1917. Although, as noted above, Brand was not a minister at the embassy and did see himself as the ambassador's adviser on financial matters.[41] Brand believed it was important that the Treasury representative 'should be not only directly responsible to the Chancellor but directly responsible also to the ambassador without any other official intervening'.[42] This Treasury Delegation connection with the embassy was an important part of the post-war set-up in Washington. This was not only because financial issues assumed such importance, but also because it enabled the British to approach the Secretary of the Treasury directly on such issues. In ordinary circumstances, etiquette dictated that the embassy could only approach the Administration through the Department of State.

Brand's successor, Gordon Munro, moved to Washington from Canada where he was the Financial Adviser to the UK High Commissioner. Before that, he was a merchant banker with the firm of Henry Wagg, which he had joined after having been invalided out of the Army. Munro was educated at Wellington and the Royal Military College, Sandhurst.

Munro worked closely with both Makins and Magowan and this cooperation facilitated the merging of the embassy's economic side and commercial side, referred to above, thus allowing Makins to eventually return to the Foreign Office.[43] Munro also took on additional responsibilities, being appointed to replace Makins on the Combined Policy Committee referred to above. Munro played an important role not only in the financial aspects of the embassy's work – for example, the interpretation of the terms of the American loan to Britain negotiated under the Financial Agreement – but also in the negotiations with regard to atomic energy. In 1949, Munro left the embassy and became the Financial Adviser to the Government of Southern Rhodesia.

If the scarcity of dollars raised the importance of the economic side of the embassy, then the need to persuade Congress and the American public to part with dollars raised the importance of the embassy's information services. In 1946, Halifax observed: 'I am convinced that we shall need all the work that can be done on the press and the radio for the next few years if we are to hold our own.'[44] By 1946, the Foreign Office had inherited the British Information Service (BIS) from the wartime organisation the Ministry of Information. The head of the BIS was William Edwards, who had succeeded Harold Butler. Appointed in mid-1946, Edwards held the rank of Counsellor and worked at the embassy in Washington. Edwards had become a 'devoted admirer' of America since his days as a Davison scholar (a scholarship offered to members of Oxford or Cambridge universities) at Princeton University.[45] During World War II, Edwards 'was Director of Public Relations at the Ministries of Production and Supply and, in that capacity, was in charge of the public relations of the British Supply Council in Washington'.[46] Consequently Edwards had the background required to head the BIS, i.e. experience in public relations and knowledge of America. Keen to secure his services in Washington, Bevin wrote to Sir Stafford Cripps asking him to release Edwards from the role he had returned to at the end of the war, i.e. Director of the Overseas Information Division at the Board of Trade.[47] Edwards' background had been in industry and, according to him, the Foreign Office asked him to take on the role of head of the BIS because 'they thought the major post-war problems of Anglo-American relations would be economic and industrial'.[48] Edwards remained in Washington until 1949 when he was replaced by Gore-Booth who, as mentioned above, had served at the embassy during the war.

The BIS's principal offices were in New York, which acted as a production and mailing centre for the whole country, Washington, Chicago and San Francisco. There were also sub-offices, usually attached to the consulates, in Los Angeles, Boston, Seattle, Detroit and Houston.[49] The work of the BIS included, firstly, 'distributing guidance on current events' to embassy and Consular staff. This was an important task since it 'enables our people to have a party line for conversations with Americans'. Secondly, it was to keep in touch with prominent editors, radio journalists and columnists and supply them with appropriate material including articles and photos. Finally, it was to prepare and distribute information about Britain. By the end of 1946, the BIS employed 283 people.[50]

Even with this contingent, it was acknowledged that 'the present organisation does not permit us to cover more than a section of the press and radio'. There were approximately 800 correspondents of American newspapers in Washington. It was further acknowledged that the offices in Chicago and Los Angeles were not large enough to cope with the large-circulation Midwestern and Hollywood newspapers.[51] It is also possible that the work of the BIS was hampered by the lack of interest in public relations by the people at the top of the embassy. Edwards suggests that Inverchapel, the Foreign Office and Oliver Franks all failed to appreciate the need for the public relations side of things. According to Edwards, he did manage to get Inverchapel and Balfour to lunch with Walter Lippmann (a prominent American columnist) once, but he suggests that, more often than not, he had to deal with him alone.[52] It is doubtful that the Foreign Office displayed a lack of interest in public relations; there are too many examples of Foreign Office officials stressing its need.[53] It is, however, quite plausible that Inverchapel showed little interest in public relations.

The Consular section of the embassy was a significant operation and in mid-1946 there were '31 Consular posts with a staff of 350 persons, including 83 Consular officers'.[54] These numbers are in addition to the 400 staff at the embassy, who were mainly situated in Washington. The posts were spread across America and covered all of the major cities and ports. Whilst Consular officials had specialised functions such as registering births and deaths of British citizens in their area, officiating in any British merchant ship disputes and issuing passports, they also had a representational and reporting function. The consuls' work included reporting the political, economic and social developments taking place in one part of the country. Consuls were (and still are) freer than the diplomats in Washington in that they were able to represent their views or present their case to a range of local official institutions including, for example, the civic authorities and the police; they were not restricted to making representations only to the Department of State.

One of the most important roles of the consuls, however, was countering the anti-British feeling that existed in large parts of America. As Balfour noted:

> It must not be forgotten that, excepting in a few east coast areas, there is a traditional and deep seated suspicion of British political motives and the majority of newspaper editors, as well as a high proportion of columnists and commentators, are in greater or lesser degree anti British... We naturally do our utmost to neutralise as much of this as possible at the source, either here in Washington or in New York. But there is a strict limit to what we can do and we must largely rely on Consuls in the field to supplement our efforts.[55]

This aspect of the consuls' work was heightened by the fact that America was a country in which the appeal to public opinion was so openly accepted: 'the United States Government accepts as a matter of course that British Foreign Service officers should speak directly to American voters and pressure groups'.[56]

With a view to saving dollars, there was an attempt by the Foreign Office to close down five consulates that had been opened during the war. The embassy, which clearly understood the importance of the consulates, managed to resist these attempts and consequently the Atlanta, Cincinnati, Denver, Kansas City and St Paul, Minneapolis consulates

remained open. The consular network provided an additional counter to anti-British sentiment at a time when good Anglo-American or
even Anglo-Congressional relations were crucial.[57]

The final aspect of the embassy's work was that of the Defence
attachés. Military collaboration had been close during the war and,
although such collaboration cooled after the war, the Combined Chiefs
of Staff, formed in February 1942, continued although it was eventually merged into the NATO military machinery. Hence there was
a mechanism for military representations to be made at the highest
level. The Defence attachés, however, were a part of the embassy and
were there, at least in part, to advise the ambassador on military matters. They did, however, have their own offices and staff and corre-
sponded directly with their respective departments.

The embassy in Washington, in common with other institutions,
needed to adapt to the post-war world and the period 1945 to 1948
can perhaps be characterised as one of transition. Whilst the structure
of some parts of the embassy – for example, Chancery, the Registry
and the administrative sections – did not appear to change a great
deal after the war other parts of the embassy did. The economics side
needed to adapt to the growing importance of economic issues, issues
which the Foreign Service were increasingly being asked to deal with.
The embassy also needed to absorb personnel from some of the wartime
missions and respond to other structural changes such as the transfer of
the BIS from the Ministry of Information to the Foreign Office.

In the midst of this transition, the embassy faced another problem,
as Halifax pointed out:

> At present a great deal of work which normally falls on the
> embassy is discharged by individuals of special ability and com-
> petence who are employed by the embassy or associated with it
> but who in most cases wish to return to their ordinary peacetime
> employments at the end of the war.[58]

Halifax probably had in mind Isaiah Berlin, a First Secretary in the
Reports Section, Arthur Salter of the Shipping Mission, Harold Butler,
head of Information Services, Robert Brand, and even himself. All were

talented individuals, all one-time Fellows of All Souls and all keen to move on from Washington. The pressure for relief came not only from the wartime draftees. The regular members of the Foreign Service were becoming exhausted. Makins protested in 1946 that he had been 'working at full stretch and without any real break since 1939, and that he has now reached the point at which his work and general performance are, without question, beginning to deteriorate as a result of accumulated fatigue'.[59] Makins could not have been alone in this.

It was a difficult period for the embassy and in a letter to the Foreign Office written shortly after he had arrived, Inverchapel expressed his frustration:

> The prospect is not too rosy on the staff side. Magowan leaves shortly on a visit to England and will be away about two months. On his return Summerscale will go to England...there has as you know been a major change in Treasury Representation where Gordon Munro is replacing both Brand and Lee, a task which will take him some time to accomplish...The embassy has been pulled about in other directions. The abrupt departure of Michael Wright, and the changes in the Reports Section and the B.I.S., with the inevitable time lag in replacements...have naturally thrown a heavy strain on the whole machinery, and have given us no reserves to meet emergencies.[60]

Awareness of the embassy's problems was not restricted to the Foreign Service. The Lord President of the Council Herbert Morrison raised the issue in Cabinet and confirmed Inverchapel's diagnosis:

> We have extremely few officers left there [economic section of embassy] with real experience and contacts, and those few are melting away week by week...No doubt this has been inevitable in the immediate post war phase, but a new stability is badly needed now.[61]

Countering these dual problems of transition and transient personnel, however, were other factors. Notwithstanding the points made above, there was still a pool of very talented people left in Washington, many of whom went on to reach high office in the Foreign Service. These people also had experience of America; many of them had served in Washington or on the North American desk earlier in their careers. This movement between the North American desk and Washington and vice versa facilitated communication between the two and enhanced the pool of knowledge available. The embassy also tried to adapt its structure to make the best use of resources. The specialisations within Chancery were designed to reflect those in the State Department, facilitating a continuing dialogue and closeness between the Chancery diplomats and their counterparts in the State Department. The principle was applied to the organisation of work on the economic side of the embassy, where it was acknowledged that such organisation should correspond 'precisely to Mr Clayton's [Assistant Secretary of State for Economic Affairs] area of responsibility in the State Department'.[62]

Notwithstanding these positive aspects, however, the embassy was creaking under the weight of post-war transition. The extent to which this affected the performance of the embassy is difficult to discern but it is certainly something which needs to be considered when evaluating the role of the embassy. For the moment, however, the position of the embassy in this post-war period was perhaps neatly summarised by Inverchapel:

> It seems to me that the dissolution of the Supply Council, the assumption by the embassy of responsibility for much of the residual work of the missions, and the turnover of personnel make the first eight or nine months of this year one of transition. I have no doubt [however] that this organisation, which seems soundly planned, can absorb these changes.[63]

The above discussion is, of course, incomplete. Of crucial importance, both to the functioning of the embassy and to Anglo-American relations, was the head of the embassy, that is, the ambassador. The two ambassadors who served in the embassy between 1945 and 1948 are discussed below.

During the twentieth century, 27 ambassadors served in the British embassy in Washington. The average tenure was just under four years and ranged from nine years for Sir Ronald Lindsay (1930–1939), the longest-serving ambassador, to under two years for Edward Grey (1919–1921),[64] one of the shortest-serving ambassadors. Ambassadors were, of course, different, but they tended to fall into two main categories: the professional diplomat and the professional politician. As Max Beloff pointed out, 'the alteration between the professional diplomat and the statesman or man of letters, which began with Bryce...has remained characteristic of Britain's handling of the Washington embassy down to the present day'.[65] Two men appointed in the middle of the twentieth century were to epitomise this division. They were Lord Halifax and Lord Inverchapel. Halifax was the consummate statesman; Inverchapel the accomplished diplomat. For these two men, born within a year of each other, the ambassadorship at the Washington embassy was to be their last significant appointment. These two men were also joined by another quirk of fate; both, albeit in different ways, owed their presence in Washington to Winston Churchill.

Halifax was born in 1881 in Devon into a well-connected and very wealthy family. The loss of three elder brothers meant that Halifax, or Edward Wood as he was then called, would inherit both his father's title and estates. He also inherited his father's religious devotion and Halifax was a lifelong practising Christian. After Eton, he went up to Oxford, where he was awarded a first in Modern History and was elected as a Fellow of All Souls. Edward Wood entered Parliament as a Conservative in 1910 and remained there until 1925. Wood's first ministerial appointment in 1921 was as Churchill's Under-Secretary for the colonies; his first Cabinet appointment came in 1922 when he was appointed as President of the Board of Trade. Wood gave up his commons seat in 1925 in order to become the Viceroy of India and at the same time he was appointed Baron Irwin of Kirby Underdale. After his five-year term in India, which was generally viewed as a success, Irwin returned to British politics.

Irwin was offered and turned down the position of Foreign Secretary but in 1932 took up the position of President of the Board of Education.[66] In 1933 he also became Chancellor of the University of Oxford and with the death of his father in 1934 took the title of Viscount Halifax. After the November 1935 election, Halifax became the Leader of the House of Lords and Lord Privy seal; in 1937 he became Lord President of the Council. In 1938, following Anthony Eden's resignation Halifax became Foreign Secretary. He remained in this position until Churchill asked him to take up the ambassadorship at the Washington embassy in January 1941. It is beyond the scope of this book to debate Halifax's role as Foreign Secretary and his part in the outbreak of World War II and Churchill's succession to the premiership in May 1940 but, if the judgement of Andrew Roberts is to be accepted, it was during this period that Halifax, in refusing the Premiership in favour of Churchill's succession, perhaps performed the greatest service for his country.[67]

Halifax then was firmly in the category of statesman. In modern-day parlance, he was a professional politician, although he would probably have recoiled from the term. He was, however, a reluctant diplomat. Shortly after the death of Lord Lothian, who had been appointed to the position of ambassador in Washington by Halifax in 1939, Churchill pressed Halifax to take the position himself, saying 'I have no doubt whatever that the National interest will be best served at this juncture by your becoming our ambassador to the United States'.[68] Not wanting to 'leave London while things were as they were with the war', Halifax tried to dissuade Churchill.[69] He failed and on 14 January 1941 Churchill escorted Halifax to Scapa Flow, where Halifax boarded the newly commissioned battleship, *King George V,* to begin his trans-Atlantic passage.

It is sometimes suggested that Churchill wanted Halifax out of the higher echelons of British politics and in a place where Halifax was not able to impose the 'restraint and checks' that he had placed upon Churchill's premiership.[70] But Churchill may also have been thinking of Franklin D. Roosevelt's remarks in 1938 when a replacement for Lindsay (Lothian's predecessor) was being considered. Roosevelt suggested that the replacement was 'enormously important' and, the President added, 'a career diplomat is not the proper choice at this time'.[71] Some support for the argument that Churchill's offer of

Washington to Halifax was not only about his removal from British politics is given by the fact that Churchill offered the ambassadorship to Lloyd George first. Whatever the motivation, Roosevelt signalled his approval of Halifax by paying him the compliment of travelling down Chesapeake Bay in the presidential yacht to meet him. It was a symbolic act but one which put Halifax on good terms with the President from the beginning.

Notwithstanding this initial fillip, Halifax's term in America got off to a shaky start. Halifax made a number of gaffes. At the end of January 1941, shortly after he had arrived, Halifax visited Senator Walker George, Chairman of the Senate Foreign Relations Committee, and on leaving, Halifax told pressmen that they had discussed the timetable of the Lend Lease Bill. The headline the next day, albeit in the isolationist newspaper *The Chicago Tribune*, was 'Halifax Steers FDR Bill'. In another incident, Halifax suggested that 'America's aid to the Soviet Union amounted to help for Germany', a remark that 'caused great offence'. Finally, leaving a Chicago White Sox baseball game early and then asking if the fielders were 'throwing the ball at the runners' did not help Halifax's popular appeal.[72] Halifax's early views on the Americans, such as 'they strike me as very crude and semi educated', and 'they think that everything can be resolved on the emotional level', did not encourage any rapport between Halifax and his host nation.[73] In October 1941, Isaiah Berlin commented 'the Halifaxes are very remote & viceregal, equally distant from English & Americans, she [Lady Halifax] quite popular locally in the Washington ambit, he neither known nor liked'.[74]

Gradually, however, Halifax became, at least outwardly, more in tune with American culture and its attendant informalities. Halifax ventured out of Washington; in fact, he was the first British ambassador to visit every state in the United States and, with the help of new advisers, his popularity began to improve. America's entry into the war and the stoicism with which Halifax bore the death of one son and the serious injury of another helped cement the goodwill that was gradually developing between Halifax and the Americans.[75]

If good relations with the American public were important, good relations with the US Administration were essential. The cordial start to relations between the President and Halifax continued until Roosevelt's death. As Birkenhead relates, 'the ambassador was told that he could make direct contact by telephone with the President... whenever he wished... and could enter the White House through a private door, and thus escape the attentions of the ubiquitous American press'.[76] Halifax struck up a close relationship with Cordell Hull, Roosevelt's Secretary of State. Halifax noted that 'he talks very freely to me'[77] and Hull commented that 'while I keenly regretted Lothian's death, I saw at once that I could work on the same effective cordial terms with his... successor'.[78]

Halifax cultivated good relations with other important members of the Administration, men such as Hopkins, Acheson, Forrestal, Lovett and Marshall. Halifax made some long-lasting friendships during his tenure at Washington. George Marshall wrote in 1947 'Lady Halifax and you gave Mrs Marshall and me great pleasure during the troubled war years. I don't know any two people who Mrs Marshall and I admire more.'[79] Halifax, however, never managed to quite shake off his cold aristocratic manner. Acheson commented: 'Tall and gaunt Lord Halifax... an English aristocrat reminiscent of the second quarter of the nineteenth century, might have been Lord Melbourne... if he had been a bit handsomer, lighter and more amusing'.[80]

A factor which seriously affected Halifax's role as ambassador was the relationship between Churchill and Roosevelt. Churchill's desire to mix up British interests with those of America with a view to forging a strong Anglo-American relationship is well documented. So strong was the desire that he was not prepared to leave its nurturing to the Foreign Office or mere diplomats. Churchill sent Roosevelt hundreds of personal messages and crossed the Atlantic six times during the war to meet with the President. This level of activity between leaders is bound to have an effect upon normal diplomacy. When Churchill visited Washington, he had meetings with Roosevelt; it was often the practice to exclude Halifax and, indeed, members of the Department of State. The consequence was that often decisions were made on Anglo-American issues about which Halifax had not been consulted. Halifax often had to rely on his closeness to Harry Hopkins, a confidant of the President, to get an account of these meetings. Dean Acheson observed 'how difficult the ambassador's position was rendered by these private meetings'.[81]

Notwithstanding the Churchill–Roosevelt relationship, however, there was work to be done by Halifax. He made at least 65 major speeches across America during his tenure.[82] Many of these speeches echoed the advice that Ernest Bevin had given Halifax before he left for America: 'I have always believed that once America was really awakened they would feel that what we were fighting was a common cause. I think we have talked a little too much of "Aid to Britain" and not enough of the contribution to our common victory'.[83] Halifax was, of course, unable to suggest directly that America enter the war but he was able in his speeches to present Bevin's sentiment that 'these decisions [for example American aid] have been primarily and rightly inspired by your own conception of your own defence needs in the face of Hitler's threat, not less grave to the new world than the old'.[84] After America entered the war, and as it progressed, the sentiment expressed in Halifax's speeches altered. Initially the speeches were concerned with support for what Bevin called the common cause and also pleas that Britain was worth fighting for. As the war was ending, however, an expression of the need for Britain and America to prepare for the new world order was made. This not only referred to the United Nations but also to the continued collaboration between America and Britain. One of Halifax's final broadcasts called for Anglo-American economic cooperation.[85] (The broadcast was made in anticipation of forthcoming Loan Agreement negotiations.)

Aside from touring the country promoting Britain's cause and liaising with members of the US Administration, during his time in Washington, Halifax also presided over the 'mini Whitehall' that existed there during the war. As noted above, at one time during the war, there were over 9,000 British citizens in Washington. Halifax was the titular head of this group. He was also called upon to chair a number of meetings of its various representatives, for example the heads of Missions. Halifax, in fulfilling this role, was 'always calm, efficient, quiet and judicious; never wasting a word and only intervening when absolutely necessary'.[86]

The death of Roosevelt signalled changes in Washington to which Halifax would have to adapt. Although Halifax liked Truman, saying 'he is sensible, honest, straightforward with principles and not, I should judge, lacking in courage', initially, at least, he was not as close to him as he had been to Roosevelt.[87] Truman's succession led to other changes in the Administration. People to whom Halifax had been close began to lose influence. Edward Stettinius (Secretary of State) left in June 1945; Harry Hopkins no longer had the ear of the President and Cordell Hull had left the previous autumn. Halifax needed to establish contacts with the new members of the Administration. A further effect of the Truman presidency was a resurgence in the influence of the Department of State. Byrnes replaced Stettinius; an appointment that was lauded in America but about which Halifax had reservations. However, the effect of Roosevelt's death or Byrnes' appointment on diplomacy in Washington was probably not as great as that of the ousting of Churchill from office by the British electorate in July 1945.

Whilst Churchill did not have the personal rapport with Truman that he had with his predecessor, he continued 'to fill the airways with messages' to the new President. Churchill sent 44 wires to Truman during his first month in office; more than Attlee did in an entire year. As Robert Hathaway pointed out, 'while FDR's death may have snapped a unique bond tying two nations together, it was actually Churchill's subsequent defeat which resulted in the new and less personal tone which came to mark the Anglo-American relationship'.[88] This new tone led to a more active role for the ambassador. Halifax played a significant role in the Loan Agreement negotiations, discussions on atomic energy collaboration and the formulation of Anglo-American Palestinian policy. Although one cannot be certain, it is doubtful if Churchill would have left these matters almost entirely to his ambassador in the way Attlee did.

Halifax first raised the idea that he should leave Washington in March 1943. In a conversation with Eden, he suggested that the work of the ambassador had declined in importance since America had entered the war and that Churchill's visits reduced the responsibility and function of the ambassador.[89] Perhaps this was simply Halifax's way of expressing his displeasure; in any event the issue does not seem to have been raised again, in earnest, until March 1945. Halifax wrote to Eden: 'I should ask you to let me give up here, at such a date as may be convenient to you, this year.'[90] In addition to citing personal reasons for wishing to leave, Halifax also suggested that the timing was right, because Roosevelt was firmly back, stage II negotiations had been completed and there were good relations with the State Department. He also pointed out that 'growing importance is going from now on to attach to matters financial and industrial on which I have not much to put into the pot'.[91] Eden's answer was non-committal.[92] Halifax changed his mind after the death of Roosevelt and in a letter to Churchill suggested he stay on until the spring of the following year.[93] It was an arrangement which Churchill fell in with and one which Bevin was more than happy to honour. In a meeting with Halifax, Bevin said 'I hope you are going to remain on in Washington. I am a great believer you know in the necessity for continuity in foreign policy.'[94]

Halifax went to Washington under protest. He arrived with the whiff of appeasement about him and with virtually no experience of America. He made a poor start. He did nevertheless manage to overcome these setbacks. Whilst labouring under Churchill's shadow, he managed to build some strong relationships with members of the US Administration. He also set about travelling the country in an attempt to convert Americans to be supportive of Britain's position. He was, however, a victim of his upbringing and never quite managed to shake off the aristocratic demeanour which it was so easy for Americans to misinterpret as pomposity and arrogance. Nor did Halifax ever completely come to understand Americans. Two years after he arrived, he was still making comments such as 'the trouble is one always thinks of these people as English and expects them to behave the same'.[95] Halifax left Washington on 13 May 1946; he had served for over five years. It was to make him the second longest serving UK ambassador to America of the twentieth century.

As explained in the Introduction, Halifax's ambassadorship tends to be seen as a wartime one and the commentary by Harold Ickes (Secretary of the Interior) on Halifax when he left Washington seems to support this view:

I am bound to say that during the war Lord Halifax did an outstanding job here. He performed wonders in helping to bring about a better understanding between our two countries and an appreciation here of what Great Britain stood for and what her place in the post war world would mean to civilisation as well as to the United States of America. The effect of his services here, in my judgement, will be felt for many years to come.[96]

The focus here, however, is on the post-war period when, as suggested above, Halifax took a more active role. It is a period of Halifax's ambassadorship which is infrequently discussed in the literature. It is a gap which, in part, this book seeks to fill.

Halifax's successor was firmly in the camp of professional diplomat; according to Hugh Dalton he was 'one of our very best diplomats'.[97] He was also a contrast to Halifax. Halifax was staid and measured in almost everything he did, whereas Lord Inverchapel could be flamboyant and on occasions eccentric. Halifax went to Washington under protest; it was for him a form of banishment from British politics. For Inverchapel, it was the crowning moment of his career. Halifax grew to accept if not enjoy life in Washington.[98] Inverchapel came to dislike Washington and became bored with the lifestyle there.

After the first conference of foreign ministers in London in September 1945, Sir Archibald Clark Kerr, as Inverchapel was then known, the then British ambassador in Moscow, wrote to Ernest Bevin: 'You have now had a close up of Molotov for three weeks. I have had three and a half years of him and I should like to persuade you to agree with me that three and a half years of that rigid, stubborn and not always honest man are enough.' Clark Kerr continued, perhaps mindful of not wanting to appear washed out, 'I cannot claim the easy refuge of many – ill health, for my health is good, nor fatigue, for I am not tired, but...the time has come for a fresh mind in Moscow'.[99] There was only one position that could be regarded as promotion for Clark Kerr: the ambassadorship in Washington.

Bevin admired Clark Kerr's work in Moscow.[100] On 16 January 1946 Bevin met with Clark Kerr in the Foreign Office. Bevin offered him the post of ambassador to the United States of America. Clark Kerr's obvious delight was greeted with 'Ah, Archie, I know you want the job, but you needn't think you're the best man for it. What you are is a member of the Union and I'm the General Secretary. So you're going to get it'.[101] After the political appointments of Lothian and Halifax, Bevin was reverting to the practice of sending a professional diplomat to Washington. The 'General Secretary' was to reverse this closed shop practice two years later with the appointment of Oliver Franks.

Archibald John Clark Kerr was born in Australia in 1882. His father, John Clark Kerr, owned a sheep station near Sydney, and his mother was the daughter of Sir John Robertson, Prime Minister of New South Wales.[102] The family returned to England in 1889, in part to educate the children. Clark Kerr attended Bath College and afterwards toured Europe in order to study languages. In 1906, after the second attempt, he succeeded in passing the examinations necessary for entry into the diplomatic service. Clark Kerr's first posting was to Berlin, where he remained until 1910 after which he spent a short spell in Buenos Aires. In April 1911, by which time he was a Third Secretary, he was sent to Washington. Washington at that time was a small mission with only nine diplomats and the ambassador was the Liberal politician James Bryce. Clark Kerr came to admire Bryce and began to adopt more liberal views. After Washington came promotion to Second Secretary and postings to Rome and Tehran before his return to the Foreign Office in 1916.

In 1922, Clark Kerr was posted to Cairo, where he served as the deputy to Lord Allenby the High Commissioner. Egyptian politics were a source of controversy at the time and Allenby's temperament did little to resolve the situation. The Foreign Office blamed Clark Kerr for some of Allenby's more rash actions and, given that Clark Kerr had already fallen out with Sir William Tyrell, Under-Secretary in charge of staffing at the Foreign Office, a black mark was established against his name. It was Churchill who rescued Clark Kerr's career. This was somewhat ironic since Clark Kerr disliked Churchill and his politics.[103] Churchill had approved of Clark Kerr's actions in Egypt and after conversations with both Austen and Chamberlain managed to get the black mark against Clark Kerr's name lifted.

Clark Kerr's next posting was to Central America where, with the rank of minister, he was to head the tiny mission in Guatemala, although he also presented his credentials to several other small Central American countries. In 1928, he moved to Chile and it was here that he met and married Tita Diaz Salas, a woman 29 years younger than himself. In 1935, after a posting to Sweden, Clark Kerr was appointed ambassador to Iraq. From here, having reached the highest rank in the Foreign Service, Clark Kerr consolidated his position, firstly by being appointed ambassador to China from 1938 to 1942 and then as ambassador to the Soviet Union.

It was, of course, a difficult time to represent British interests in the Far East but as a firm opponent of appeasement Clark Kerr did all he could to pursue policies that would deter Japanese aggression. Britain, however, was in no position to offer practical support. A devastating blow for Clark Kerr during this period was that his wife left him to go and live in New York. This was to become, in due course, a significant motivating factor in Clark Kerr's attempts to persuade Bevin to send him to Washington. Clark Kerr was knighted in recognition of his notable successes in China and sent to Moscow, where he established his reputation as a brilliant diplomat.[104]

In Moscow, as Clark Kerr pointed out, 'the chiefest of my duties has been to smooth over rough places while the war was going on'.[105] The rough places were not only of Soviet origin. It was left to Clark Kerr in 1942 in Moscow to persuade Churchill to return to a meeting with Stalin and sign a joint communiqué after Churchill had taken umbrage at Stalin's behaviour. It was described by Clark Kerr's biographer as 'probably the most important diplomatic coup of his career'.[106] Several other successes followed, including the foreign ministers conference of 1943. Reporting on the conference to the House of Commons, Eden said 'I must pay a special tribute to the work of Sir Archibald Clark Kerr. Much of the preparatory laying of the ground that is necessary for such a conference fell to him and he has rendered already remarkable services to Anglo-Soviet understanding.'[107] The various successes in Moscow were recognised in 1944 by Clark Kerr's appointment as a Privy Councillor.

Clark Kerr left Moscow for the last time in January 1946. Before he took up his appointment in America, however, Bevin asked him to accept a one-off assignment to act as the mediator in talks between the Dutch government and the Indonesian Nationalists in the Dutch East

Indies. Through no fault of Inverchapel's, however, the mission was unsuccessful and after an 'exhausting ten weeks in SE Asia' Clark Kerr 'came back to London really very tired'.[108] This was not the best way to embark upon a demanding posting to America.[109]

After being introduced into the House of Lords, Lord Inverchapel, as Clark Kerr was now called, sailed for America on 23 May 1946. Walter Bell, his private secretary, who accompanied Inverchapel, recalls: 'On our journey to America Lord Inverchapel was obviously very depressed and daunted by the prospect. He was a bad speaker with rather inaudible delivery. He hated facts and figures... similarly he had no interest or understanding of economics. The American press were naturally deeply interested in such subjects.'[110] It was noted above that Halifax had identified the growing importance of an appreciation of financial matters. In the same letter, Halifax also noted that 'the work that the ambassador can do here has... developed... into that of super public relations'.[111] Inverchapel did not seem entirely suited to the evolving role the ambassador was expected to play. Additionally, America was the first democracy in which Inverchapel had served as an ambassador and consequently it was 'the first post where the media was off the leash'.[112]

Inverchapel was perhaps unsuited to the posting in other ways. He exhibited a number of eccentricities, some of which were relatively harmless such as continuing to write his dispatches with a quill pen and having his own piper play the bagpipes at 8 am underneath his guests' windows.[113] Others were not so harmless, such as a tendency to make shocking and controversial remarks. For example, when, arriving in the United States, he was asked what comment he had for the American people. He replied 'just tell them I have a red face and a big nose'.[114] Another event was to raise eyebrows. Inverchapel took Evgenii Yost, a Soviet national, to Washington as his valet. This was only a matter of months after the Gouzenko spy story [115] broke and it was revealed that Soviet espionage had been undertaken within the Manhattan programme in America. Yost was Inverchapel's servant in Moscow, and when Inverchapel left, he was given Yost by Stalin. Not only did the issue cause dismay in the FBI and the American press, but it also led to the matter being raised with Foreign Office ministers in

London. Bevin, whilst attending the conference in New York, had to write to Inverchapel to instruct him to part with Yost.[116] It is perhaps not surprising that Halifax, when debating his successor with Eden, said in respect of the suggested appointment of Inverchapel, 'I have a shade of doubt about it'.[117]

Against these failings and eccentricities must be placed the very real ability that Inverchapel possessed. Isaiah Berlin observed 'a charming man, full of wit & cleverness [and] is very persuasive'[118] Bevin, initially at least, regarded him as 'one of our very best men'.[119] He was highly experienced and someone who could, according to Nicholas Henderson, get something for nothing from a foreign government.[120] Whilst Inverchapel was not the best ambassador when it came to operating in the public domain, he was nevertheless very effective on the private side of Washington. 'He did . . . court opinion in Congress and established good relations with . . . the State Department'.[121] Marshall, when he was Secretary of State, was frequently absent from Washington but Inverchapel established good relations with the Under-Secretary Dean Acheson and his successor Robert Lovett. Inverchapel had also retained many friendships from his earlier days in Washington, including men such as Felix Frankfurter, an Associate Justice at the Supreme Court. Additionally, although 'Inverchapel did not take a very close interest in the machinery of the embassy'[122] he did manage to hold it together in the difficult post-war transition period.

Notwithstanding Inverchapel's aversion to public speaking, he toured the country delivering speeches on behalf of Britain. It must have been gruelling work. There are over 45 major speeches amongst Inverchapel's papers and nearly all of them contain the dual themes of defending the concept of the British Empire and explaining the nature of the new Labour government. A speech given to the Foreign Policy Association is not untypical. In defending the Labour Party, Inverchapel says 'there are those that suggest of late we have trifled with our heritage, because the Government now in power in my country was elected to take control of a large part of our economy . . . there will always be a few who see the threat to liberty wherever the State puts its hand . . . I should like to dispel any misgivings'. Referring to the Commonwealth in the same speech, he said 'all these territories are in different stages of development. Long ago we ceased to regard them as fields of exploitation... We see the British Empire... transformed into, one great free association of peoples.'[123] Defending Britain was a key part of the ambassador's role, particularly at a time when Britain was asking so much of America.

The summer of 1947 was a critical time for Anglo-American relations, yet notwithstanding this Inverchapel decided to return home to Scotland for two months during that summer. In October 1947, Bevin wrote to Inverchapel 'things are getting tough here and I want you to know how much my colleagues and I are relying on you to put things across in Washington to the utmost of your ability'.[124] Inverchapel's reply was feeble.[125] Shortly afterwards Bevin wrote again to Inverchapel:

> When the legislation for Marshall Aid has gone through we shall enter into a new phase of Anglo-American relations. Such a phase is likely to last for a number of years... it would be in the national interest that we should try to maintain the same ambassador in Washington throughout that period... Prime Minister and I therefore have decided to make a change.[126]

Inverchapel replied 'I am only too glad to fall in with your plan'.[127] Inverchapel was to leave when the Marshall Plan legislation had gone through Congress, i.e. in the middle of 1948. He was, according to William Edwards, 'very angry at the Foreign Office for the way he was treated'.[128]

Henry Brandon, who was the *Sunday Times* correspondent in Washington during Inverchapel's tenure, suggests that he was the wrong choice for Washington. Further, he says 'he came to Washington for the wrong reasons, one of them was he assumed it might persuade his estranged wife to remarry him (which she did) and another that he wanted to crown his career there'.[129] These, however, do seem to be particularly inappropriate reasons. A better explanation as to why he may have been an inappropriate choice is that he found it difficult to adapt to post-war Washington, where the nexus of diplomacy was moving from the political to the economic. It was a much harsher place than the Washington he had left over 30 years before. The city demanded an adherence to convention both politically and socially; Inverchapel could not oblige. Also, in common with many in the post-war world, he was tired. John Hersey, an American journalist who had known Inverchapel in China and the Soviet Union, commented 'I remember, at a dinner at the embassy, seeing the look of an unhappy man; the zest of other times was just not there'.[130] Reflecting on his two years as ambassador, Inverchapel said 'They have been two uncommonly lively years, brawly, ugly, with some shining exceptions. A multitude of unhappy events have scarred and disfigured them.'[131]

Having looked at the structure of the embassy and the background of some of the key personnel within it, we now consider the environment within which the ambassador and the embassy operated; that is, the American political system. It was a system that vexed British diplomats. Robert Brand commented 'In many ways [America] is exasperating to deal with. That is made certain...by the endlessly unfortunate consequences of the Constitution which the Founding Fathers gave it.'[132] It was nevertheless a system within which the embassy needed to manoeuvre and one which it needed to understand. Of particular interest to the embassy was the conduct of foreign policy. The American Constitution, informed by the principle of the separation of powers, does not allow for one focal point for the conduct of foreign policy: 'there is no single source of authority in Washington for the conduct of foreign affairs'.[133] Given that one of the roles of the embassy was to influence American foreign policy, it needed to be mindful of where it brought that influence to bear. The principal options were the executive, the legislature and the public.

The apex of the pyramid and the single person with the most influence on foreign policy was the President. Although constrained by Congress he did, and still does, nevertheless have considerable powers. It was, of course, important for the embassy, if possible, to maintain close relations with the President. It was noted above how close Halifax was to Roosevelt, and he also developed a good relationship with Truman. Halifax met with Truman on many occasions and knew him from the time when he had been Vice President. The embassy, conscious of the effect of Roosevelt's death on embassy relationships,

had within days of the President's death set out the possible consequences for Anglo-American relations and additionally suggested that
'new ties are forged to replace those which [the] death of Mr Roosevelt
so tragically snapped'.[134]

There is no evidence at all that Inverchapel was close to Truman.
He met with Truman on four occasions in 1946, once to present his
credentials on 5 June, once to introduce the Archbishop of Canterbury
to the President on 20 September and twice to accompany ministers
to meetings with the President: Dalton on 2 October and Bevin on
3 December.[135] Whether the ambassador was close to the President or
not, a strategy used by the embassy was to attempt to influence those
who were close to the President.

In addition to the White House staff, there were 'special presidential agents'; men who were close to the President and who had
considerable influence over him.[136] The classic example of a special
presidential agent was Harry Hopkins, who carried out missions for
both Roosevelt and Truman. Others in this category might include
Bernard Baruch, 'a counsellor to six Presidents', Samuel Rosenman,
who worked for both Roosevelt and Truman, and even former
President Herbert Hoover, who Truman sent to Germany in 1947 to
ascertain German food requirements. The embassy, in particular the
ambassadors, sought to develop close relationships with these agents
and use them as appropriate. Halifax was very close to Hopkins until
his death in January 1946 and both Halifax and Inverchapel knew
Baruch and Rosenman.

The White House staff could also exert considerable influence on
foreign policy. This was obviously the case with people such as Fleet
Admiral William D. Leahy, Truman's chief of staff, but less clearly
so with more junior staff; for example, David Niles, Administrative
Assistant to the President.[137] Niles played a crucial role, as described in
chapter 4, in the President's Palestinian policy. The embassy attempted
to constantly monitor the people who were close or became close to the
President. For example, under the heading 'The New Power behind the
Throne' the embassy, in a supplement to its Weekly Political Report,
identified Clark Clifford, a recently appointed special counsel to the
President, as Truman's new and 'most intimate adviser'.[138]

The embassy clearly understood the importance of the individual in American politics. The Reports Division produced a publication entitled *Leading Personalities in the United States* which listed, with biographical details, approximately 300 people who were thought to be of importance to Britain. In addition to certain Congressman and White House staff, the list included officials in other government departments, members of the Judiciary, senior officers in the military, State Governors, Trade Union officials, businessman, economists and important religious leaders.[139]

The body within the executive branch that had 'the principal responsibility, under the President, for the determination of the policy of the Government in relation to international problems' was the Department of State.[140] It was also the department with which the embassy had the most contact, being the first port of call if the embassy needed to communicate officially with the American government.[141] The Department of State then assumed considerable importance for the embassy in the conduct of its relations with the US Administration. Like the embassy, the Department of State underwent considerable change in the immediate post-war period. 'The department and its autonomous arm the Foreign Service...quadrupled their personnel from 5,250 in 1939 to 20,000 on July 1 1947'. The department itself grew from 2,755 employees in 1938 to 7,290 by March 1947.[142] The increase in size was a reflection of the growing importance of America's worldwide role and the fact that Truman felt that some wartime agencies should have a permanent role in federal government.

Other than a short period when Edward Stettinius was Secretary of State, the department during the period under review was led firstly by James Byrnes and then by George Marshall. Byrnes was appointed Secretary of State in July 1945. He was elected to the House of Representatives in 1910 and the Senate in 1930. In 1941, Roosevelt appointed him to the Supreme Court; a year later, at the President's request, he resigned to become first the Director of the Office of Economic Stabilisation and then the Director of the Office of War Mobilisation and Reconversion.[143] According to David Anderson, 'Byrnes was one of the most powerful politicians in the United States in the 1930s and 1940s. His former Senate colleagues approved his appointments to the Supreme court and as Secretary of State unanimously without even conducting hearings.'[144] Byrnes was favourably disposed towards Britain: 'He delivered more than one vigorous speech in favour of aid to Britain and it is now established that the Lend Lease Law came through the Senate as well as it did because of his able sponsorship'.[145] At the time of Byrnes' appointment, Halifax observed that 'he promises to be a tactful, friendly, reasonable and accessible Secretary of State, but one liable to oscillate under strong political pressure'.[146] Whether as a result of ill heath[147] or because of policy differences with Truman over the Soviets,[148] Byrnes resigned in January 1947.[149] Byrnes went on to become Governor of South Carolina from 1951 to 1955. He eventually broke from the Democratic Party completely, endorsing Nixon in 1960 and Goldwater in 1964.

Byrnes was succeeded by George Marshall, the first military man to occupy the post. Marshall graduated from the Virginia Military Institute in 1901 and after distinguished service in France in World War I, he progressed gradually through the Army ranks until he was selected by Roosevelt, in 1939, to be his Chief of Staff at which time he was also promoted to the rank of General. Marshall became the unofficial leader of the Joint Chiefs and the first among equals within the Combined Chiefs. To Churchill, he was by the war's end the true organiser of victory. Marshall had considerable experience in international relations. He attended all ten Anglo-American and three Anglo-Soviet-American summit conferences during the war as well as undertaking a mission to China on behalf of Truman.[150] Marshall's two-year tenure as Secretary of State was characterised by increasing Soviet truculence and acceptance by America that she needed to take a major role in international affairs. Marshall had the virtue of being admired and respected by Congress and had 'convinced the public that as Secretary of State he [was] non partisan and above politics'.[151] Marshall retired from the Department of State in 1948. He was recalled by Truman during the Korean crisis to become Secretary of Defence. In 1953, he became the first professional soldier to be awarded the Nobel Peace Prize, in recognition of his part in the European Recovery Plan.

It is perhaps interesting to note that the relationship between the British ambassadors in Washington, whether that be Halifax or Inverchapel, and the Secretaries of State, whether that be Byrnes or Marshall, was not quite as significant as might be thought. There are two reasons for this. Firstly, both Byrnes and Marshall were out of Washington for considerable periods of time attending international conferences and so it was often difficult for the ambassador to arrange meetings with them. Secondly because there was, as a result of some of these conferences, direct contact between the Secretaries of State and their opposite number Bevin, there was perhaps less need for traditional diplomacy. Halifax, who knew Byrnes during the war, had some contact with him. They met to discuss the possibility of Britain transferring bases to America and to consider the setting up of the Anglo-American Committee of Enquiry into Palestine, and they both sat on the Combined Policy Committee, which dealt with atomic energy collaboration. They were not, however, as has already been noted, particularly close. There is little evidence that Inverchapel spent much time with Byrnes, although he believed he had 'succeeded in establishing harmonious relations with him',[152] and Inverchapel only met with Marshall on six occasions in 1947 and three in 1948 – not a great deal considering the events of the time.[153] One consequence of the limited contact between the embassy and the Secretaries of State is to elevate the importance of their deputies and other senior members of the department. Four stand out: Dean Acheson, William Clayton, George Kennan and Robert Lovett.

Dean Acheson, who was himself to become Secretary of State in 1948, studied law at Harvard under Felix Frankfurter. His first government position was as Under-Secretary in the Treasury Department in 1933. He resigned after eight months, however, following a disagreement with Roosevelt. He returned to government in 1941 as an Assistant Secretary of State for Economic Affairs. In this position, he was responsible for negotiating Lend Lease terms with Britain. In August 1945 he was appointed Under-Secretary of State, a position he remained in until July 1947 when he temporarily left government in order to restore his fortunes by practising law. During Byrnes' long absences at various international conferences, Acheson developed a strong rapport with Truman and had considerable influence for an Under-Secretary. Acheson's view of the Soviets perhaps mirrored that of the Administration, with early optimism giving way to recognition that there would be a long period of difficult relations with them.[154]

William Clayton, or 'Doctrinaire Willie' as Hugh Dalton called him, was a highly successful self-made cotton trader who was independently wealthy. He entered government service in 1940 and became Assistant Secretary of Commerce in 1942. At the end of 1944, he became Assistant Secretary of State in charge of Foreign Economic Affairs and he was promoted in 1946 to the newly created position of Under-Secretary of State for Economic Affairs. Clayton was also, inter alia, a Director of the Export Import Bank, a representative on the Governing Council of UNRRA and an alternate Governor for the International Monetary Fund. Clayton was an honest and competent negotiator and, according to the embassy, 'never betrayed any anti British bias, but his hostility to Government "meddling" with the economic machine may lead him to sharp opposition towards some British economic policies'.[155] Clayton played a significant role in the negotiation of the Financial Agreement between Britain and America in 1945 and he was very influential in the formulation of the Marshall Plan.[156]

George Kennan was a Foreign Service Officer who specialised in Soviet Affairs; he is acknowledged to be the originator of the policy of containment that was practised during the Cold War. Kennan was Averell Harriman's (American ambassador in Moscow 1943 to 1946) right-hand man in Moscow between 1944 and 1946. His service therefore crossed with that of both John Balfour and Lord Inverchapel. In 1947, Kennan was appointed by Marshall to head up a new unit in the Department of State, the Policy Planning Staff. It was this unit which nurtured the various proposals which led eventually to the Marshall Plan. Kennan later served as the American ambassador in both Russia and Yugoslavia.[157]

The other personality who had considerable contact with the embassy during this period was Robert Lovett. After a successful business career, Lovett joined the Administration in 1940 becoming a special assistant to Henry Stimson, who was then Secretary of War. Lovett was quickly promoted to the position of Assistant Secretary of War for Air in 1941, a post he held until 1945 when he temporarily returned to business. He returned to succeed Acheson as Under-Secretary of State in July 1947. He remained in the Department of State until 1949. The embassy noted that Lovett was 'exceedingly friendly to Great Britain' and was 'an excellent man to do business with'.[158] Lovett worked with the embassy to remove the obstacles which stood in the way of a successful passage of the Marshall Plan proposals through Congress.[159]

The structure of the Department of State as at August 1947 and one year prior to that is given in Chart II. The chart shows the top level within the department at different times and the positions occupied by the people mentioned above.[160] Beneath this top level and common to both periods there were the political departments: over 20 of them, grouped into regions. Two important regions for the British were the Office of European Affairs, headed by John Hickerson, and the Office of Near Eastern and African Affairs, headed by Loy Henderson.[161] The Chancery section of the embassy, as noted above, attempted to tailor its political specialisations to these departments.

The closeness of the embassy to officials in the department is evidenced by, for example, a letter written by Jock Balfour to Neville Butler at the Foreign Office. In the letter, Balfour records a post-dinner conversation between himself, Chip Bohlen (Counsellor to George Marshall) and Dean Acheson, where the department officials were ruminating about the problems in the Department of State and the need for a reorganisation. Acheson grumbled about the 'inadequacy of meetings of departmental chiefs' and the tendency for officials to 'concentrate their efforts on expressing their own views as to how US policy should be conducted, instead of confining themselves to the task of presenting to their superiors balanced appreciations of the matters in which they specialise'. Interestingly, Bohlen, who was an ex-foreign service officer rather than someone brought into the department on a temporary basis like Acheson, 'expressed the opinion that difficulties in the way of establishing a coordinated US foreign policy lay in the American system of government rather than in any defect of organisation within the State Department itself'. It was an interesting conversation to be having in front of a foreign diplomat; Balfour must

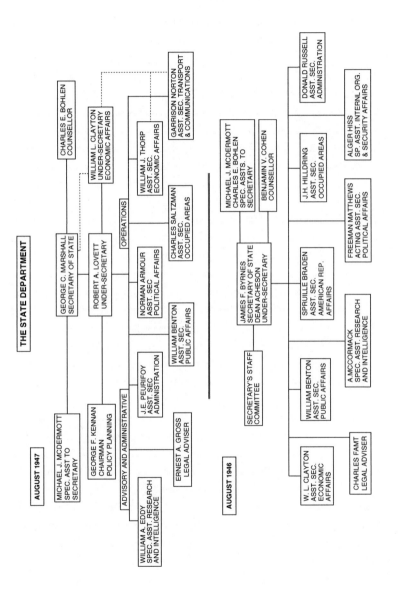

THE STATE DEPARTMENT

AUGUST 1947

GEORGE C. MARSHALL
SECRETARY OF STATE

CHARLES E. BOHLEN
COUNSELLOR

ROBERT A. LOVETT
UNDER-SECRETARY

WILLIAM L. CLAYTON
UNDER-SECRETARY
ECONOMIC AFFAIRS

MICHAEL J. MCDERMOTT
SPEC. ASST TO
SECRETARY

GEORGE F. KENNAN
CHAIRMAN
POLICY PLANNING

ADVISORY AND ADMINISTRATIVE

OPERATIONS

J.E. PEURIFOY
ASST. SEC
ADMINISTRATION

NORMAN ARMOUR
ASST. SEC
POLITICAL AFFAIRS

WILLIAM J. THORP
ASST. SEC.
ECONOMIC AFFAIRS

GARRISON NORTON
ASST. SEC. TRANSPORT
& COMMUNICATIONS

WILLIAM A. EDDY
SPEC. ASST. RESEARCH
AND INTELLIGENCE

ERNEST A. GROSS
LEGAL ADVISER

WILLIAM BENTON
ASST. SEC.
PUBLIC AFFAIRS

CHARLES SALTZMAN
ASST. SEC.
OCCUPIED AREAS

AUGUST 1946

JAMES F. BYRNES
SECRETARY OF STATE
DEAN ACHESON
UNDER-SECRETARY

MICHAEL J. MCDERMOTT
CHARLES E. BOHLEN
SPEC. ASSTS. TO
SECRETARY

BENJAMIN V. COHEN
COUNSELLOR

SECRETARY'S STAFF
COMMITTEE

SPRUILLE BRADEN
ASST. SEC.
AMERICAN REP.

J.H. HILLDRING
ASST. SEC.
OCCUPIED AREAS

DONALD RUSSELL
ASST. SEC.
ADMINISTRATION

W. L. CLAYTON
ASST. SEC.
ECONOMIC
AFFAIRS

WILLIAM BENTON
ASST. SEC.
PUBLIC AFFAIRS

A. MCCORMACK
SPEC. ASST. RESEARCH
AND INTELLIGENCE

FREEMAN MATTHEWS
ACTING ASST. SEC.
POLITICAL AFFAIRS

ALGER HISS
SP. ASST. INTERNL. ORG.
& SECURITY AFFAIRS

CHARLES FAMT
LEGAL ADVISER

have been trusted.[162] On another occasion, Bohlen commented on 'the extraordinary place in the confidence of the State Department and of Congress that Jock Balfour has enjoyed'.[163]

The Department of State was not the only body within the executive that played a part in foreign policy making. Almost all the other departments would have had an influence, particularly the military, but perhaps the most significant outside of the Department of State was the Department of Treasury. The Treasury, through men such as Harry Dexter White, special assistant to the Secretary of the Treasury, was instrumental in the formation of the International Monetary Fund and the International Bank for Reconstruction and Development, both instruments of American foreign policy. The Treasury, too, was in the vanguard of the British Loan Agreement and other bilateral negotiations with Britain. The embassy, through its connection with the UK Treasury Delegation and eventually its own Finance Minister, maintained close connections with firstly Fred Vinson and then John Snyder, the two Treasury Secretaries in the Truman Administration.

Whilst the Department of State was the central foreign policy making body in Washington and the one with which the embassy had the most contact, it was not without a rival. Congress, which neither liked nor trusted the Department of State, frequently sought to subvert or modify the department's proposals.[164] Congress had the power to tax and appropriate funds. The increasing use of economic policy as a tool of foreign policy in the post-war period thus led to an increase in the power of Congress over foreign policy. Conflict often arose between the Administration and Congress, not only because of straightforward political differences between Democrats and Republicans, but also because 'public opinion presses in different ways upon Congress and President. The President has reason to look upon the nation as a whole, whereas Senators and Representatives feel the concentrated opinion of their smaller constituencies.'[165] A further factor that could lead Congressmen to subvert the Administration is that they were 'not actuated by the fear of bringing their Government down' in the way Members of Parliament are.[166]

The task for the embassy was, more often than not, twofold; firstly to convince the US Administration of a particular course of action and then to convince Congressmen. As Brand pointed out: 'Washington negotiations are always difficult. That is determined by the character of the United States Constitution.'[167] The embassy could not involve itself directly in American politics and lobby directly. It therefore fell back on more indirect methods such as appointing a Congressional liaison officer, as noted above, and by the ambassador and others entertaining Senators and Representatives directly. Halifax had regular weekly lunches with different Congressmen throughout his time in Washington. Keynes during the British loan negotiations believed that he would meet with a quarter of all Senators before he left Washington.[168]

The embassy and the Foreign Office monitored Congressional behaviour closely. For example, a chart was produced which gave the detailed voting record of Congressmen on the four key Congressional committees (i.e. both the Senate and the House Foreign Relations and Appropriations committees), in respect of foreign aid and economic policy issues. The chart detailed the voting record in respect of the Lend Lease, Reciprocal Trade Agreements, Bretton Woods Agreement, UNRRA Participation, British Loan Agreement and Greco-Turkish Aid.[169] Lists of Senators regarded as holding isolationist views were also maintained by the embassy. All of this information would have been enormously helpful when meeting with Congressmen and in trying to influence them.

Congress operated through over 80 committees. As suggested above, one of the most important was the Senate Committee on Foreign Relations.[170] The committee had strong powers and if it disapproved of a measure, there is little chance that the Senate would adopt it. The Chairman, too, was powerful. Not only was he listened to in the Senate and the country, he had the power to ignore the President's recommendations and not to bring a particular measure before the committee. The committee had 23 members selected from different parties in accordance with their strength, and the Chairman was chosen from the majority party. The Chairman in the 79th Congress, i.e. from January 1945 to December 1946 was Tom Connolly (Democrat, Texas). He was succeeded in the 80th Congress by Arthur Vandenberg (Republican, Michigan).[171]

A great deal of the embassy's time was taken up with analysing and reporting upon the differences between the Administration and

Congress. Where the Congressional attitude resulted in an adverse affect upon British interests the embassy would also, through education or other means, seek to convert Congressmen. This was a difficult and delicate task since the embassy could not be seen to be lobbying. One area, however, where it was possible to influence Congress was by influencing public opinion.

Public opinion was particularly important in America, partly because it was so open to influence by both domestic and foreign lobbies and partly because it was taken so much notice of by both the executive and the legislature. Public opinion can have two meanings in this context. Firstly, there is the opinion of the public at large, i.e. independent individuals spread throughout the population. The opinions of this group were often gathered through polls. Secondly, there is the opinion of groups of ordinary citizens who formed themselves into groups or organisations and who, by so doing, had considerable influence over foreign policy. The opinions of these groups which sometimes represented special interests were usually presented directly to the Administration or Congress.[172]

The courting of public opinion in America was almost institutionalised. In January 1944, the Department of State established the Office of Public Affairs. Its tasks included measuring public opinion, answering questions from the public on foreign policy and attempting to 'attract friendly public opinion to the projects in foreign policy which the Administration considered sound'.[173] It went further:

> When the General Assembly of the United Nations held its first meeting in London in January 1946, the Public Affairs Office sent the American delegation special surveys of public opinion. The delegates could and did modify their position when it was out of line with opinion at home. This daily reporting service helped guide Secretary of State Byrnes at the Paris peace conference in the summer of 1946.[174]

The groups or organisations such as the Chamber of Commerce, National Association of Manufacturers, the American Bar Association, the American Jewish Conference and the League of Women Voters,

to name a small selection, were extremely influential in the formation of foreign policy. For example, the Department of State invited
42 of them to send representatives to attend the international conference at San Francisco in the spring of 1945, which set up the United
Nations.[175] The Department of State also suggests that the British
Loan Agreement would not have been approved by Congress without
them. 'The majority of letters which members of Congress received on
the matter came from opponents of the credit. But many of the leading
organisations vigorously supported the credit and successfully urged
the House and Senate to vote in favour of it.'[176]

It is no surprise, then, that William Edwards wrote:

Public opinion counts for everything in this country. It is not sufficient for us merely to secure the support of the Administration
for any particular British policy through the ordinary processes
of diplomatic negotiation. It is essential also to secure the support of the American people and through them the American
Congress. The work therefore which our Information Services
do with the American public is the essential counterpart of our
strictly diplomatic work.[177]

Much of the work that the BIS did in America was effected through
the press. The press was probably the single most important factor
in the formation of public opinion. In the field of foreign affairs, the
important opinion-forming elements of the press were the correspondents abroad and the columnists in America; columnists such as Walter
Lippman, Drew Pearson and the Allsop brothers. Their articles could
appear in 600 to 800 newspapers throughout the country.[178] Although
the BIS was a large part of influencing American public opinion, there
was also another 'counterpart' to the 'strictly diplomatic work' and
that was the work other parts of the embassy already did to influence
American public opinion outside the press. It has already been noted
that both Halifax and Inverchapel spoke extensively to the organisations referred to above, that the attaché for Women's Affairs toured
the country speaking to women's organisations and that the Consuls
were aware of their obligation to court the public. The important

point, of course, is that the role of the embassy entailed communicating not only with the organs of state but also with ordinary citizens. This was a slightly unusual role to perform at the time and perhaps it was one that was peculiar to America. It was, however, an important role because, as Brand pointed out, the American government and the departments of the American government 'are more directly and immediately influenced by public opinion than any other Government in the world'.[179]

This chapter has pieced together the structure of the embassy in the immediate post-war period. At the same time, it has described the backgrounds to some of the important diplomats who operated in Washington at that time. A picture which emerges is that of an institution responding to change. It was not only changing personnel and structures which the embassy had to contend with but also a series of external changes as well. The death of Roosevelt, the election of a Labour government in Britain and a rapidly growing Department of State were all events which the embassy had to respond to. The chapter also briefly considered the various options open to diplomacy within the American political system. The embassy needed to operate on a broad front in America in order to get its message across. In the subsequent chapters, these issues are put together in the context of a number of events. The next chapter starts with a consideration of the Financial Agreement between Britain and America signed in December 1945.

CHAPTER 2

THE FINANCIAL AGREEMENT

The dollar sign is back in the Anglo-American equation.[1]

One of the first challenges faced by the embassy in the post-war period was the termination of Lend Lease. The concept of Lend Lease was introduced by President Roosevelt in 1940. In the period from the approval of Lend Lease through to 30 June 1945, America handed out over $42 billion. Of this Britain, received $13.5 billion but reciprocated $3.8 billion.[2] Congress allocated the funding for Lend Lease on the basis that it was to promote the defence of the United States.[3] Once the war had ended both in Europe and in the Far East, the purpose for which Lend Lease was did not exist any longer. Although this was debatable, Truman felt that he no longer had the authority to continue with the aid. Accordingly on 21 August 1945, the President announced that he 'had directed the Foreign Economic Administration to take steps immediately to discontinue all Lend Lease operations'.[4] This early action by Truman, which was against the advice of some of his closest advisers, demonstrates the Administration's wariness of the Congress.

The cancellation of Lend Lease, which, as Dell points out, was a 'surprise only to those in London determined to be surprised',[5] created for Britain an urgent need for American dollars. The only source of these dollars in the post-war world, other than Canada, was the United States itself, and because of the severe impact the war had upon Britain's export capabilities the only method of obtaining these dollars, in the short term, was by way of a grant or a loan. It was this shortage of dollars that led to America affording Britain a credit of $3.75 billion. This credit, together with its terms and conditions, became known as the Financial Agreement between the Governments of the United States and the United Kingdom (henceforth Financial Agreement or Loan Agreement) and was dated 6 December 1945. The Financial Agreement, however, was not approved by Congress until 15 July 1946. How, then, was this credit obtained? Who decided the terms and conditions? Who was responsible for negotiating the credit?

Traditionally, at least in Constitutional terms, it is the Cabinet, acting through Parliament, which determines Britain's policies. Domestic policy requires, and only requires (other than the royal prerogative), the will of Parliament to turn a policy into an action. Foreign policy, short of war, however, normally requires the approval or agreement of another government. The execution of foreign policy, i.e. turning it from a policy desire into an action, is dependent upon on a number of factors. One of these factors is negotiations with one or more other governments. These negotiations are often carried out by diplomats and other officials. A further factor influencing the execution of foreign policy is an appreciation of the environment and circumstances in which any policy desire is likely to be accepted. Put another way, a government is likely to maximise its chances of success by tailoring the presentation of its case to the prevailing climate at the time. The information needed to do this is often provided by the British embassy in the foreign country concerned.[6] An embassy, then, can play a significant part in the implementation of foreign policy. The embassy in Washington certainly played a major part in the securing of the $3.75 billion credit from the Americans in 1945.

The role the embassy played in both the pre-negotiation stage and the negotiations themselves in determining the terms of the Financial Agreement is considered below. Once the terms of the Financial Agreement had been settled, it was necessary for the US Administration to present them to Congress for approval. The part the embassy played in influencing Congress is also considered below.

The build-up to the loan negotiations had a significant impact on the outcome of the negotiations themselves. In any negotiation, it is important for both the negotiators and the principals to understand the negotiating environment, how it is changing and the pressures on the opposing team. The embassy was involved in providing this information in a systematic way. The negotiating teams and the dynamics within them and between them are also crucial in discussions of this nature. Members of the embassy were part of the negotiating team and in a variety of ad hoc ways were involved in the dynamic that existed between members of the British team and also with members of the American team. Before considering these issues, however, it is necessary to examine some of the events which took place prior to the negotiations but which had a material impact upon them. The embassy was involved in these events in a number of ways.

An event which had an overwhelming impact upon the negotiations was the circulation of Keynes' now famous paper, entitled 'Overseas Financial Policy in Stage III'.[7] By the end of World War II, Britain had lost one-quarter of its wealth, had sterling debts equivalent to $14 billion and the volume of its exports had declined by over two-thirds.[8] Before World War I, Britain was by far the world's largest creditor. By the end of the second, she had the largest external debt in history.[9]

Keynes' paper highlighted three major problems: high external debt, a weakened export industry and high government expenditure overseas. Keynes then set out three alternative solutions to Britain's financial predicament: 'starvation corner',[10] 'temptation' and 'justice'. 'Starvation corner' implied an isolationist Britain, exercising complete financial independence of America. This was a bleak prospect and one not seriously contemplated. 'Temptation' would involve a credit of some sort from the Americans, possibly up to $8 billion, in exchange for accepting an array of American conditions including sterling convertibility and the full implementation of the free trade proposals implied in Article VII of the Mutual Aid Legislation. Keynes was against temptation as a solution for two reasons. Firstly, he objected to Britain's resultant indebtedness, which if sterling balances were included amounted to a figure of some $20 billion (a figure he suggested was similar to the amount the Russians were demanding as reparations from Germany). Secondly, he objected on the grounds of fairness. According to Keynes, it was not that 'a settlement would ... be unduly onerous financially or economically' but because such a settlement would fail 'to measure up to the criterion of Justice'.[11] 'Justice' was Keynes' third alternative.

'Justice' to Keynes entailed an approach that was based upon 'a general reconsideration of the proper burden of the costs of war'.[12] Keynes suggested that the post-war burden borne by the UK was 'disproportionate to what is fair'. With justice, the United States would be asked to take account of the estimated $3 billion spent by the UK in America when she fought alone at the beginning of the war; i.e. the United States was to refund the UK with a 'sort of retrospective lend lease'.[13] Additionally the United States was to provide the UK with a call of up to $5 billion over a ten-year period. Further, Britain would approach the holders of sterling balances estimated, at that time, to be some $12 billion at the end of the war and, in overall terms, ask them to contribute, i.e. write off 25% of their balances.[14] (Of the remaining balance, 50% would be funded and 25% would be fully liquid and convertible.) Canada was also to contribute $500 million. In exchange for all of this, Britain would cooperate with the Americans to create a world economy based upon multilateral trade.

Keynes' paper ends with an analysis of how 'such proposals be presented with the best hope of conviction to the people of the United States and to the countries of the sterling area'.[15] These proposals are the essence of Keynes' anticipated negotiating stance. Britain fought the war alone for a period, spent considerable sums of money on munitions and other goods in the United States and consequently shouldered an unfair burden for the costs of the war. If Britain was asked to continue to carry this burden, then she and others in the sterling area would be unable to participate in the free international economy, something on 'which the Americans have set their hearts'. Keynes pointed out that the Americans had a surplus which they would need to recycle and, in any event, the amounts proposed were small for the Americans: 'The contribution proposed ($3 billion) is the cost of the war to the United States for a fortnight.'[16] The essence of Keynes' proposal, then, was that America would provide Britain with grant aid; i.e. America would give Britain billions of dollars in exchange for Britain liberalising its currency and trading constraints and in consideration of Britain's unfair share of the cost of war. The document, together with variations upon it, formed the basis of the British approach to the Loan Agreement negotiations. To what extent did the embassy influence or seek to influence this document? The official in Washington who had the most contact with Keynes was Robert Brand. Brand corresponded with Keynes nearly every day from Washington for the last two- and- a-half years of his life.[17] The correspondence included not only commentary upon Keynes' economic proposals but also advice on how those proposals might be received in America. Brand was against any talk of justice. In his first letter to Keynes after he had read 'Overseas Financial Policy in Stage III', Brand warned that Justice 'will never be a popular argument here or one which is desirable to stress or one we can carry far without provoking serious reactions'.[18] In the same letter, Brand also says 'I do not think it will be easy to get a free grant of money as a sort of restitution'. Brand was consistent in his view that a free gift would not be available and that words like 'justice' should not be used in any negotiations with the Americans.[19] Another issue which Brand was consistent about was the need for Britain to enter into commercial negotiations at the same time as the financial discussions were taking place. Keynes was hoping to, at least in part, divorce the two so as not to be pressured into an agreement on trade because of the need for a credit. Brand, however, advised him that he could not 'conceive that the financial negotiations will be altogether divorced from the commercial negotiations'.[20]

Keynes wrote his paper when Roosevelt was still in office, and he seemed to predicate his tactics on Roosevelt remaining in office. In a letter to Brand, Keynes suggested that the arrangement between Britain and America with regard to Stage III assistance 'ought to come as a coup d'état from the President'.[21] Keynes' tactics, however, did not seem to alter significantly with the arrival of Truman in April 1945. Brand felt differently: 'The advent of a new President, of course, changes the picture a great deal. His personality and background and his relative lack of experience, all indicate that the role of Congress will be very important.'[22] Brand went on to amplify the point, suggesting in the same letter that a campaign of educating the American public about Britain's plight and requirements in the post-war period should be undertaken. He even suggested the method:

> my idea would be to get some articles written in, say, Foreign Affairs, Atlantic Monthly, Yale Review etc which will indicate to those who can easily understand the character of our problems. If the elite understand, the knowledge will fairly soon trickle down over a wide area covering many of those, who make public opin-ion...In addition one could stimulate Walter Lippmann and a few others to take the right road and take steps to see some lead-ing Congressmen and Senators.

Brand was well aware that power had shifted from the Administration to Congress and that this would have consequential effects on the Financial Agreement negotiations. The embassy then, in the form of Robert Brand, gave a very clear indication that the strategy being developed by Keynes would not go down well in America.

Aside from Keynes' memorandum, other key events in the pre-negotiating period were the visits to London by prominent officials and advisers from the American Administration. The importance of the embassy's closeness to the 'special Presidential agents' referred to in chap-ter 1 is underlined by the fact that both Rosenman and Baruch were sent to Britain by Roosevelt to discuss post-war financial aid, among other topics. Rosenman met with Keynes and other Treasury officials and indi-cated to them that he had been charged by Roosevelt to enquire into the 'UK's need for financial assistance from the USA in Phase (Stage) III'.[23] Rosenman met with both Halifax and Brand prior to his departure.[24] Consequently, Keynes and the other officials were briefed before the meet-ing. As Brand put it, 'I felt sure that it would be regarded as most valu-able that a man in his important position, should learn at first hand the problems...of the United Kingdom and the British Commonwealth'.[25]

Baruch also visited Britain in early April 1945 at the behest of Roosevelt, because as Baruch says 'having in mind my long and inti-mate friendship with the Prime Minister [Churchill] extending over thirty years President Roosevelt felt that a frank, candid interchange of thoughts between us would be mutually helpful for our two countries'.[26]

In his report to the President, Baruch indicated that Keynes and the Bank of England were to ask America for a gift of $5 to $8 billion, something which Baruch was very much against. Baruch's report, although originally envisaged for Roosevelt, was actually sent to Truman and Stettinius. Truman asked for it not to be circulated other than to Will Clayton.[27] Churchill's and the embassy's closeness to Baruch was to prove to be important as the Financial Agreement was passing through Congress, a subject which is discussed further below.

Clayton, who was discussed in the previous chapter, was a crucial figure in post-war Anglo-American relations. As the embassy reported, 'the appointment of Mr Clayton to the newly created post of Assistant Secretary of State for Economic Affairs may prove to have been one of the most important appointments in recent times'.[28] Clayton foresaw that the end of the war offered a good opportunity to liberalise American trade policies. He also foresaw the dangers, however: 'My conclusion is that the most careful and intelligent plans on a community or industry basis can easily prove to be of little if any help in providing a satisfactory level of employment if we make a mess of our international economic and financial relationships as we did in the last peace conference and during the interwar period.'[29]

Brand visited Clayton in the State Department in January 1945. He had known Clayton for many years and thought highly of him. He indicated that 'Clayton will be fundamentally a much sounder guide as to what is and is not possible here'.[30] Brand also took the opportunity to educate Clayton about Britain's predicament, going as far as sending him copies of papers and reports on Britain's position. After enquiring into Clayton's new role, Brand concluded that 'Clayton will, under the new regime, have much more authority than [his] predecessors'. Interestingly, in response to a statement by Brand that he assumed that all financial problems between the American and British governments were a matter for the Treasury, Clayton countered with: 'under the American system of government all problems relating to foreign governments came first to the State Department. If, therefore, there was a question of a loan or credit facilities to a foreign government that would be a matter, in the first place, for the State Department.'[31] Brand had perhaps touched on a

sore point here. It is interesting to note that by August 1945 Fred
Vinson (Treasury Secretary) felt compelled to write to Truman referring to Clayton's talks with the British Treasury. 'It is my opinion
that we should not make any further commitments in London but
should hold discussions among ourselves and arrive at a position to
be taken when the British come here in September.'[32]

Brand wrote to Keynes in April 1945 reporting that Clayton was
regarded as a 'Manchester free trader' and, although his views were held
sincerely, 'he can and is likely to be rigid and obstinate'.[33] Brand also
reported that there was a wide gulf between the views of Clayton and
those of the American public and Congress. Brand dined with Clayton
in early June 1945 and again discussed with him Britain's position and
the timing of any Stage III talks. With Britain's problems looming
large and the possibility, at least, of the Japanese war ending quickly,
both Clayton and Brand agreed that they should wait no longer than
September to begin Stage III talks. At their meeting, Brand discovered that Clayton would be in London in early August; this would
be an ideal occasion to have pre-talk discussions. The information on
Clayton and his views, of which the above is only one example, could
have been of considerable help to Keynes and others in attempting to
formulate a negotiating strategy for the Financial Agreement.

Clayton arrived in London in early August with very clear views as
to what he wanted. In a memorandum to Vinson, he indicated that
Britain's financial problems were the greatest barrier to multilateral
trade and that it was therefore 'definitely in our [America's] interest
to give Britain the financial help required to bridge the transition
to peacetime equilibrium'. In the same memorandum, however, he
indicated that an outright gift would be unwise, as would any form
of credit without 'laying down conditions that would ensure a sound
advance towards our [America's] post war objectives'.[34]

There were several meetings in London during August, the importance of which was not lost upon the British. Hall Patch offered a 'word
of warning to those who will conduct these initial discussions with Mr
Clayton. We shall be playing for large stakes and these initial discussions
may set the tone for the all important discussions on Stage III which are
at present arranged to take place in Washington in the autumn.'[35]

Perhaps it was a pity, then, that Keynes set out virtually the whole of the British case for funding and got in return a frank view of what the Americans were prepared to offer.

In pursuing his concept of justice, Keynes suggested that the Americans offer the British a gift of around $5 billion in return for which Britain would ratify Bretton Woods, liberalise the sterling area and move towards convertibility. If the Americans failed to accede to this request, Britain would be forced to insulate herself in the sterling trading bloc with all the repercussions that implied for Britain and, indeed, America. Clayton's response was that 'the British should not expect to get financial assistance in the form of free grant'.[36] Further, he indicated that there would be no financial assistance at all without a clear commitment to multilateral trade and a substantial removal of the barriers to it. Whilst the Americans were concerned that Britain might go down the bilateral trading route, they also saw through Keynes' position: 'to cover a basically very weak financial position with a very serious outlook the British are putting up a very determined front'.[37] The advice the embassy had given earlier in the year was consistent with the position being taken by Clayton.

Whilst the above-mentioned deliberations between American and British officials were taking place, the embassy continued with a pivotal part of its work, i.e. the reporting of the American mood and atmosphere to London. As a correspondent of Keynes noted: 'explaining a foreign country to your own country is now the hardest and yet the most important part of diplomacy'.[38] It was a task made considerably more difficult for the embassy by the pace of events in 1945. At the time Keynes wrote his memorandum neither he nor anyone else could have imagined that in six months' time there would be a Labour government, the war would be over, Lend Lease would have stopped and he would be negotiating in Washington with a new administration.

As noted in chapter 1, the embassy produced Weekly Political Reports and supplements thereto. These reports were based upon surveys from the American press, as well as

consular reports from various key posts in the country and those of the BIS offices in New York and several other important cities

and, not least, exchanges with well informed observers of the
Washington scene – officials, politicians, journalists, diplomats – as well as such information as members of the British
Embassy and other British missions came by in the course of
their regular work.[39]

A further source, not mentioned by Isaiah Berlin in his introduction to
Washington Dispatches but frequently used by the embassy, was Gallup
polls. They were useful for a number of reasons, an important one
being to track American opinion of the British.

The position of America at the end of the war contrasted sharply
with Britain's. American national output had more than doubled in
real terms. America's GNP rose from $91 billion in 1939 to $219 billion in 1945. Manufacturing volume trebled and exports flourished.[40]
This affluence, however, did not necessarily mean that America was
prepared to hand out unconditional aid to Britain. After four years
of war, the US Administration, as Brand and Halifax implied, also
needed to be mindful of the mood of the American population and
that of the Congress. America had made a significant contribution
during the war and there were those in Congress who felt no more
overseas aid should be given.

One strand of opinion which the British always needed to be mindful of was isolationism. In March 1945, the embassy reported: 'As for
Isolationism it has . . . shifted from the political front . . . and moved to
economic fields where it can operate in a much more disguised if even
more destructive fashion.'[41] A further change that was taking place
with the war ending was that Congress was beginning to reassert
itself. In April 1945, the embassy in a supplementary political report
warned that 'the Lend Lease Bill, like all economic issues at present,
aroused a real opposition to the Administration'.[42] In the same supplementary report, the embassy reported the results of a 'confidential
unpublished Gallup poll', which indicated that '30% think that the
United States has "nothing" or "not much" to gain from England after
the war'.[43]

In addition to the regular political reports, individual members
of the embassy also provided their own analysis of events. A notable

contributor in this category was John Balfour. In a report written to the Foreign Office in August 1945, Balfour sought to put Britain's position in some perspective. 'During recent months the concept has steadily gained ground in this country that Great Britain has come to occupy a position on the world stage which in terms of power and influence is inferior to that of the USA and the USSR.' Elsewhere in the report, Balfour says: 'In our own bilateral dealings with the United States Government we should be careful to formulate requests for their support in such a manner as to avoid the appearance of teaching the Americans where their best interests lie.'[44] Perhaps this was an attempt to tone down some of the perceived arrogance in the Foreign Office and elsewhere in the Civil Service.[45]

The embassy did not restrict itself to analysis; it was prepared to offer advice. Balfour provided clear advice in another despatch which analysed the reasons for the abrupt termination of Lend Lease in August 1945:

> The conclusions which this picture suggests are: First, that Clayton should come back as soon as possible and use his influence to stiffen Byrnes...Secondly, it seems important that the main discussions on Stage III should be opened here as soon as possible. Thirdly, as regards tactics it is evident that, from the point of view of personalities, the worst position for us is to have Crowley in sole charge of the negotiations about Lend Lease on the American side.[46]

Balfour warned that 'You should be aware that with the passing of time and the changes of personnel here, there is a certain contraction of view in the Administration on some of the broad issues affecting our relationship. The dollar sign is back in the Anglo-American equation.'[47] It is possible that Balfour's messages in addition to the termination of Lend Lease inculcated London with a sense of urgency precipitating the meeting of ministers on 23 August.

It was this meeting that perhaps cemented the approach to be taken in the Loan Agreement negotiations. Attlee stated that the purpose of the meeting on the 23rd was to consider 'the lines on which...the negotiations should be handled'.[48] The meeting was attended by several ministers (Dalton, Bevin, Cripps, Morrison and Lord Pethick-Lawrence) and by Halifax, Brand and a number of other officials. The mere presence of Halifax and Brand at the meeting is, in itself, suggestive of the embassy's role and the importance placed upon it by ministers. At the meeting Keynes suggested that:

> the terms offered might vary from an out and out grant in aid, to a commercial credit. He thought that he should not be authorised to agree to anything except an out and out grant. Help on any less favourable terms should not be accepted except after very long thought on the part of ministers in London.[49]

Keynes made the above remark (that he should in essence pursue the option of 'justice') notwithstanding the fact that he had been advised by the embassy and told by the Americans (even after he had threatened the bilateral trading route) that they would not provide grant aid. Brand commented that

> it would be undesirable that the United Kingdom representatives should ask for a grant in aid. There was a danger that if we did, there would be a leakage and that it would be stated in the United States Press that we had made such a request. This might well be represented to our disadvantage.[50]

This comment was consistent with Brand's correspondence with Keynes and the Treasury.

Whilst Brand had kept Halifax informed in the pre-negotiation period, there does not appear to be any evidence that Halifax had any strong or even informed views on the Stage III discussions. The only significant intervention Halifax made was to state that 'getting a large sum from the Americans depended less on the size of the sum, than on being wrapped up in attractive appurtenances', and, in that vein, he resurrected his old idea of giving the island of Tarawa to the United States.[51] Halifax also suggested at the meeting of ministers that Britain take an 'unselfish attitude about bases'. This latter point is an interesting one in that the nearest the Financial Agreement came to being defeated in Congress was as a result of the McFarland amendment, which proposed that the Financial Agreement only be voted through if Britain transferred certain bases to America. Halifax was perhaps more concerned with the selling of any deal that was struck rather than with the terms of the deal itself – something it seems he was prepared to leave to others.

Notwithstanding the remarks made by Halifax and Brand, the conclusion of the meeting was that the matter should be 'handled by Lord Keynes and his colleagues on the basis that he had outlined that evening'. Further, it was acknowledged that the discussions should be ad referendum, with reports being made to ministers in London as and when necessary.[52] The question as to why ministers seemed to be taking Keynes' advice over that of representatives of the embassy is considered further below.

It was noted above that one of the principal roles of the embassy, in addition to its reporting function, was to attempt to persuade America to adopt policies that Britain wanted. In this particular case, it was to negotiate a large dollar credit in the form of a grant. The negotiating teams and the dynamics within and between them were important. The embassy was involved in this dynamic in a variety of ways. The British negotiating team, initially at least, consisted of Halifax, Brand, Keynes, Henry Self and Hall Patch. Halifax led the British team in Washington.

The Keynes–Halifax axis was an important element in the Washington negotiations. Although they had met when Halifax was minister of Agriculture in 1925 and they had overlapped at Eton, their relationship did not develop until Keynes visited Washington in 1943. In July of that year, Halifax noted in his diary 'He [Keynes] has got a very acute but obstinate mind. He is a good fellow to do business with, and in spite of one or two tiresome qualities, I like him.'[53] They met again in 1944 when Keynes was in Washington to discuss the extension of Lend Lease into Stage II. At these negotiations, Keynes would become anxious and would call on Halifax who would provide a 'calming influence in moments of stress'.[54] This modus operandi was to continue in the 1945 negotiations. Keynes would often become exasperated with both the Americans and the British in London and on several occasions threatened to resign. Halifax, whether rightly or wrongly, would dissuade him and calm his nerves. Keynes wrote to his mother, 'Halifax and I work together like brothers'.[55] Their roles divided naturally. Keynes led on technical financial issues and Halifax, who claimed ignorance of financial matters, dealt with the personal and political relationships.

Keynes hoped to meet with Halifax before the crucial meeting of ministers on 23 August. In mid-August, however, Halifax left London in order to take a long break in Yorkshire.[56] This deprived Halifax of the opportunity to discuss the negotiations with Keynes prior to the ministers' meeting, which Halifax was flown down for. Keynes also expressed to Halifax his disappointment that he would not have Halifax's 'comfort' and 'counsel' in the early stages of the negotiation. Keynes was aiming to arrive in Washington on 1 September; Halifax somewhat later. Whether in connection with this or not, it is interesting to note that Sir Wilfrid Eady (Second Secretary, Treasury) wrote to Sir Edward Bridges (Permanent Secretary, Treasury): 'I ... think that Lord Halifax should be asked to return to Washington not much later than the end of the month.'[57] Eady also attached a draft letter from the Chancellor to the Foreign Secretary which stated:

> The negotiations are clearly going to be very difficult. Although many of them are highly involved the broad decisions upon them will be taken by Congress and American public opinion. It is therefore of very great importance that, at all stages from the beginning, we should have someone at Washington who can keep in touch with the progress of the negotiations and judge the effect on American opinion.
>
> This leads me to urge you very strongly to press Lord Halifax to return to Washington ... I know this may well be personally very inconvenient to him ... and I should not make the suggestion but that I believe it to be imperative in the national interest.[58]

Bevin did ask Halifax to return to Washington before the end of August. Halifax, however, told Bevin that 'I would do this if it was his wish and any use, but in point of fact it wasn't'.[59] Halifax, in fact, returned on 8 September. This indicates the strength of Halifax in relation to the ministers, the reliance Keynes placed upon Halifax and the importance the government placed on diplomats assessing the American mood.

The relationship between Keynes and Halifax was the most important one during the negotiations but other relationships were also relevant. As shown above, the relationship between Brand and Keynes was also important and, indeed, close. Brand was somewhat reverential towards Keynes, which is, perhaps, not surprising given that Brand was dealing with the world's leading economist. It was the case, nevertheless, that Brand was prepared to offer Keynes his thoughts on economic and non-economic issues.

Brand and Halifax were also on good terms not just professionally, but personally. Brand frequently briefed Halifax on financial matters both formally in writing and informally through meetings at the embassy.[60] The relationship between the two was also perhaps that of two Englishmen abroad. For example, they attended church together and gossiped about unfolding political events in Britain and elsewhere. It fell to Lady Halifax to inform Brand that he had lost his son in the final month of the war. Halifax, who had experienced a similar loss, tried to console him where he could.

The core of the British team, then, consisted of Halifax, Brand and Keynes. The core of the American team consisted of Clayton and Vinson. Vinson served in Congress for 14 years where he developed a reputation as a tax expert. A lawyer by training, he moved to the Federal Bench in 1938, where he remained until Roosevelt asked him to join the Administration in 1943. He served first as Director of Economic Stabilisation, then briefly as Director of the Federal Loan Administration and finally, under Roosevelt, as Director of the Office of War Mobilisation and Reconversion. Truman appointed Vinson as the Secretary of the Treasury in July 1945, where he remained for a year until he was appointed Chief Justice of the Supreme Court.[61] As the embassy reported, Vinson was 'on Foreign affairs a convinced internationalist, a strong supporter of Bretton Woods . . . and of other plans for international economic machinery'. He was also 'an Anglophile by origin and outlook'.[62]

Halifax first met Vinson on 14 February 1945; by 19 April he was noting in his diary that Vinson 'is now an important man in this new shake up'. On 20 July, after entertaining Vinson shortly after his appointment as Secretary of the Treasury, Halifax noted 'I am quite sure these little parties are much the best way of getting to know people whom one wants to cultivate'. Halifax continued: 'Vinson was most friendly and made great professions of his faith about the overwhelming necessity of our keeping together.' It was noted above that the embassy had identified Clayton and Vinson as important members of the new Administration. The way Halifax 'worked' on Vinson gives an interesting insight into the methods the embassy could employ to enhance British influence. Between them, Brand and Halifax had developed good relationships with the key members of the American negotiating team.

The period immediately prior to the Loan Agreement negotiations was dominated by Keynes' proposals. It was his proposals which were put to ministers and which became the basis of the British position. They not only set out the basic approach but also the financial position of the country and, therefore, the basis of the financial assistance required. Crucially, Keynes' proposals also made presumptions about American benevolence, thereby structuring the expectations of its readership: i.e. officials and ministers. It was this aspect of the negotiating strategy that the embassy sought to influence the most. The embassy was unsuccessful. The persuasiveness of Keynes and the allure of a grant were perhaps too much for Brand, a mere diplomat, to counter. It is, of course, an obvious but pertinent point that the effectiveness of any diplomat is determined, in part, by the extent to which he is listened to. Halifax, probably because he did not have much to say regarding financial matters, appeared to be content to leave matters to Keynes and Brand. It may also be that Halifax was keen not to countermand Keynes lest Dalton took it upon himself to head the negotiations. Halifax admitted that the thought of 'Hugh Dalton as Chancellor, with all the difficult negotiations with the United States ahead, fills me with gloom. I can hardly imagine a less persuasive negotiator. I hope Keynes will not feel constrained to throw his hand in.'[63]

Whilst Halifax appears to have left the overall strategy to Keynes and Brand, he was nevertheless aware that the challenge was not so much to persuade the Administration but to persuade Congress. Even in this pre-negotiation period, he tried to develop ideas that would ease the Loan Agreement's passage through Congress, in part by generating goodwill with the American public. Also, the embassy proved adept at reading the political mood in which the negotiations were to take place. Both the regular political reports and the ad hoc reports, by Balfour for example, proved to be perceptive and accurate.

Perhaps the most significant aspect of the embassy's role in the pre-negotiation period, however, was its ability to identify and then court the two key players on the American negotiating team. This crucial aspect of a diplomat's role, i.e. getting close to influential people in the Administration, is something that the embassy proved very successful at. It will be seen, however, that the failure to modify Keynes' approach, or at least to sufficiently alert ministers to its weaknesses, would cause difficulties during the actual negotiations of the Financial Agreement. It is to these negotiations that we now turn.

Halifax was appointed to head the Financial Agreement negotiations; it was, therefore, his responsibility to take overall charge of them. It has already been shown what part the embassy played in the pre-negotiation period. This section deals with the advice given to ministers on what could be achieved, the reporting of the dilemmas faced by the other side and the problems encountered by Halifax's own team during the negotiations.

The Financial Agreement extended to Britain a line of credit, which could be drawn at any time up to 31 December 1951, of $3.75 billion. The purpose of the credit was to, inter alia, help Britain 'meet transitional post war deficits in its current balance of payments' and 'to assume the obligations of multilateral trade'.[64] The credit carried a headline interest rate of 2%, which, due to the deferral of interest charges, was estimated to amount to 1.6%. The other terms of the Financial Agreement contained provisions regarding the waiver of interest under certain circumstances, the making or accepting of other lines of credit, British import arrangements and sterling balances. Additionally they provided for the convertibility of sterling on current transactions effective one year after Congress approved the credit. The credit then failed to meet the expectations generated in the pre-negotiating period, i.e. it was a loan and not a grant; furthermore, it was a loan which attracted a commercial rate of interest. Further still, the provisions with regard to convertibility were to prove onerous and ultimately led to the convertibility crisis of 1947 (discussed in chapter 5).

The part Halifax and the embassy played in negotiating the terms of the Financial Agreement began with Halifax's return to Washington on 9 September 1945. On that day, Halifax met with both Brand and Makins. He noted that Brand was 'optimistic about the atmosphere here for our main discussions'.[65] The next day Halifax met with Keynes and also convened a meeting of all the people concerned with the talks and planned his general tactics and strategy. Early warning signs of difficulties ahead were emerging even at this early stage; Halifax noted that 'a good many seemed to expect that the Americans will wish to get into more detailed discussion of commercial policy than we shall think profitable at this stage'.[66]

The Washington talks opened with a meeting of the Top Committee on 11 September 1945. The American side was represented by Clayton, Vinson, Wallace (Secretary of Commerce), Crowley (Head of Foreign Economic Administration), Eccles (Chairman of the Board of Governors of the Federal Reserve System) and McCabe (Army-Navy Liquidation Commissioner). The committee was to be chaired, in Byrnes' absence, by Clayton. The Secretary of State was attending the first post-war conference of foreign ministers in London, which was starting the same day.

The talks were to consider four main topics. Consequently, the State Department, which was responsible for scheduling and organising the meetings, formed four groups, each of which was to report to the top committee. The first group chaired by Vinson was to deal with financial problems, including the amount and terms of any financial assistance during the transitional period, sterling area arrangements and exchange convertibility. The second, chaired by Crowley, was to consider Lend Lease, which was to be wrapped up as part of the overall package. A third committee, chaired by Clayton, was, much to the disapproval of Keynes, set up to discuss commercial policy including reduction of trade barriers and cartel policy. A fourth group was set up to discuss disposal of surplus war property.[67]

At the meeting, Halifax indicated that 'he hoped that the outcome of the discussions would be such as to show a disordered world that there was still a rallying point of sanity and cooperation to which hard pressed men could turn with confidence as they faced the difficulties of the post war era'.[68] Warning shots were, however, already being fired by Congress. In an article which appeared on 12 September, the same day as Halifax and Keynes were holding their press conference, the *New York Times* reported in relation to the impending negotiations that 'many members of Congress have adopted a "show me" attitude towards any British proposals that is strictly hard boiled...Congress, as speeches today testify, reflects the view that...sympathy and understanding [for the United Kingdom] must steadily be held secondary to the interests and capacity of the United States'. The article concluded: 'a clear understanding of this attitude...should help to produce a contract which Congress will accept'.[69] Consistent with the advice, the embassy had been sending to London these warning shots should have confirmed to the British mission that sympathy for the British postwar position would not necessarily result in the Americans entering into an easy deal and that ultimately the hands of the people they were negotiating with were tied by what Congress would accept.

The opening press conference on 12 September was the British delegation's first opportunity to present its case to the public. Halifax and Keynes set out Britain's position. Halifax, opening the conference 'in a masterly way',[70] said that they had 'no intention whatever of coming to the United States as suppliants asking them to accept any arrangement merely to help us which they do not honestly feel to be in the interests of the United States and the world at large'.[71] Keynes then read a prepared statement, which set out Britain's position. In the common cause, Britain had mobilised heavily for war. This led to a dramatic decline in her exports and an adverse balance of payments, and the gap was temporarily filled by Lend Lease. Lend Lease had now ceased. Consequently Britain needed assistance to reconvert her economy to a peacetime setting. If she was to do this without resorting to bilateralism, she needed dollars. All of this would be in America's interest. Keynes also pointed out that 'after a full six years of war accompanied, not only by intense effort and sacrifice, but also by considerable privation, people in England were expecting a little relaxation'. Keynes added in reference to the idea of a loan: 'We are not in the mood, and we believe and hope that you are not in the mood, to repeat the experiences of last time's war debts.'[72] That same evening Brand organised a dinner attended by both Keynes and Acheson. The embassy lost no time in using its 'soft power' to work on the Administration outside of the main talks.[73]

After the press conference, the presentation of the British case to the top committee began in earnest. The meetings which took place between 13 and 17 September gave Keynes the opportunity to explain in detail Britain's post-war position. Keynes described Britain's external financial position, covering both her indebtedness and her difficulties in covering her adverse balance of trade. At the meeting on 17 September, against all the advice given by Brand, Keynes related Britain's predicament to its war effort and related Britain's contribution to that of America.[74]

As Brand had predicted, such comments, even though made in a closed committee environment, would leak. The banner in the *New York Times* read 'British Base Plea For Aid On Justice Over War Costs' followed by 'They Quote Statistics to Show They Contributed Far More Relatively Than We Did'.[75] Hall Patch, commenting on the leak, suggested that in comparing the relative war efforts Britain made a very good showing and that 'no great harm had been done'. He even suggested the British should have published the statement anyway. However, Hall Patch did note that 'we were advised strongly by our American friends not to publish this particular document, as it would only irritate public opinion here'.[76] This is perhaps a good example of someone who is not permanently on the ground in America underestimating the strength of public opinion on certain issues.

Frank Lee, who worked with Brand at the Treasury Delegation, felt differently. He discovered from an American friend close to the American members on the top committee that, whilst the top committee had been greatly impressed by Keynes's presentation of Britain's problems and that he had given a 'comprehensive and compelling statement of our case', the one exception concerned the burden of the war effort. The comparison of the relative war efforts of Britain and America had been regarded by some members of the committee as 'partial and invidious'. Members of the committee hoped that any document published by the British would not contain material comparing the war efforts because 'publication might hamper, rather than help, the presentation of the UK case to Congress and the US people'.[77] Lee perhaps saw the issue as much from an American perspective as from a British one; something which, of course, diplomats are encouraged to do. Halifax's comment on these initial meetings was: 'One gets the impression that the Americans are fully alive to our difficulties and are anxious to meet them, but are also acutely conscious of their own political difficulty'.[78]

After two further meetings, this time of the Finance Committee, Keynes cabled Dalton informing him that after being pressed by Vinson he had: 'stated the amount of assistance required as five billion dollars plus such amount as turns out to be due from us to pay for the cleaning up of Lend Lease'.[79] The Americans at these meetings had also made it clear that they expected members of the sterling area, i.e. the major holders of sterling balances, to make a substantial contribution to any final solution agreed and they had pressed for the British proposals in this regard. Keynes set out his proposals verbally. Of the estimated balance of $12 billion, $4 billion would be written off; of the remaining $8 billion, 10% or $800 million would be made freely convertible for any current purposes and the remaining $7.2 billion would be funded at no interest, to be paid off in 50 annual instalments of 2% beginning after 5 years.[80]

Keynes' cable concluded that the Americans 'were satisfied with the proposals for liberalising the sterling area and were not shocked by the size of the sums [i.e. $5 billion] mentioned'.[81]

After the formality of the above meetings, Clayton and Vinson requested what Halifax referred to as 'a private talk behind the scenes'. During these private discussions, which consisted of several meetings, the Americans emphasised that their case with Congress must depend on the advantages to the United States of liberalising and facilitating international trade. They also indicated, exactly as Brand had predicted and Lee had intimated, that 'arguments based on our past sacrifices and especially on comparisons between [Britain] and the United States would do no good and should be advanced if at all from the American side'.[82] These discussions also confirmed that both sides were beginning to focus on assistance of $5 billion but Clayton and Vinson 'repeated in unison that neither a Grant in aid nor an interest free loan was practical politics'.[83]

At one of the private meetings between Vinson, Clayton, Halifax and Keynes, Halifax, echoing his comments made at the meeting of ministers on 23 August in London, raised the issue of bases. Halifax, indicating that he was acting personally and without instructions, asked, presumably rhetorically, whether a 'sweetener' of some sort might help the presentation of the British case to the public. In addition to welcoming the idea Clayton went on to suggest that 'it would be valuable if, as part of any general settlement at which we might arrive, such questions as telecommunications and civil aviation could be cleared between us'.[84] Halifax then raised the point that it was important that the British government should not be seen as being blackmailed on a number of unconnected matters. Mr R. Ashton of the Economic Relations Office in the Foreign Office noted that 'this is dangerous however "personally and non commitally" it is done'.[85]

He had a point; a week later Clayton informed Halifax that he had met with the three American trans-Atlantic civil aviation operators and they had asked that the State Department make an agreement on civil aviation a condition of financial assistance to Britain. Clayton added that after he had refused to give such an undertaking, 'the representatives of the airlines had stated with extreme clarity their intention to run this idea as hard as they could in Congress'.[86] Naturally Halifax protested about this but, as Vinson and Clayton suggested, this was part of American politics. This is an interesting example of the interconnectedness of issues in American politics. Not only is it desirable that the public have enthusiasm for a particular measure but also that other lobbies, for example the telecom and aviation lobbies, be on side so as not to use their power to wreck a bill even though it may not be directly connected to the issue in hand. It is also an interesting example of Halifax acting without instructions and a measure, perhaps, of the confidence he had as ambassador and indeed the confidence he had in the people with whom he was negotiating.[87]

Whilst Vinson had made it clear that grant in aid was not available, Keynes was losing another battle. Contrary to the wishes of the Americans, Keynes was seeking to avoid discussion of commercial policy until after financial policy was settled. He sought to do this by the simple but rather crude expedient of refusing to include in the mission anyone capable of seriously discussing commercial policy. As mentioned above, the Americans had insisted on setting up a committee to discuss commercial policy. Representations were made by the Americans that this committee be appointed with members who had the knowledge and status to discuss commercial policy adequately. Clayton stressed the need for 'a United Kingdom team of equal standing to that engaged on financial policy'.[88] It now became clear that commercial policy was to be discussed and London, apprehensive of Keynes' ability to negotiate commercial matters, veered towards the American viewpoint. A team led by Sir Percival Liesching (Second Secretary, Board of Trade) and including Professor Lionel Robbins (Director Economic Section of the War Cabinet Offices) was sent to Washington. They arrived on 27 September and had the status of principal advisers to the ambassador on commercial policy, thus sidelining Keynes.

By the end of September, the negotiating strategy was beginning to fall apart. The Americans were not interested in Britain's war wounds and had made it clear that there would be no grant aid and any loan would carry interest. 'Justice' was dead as a negotiating concept. The strategy of decoupling commercial policy from financial policy had also fallen apart. The position was neatly summarised by Robbins, whom Keynes had invited on to the Financial Committee:

> It is clear that a pure grant in aid is right out of the picture. It is clear, too, that Maynard accepts this completely and is beginning to be inclined to think it absurd to believe otherwise. I had no difficulty in refraining from saying I told you so. But I perceive that we shall have a great difficulty in dehypnotising London; and I think that Maynard will have to be told that, having himself made the magic passes that now hold the King's Treasurers entranced in rapturous contemplation of ideal 'justice', it will be up to him . . . to reverse the process.[89]

The extent to which the Americans had cemented their position can be discerned from a memorandum sent by Clayton to the President. In it Clayton sets out the informal British proposals: exchange controls on current transactions would be lifted on 1 January 1947, Britain would waive the Bretton Woods transition period and the $12 billion worth of sterling balances would be dealt with in a manner acceptable to America. In return for this, the 'United States would establish a line of credit of $5 billion' and, staggeringly, the 'British made no suggestions as to terms'. Keynes appears to have given the Americans the two things they wanted, i.e. convertibility and the breaking up of the sterling pool, in exchange for a line of credit without agreed terms. It is not surprising that Clayton concludes his memorandum to the President by saying 'I am encouraged by the progress of the discussions and the reasonable attitude of the British'.[90]

Keynes' assessment of the American mood in the pre-negotiating period had been wrong and the predictions made by the embassy with regard to American benevolence, talk of relative war efforts and the coupling of commercial and financial talks were accurate. The failure to adopt the embassy's analysis was to put the British mission on the back foot and sow the seeds of problems between London and the British team in Washington. There were some, for example Hall Patch, who thought that this might be an opportunity to withdraw, albeit temporarily, in order to allow the 'hard facts of life to penetrate sufficiently "the crust of ignorance" with regard to Britain's financial position'.[91] Keynes also suggested that 'if ministers feel that we can be content with nothing less than a grant in aid it may well be necessary for me to return home having chosen the right moment to break off the negotiations'.[92]

Whilst Halifax and Brand concurred with Keynes' telegram, it is more likely that the suggestion was made with a view to 'dehypnotising London' rather than as a serious suggestion to break off negotiations. There is no evidence that Halifax wanted to break off talks. Indeed, he was perhaps more optimistic than many. Halifax noted that 'it is quite plain that the Americans would like to help us, but are quite genuinely doubtful about what they can get through Congress'.[93] He understood in turn that Congress would be affected by the labour unrest in America at the time, which lowered confidence in the future, and the effect of poor relations with Russia. This latter factor could be played both ways; either Congress would be reluctant to show Britain favour for fear of alienating the Russians or Congress would, in the face of Russian intransigence, wish to secure Britain as a firm friend. In the end, as will be shown later in this book, it was the fear of Russian intransigence that led to Congress ultimately approving the Financial Agreement. At the end of September 1945, however, Halifax believed that the former view was stronger.[94]

Halifax's optimism in respect of his negotiations with the Administration might also have been strengthened by his meeting with President Truman on the morning of 25 September, where there is some evidence that he discussed the financial negotiations with the President[95] and when, as Halifax noted, the President was 'very friendly and talked quite freely'.[96] Halifax may also have been encouraged by a 'very useful small dinner' he had organised with half a dozen Senators and Keynes.[97] The group included senior Senators such as Arthur Vandenberg (Republican, Michigan), Tom Connally (Democrat, Texas) and Alben Barkley (Democrat, Kentucky). Halifax reported that although Laski and nationalisation were discussed the evening went 'fairly well and they must have enjoyed it for they stayed till 11.30'. These accounts of the meetings with Truman and the Senators are, of course, fairly bland. It is perhaps necessarily so. It is not always possible for a diplomat to express precisely, in words, how a meeting went or what the feeling is for another person's position. Diplomacy is something of a dark art; as much can be expressed by the strength of a handshake or by the expression on a person's face after hearing a certain remark as can by actual words. On occasions a diplomat may get a sense of a person's point of view rather than a specific expression of it. It is for this very reason, of course, that diplomats on the ground are so crucial and why it is important that their judgement can be relied upon.

The atmosphere within the British team was still positive towards the end of September. Keynes wrote 'The team here . . . is just about as good as one could possibly have. The ambassador is immeasurably helpful and we are working together very closely.'[98] Even a meeting between

Keynes and Liesching and Robbins on 29 September was harmonious, despite Halifax initially being concerned that there might be a 'stiff leg atmosphere'.[99] Robbins commented: 'When we arrived at Washington he [Keynes] greeted us with the utmost friendliness and at once appointed me to be liaison between the financial and commercial delegates.'[100] The only sign of tension was at a lower level. Michael Wright discovered that the Treasury Delegation had not been passing all telegrams to the ambassador but rather giving some directly to Keynes. Michael Wright wrote: 'I told him [Frank Lee] that this was quite intolerable and that he must dismiss once and for all any idea that important telegrams could pass at the Treasury level without Y.E. [Your Excellency], who was leader of the delegation, being fully informed.'[101]

It is interesting to observe that Halifax does not appear to have been weighed down by the first 20 days of the negotiations. He carried on his regular meetings with the heads of missions (including holding talks with regard to reducing their size in the post-war period), gave a coast-to-coast radio broadcast, continued to meet with his ministers on other matters, persisted with his relentless round of entertaining and still managed to read several books, continue his regular tennis matches with, amongst others, Donald MacLean and take up driving lessons for the first time.[102]

The negotiations, however, were set to become more intense and from the end of September onwards, there developed two sets of negotiations: the delegation in Washington versus the Americans and the delegation versus London. Both were to be difficult; the Americans had been given what they wanted and had no real incentive to make concessions, and London retained an expectation of justice that only time and reality would shift.

On 2 October, Dalton circulated telegrams reporting the progress of the talks, as well as a memorandum prepared by Keynes on 26 September. Ministers discussed these documents on 5 October. Keynes' memorandum confidently asserted that substantial assistance would be forthcoming conditional upon, inter alia, liberalising arrangements in the sterling area, acceptance of Bretton Woods and Britain's creditors in the sterling area making a contribution to any general settlement. He also added, however, that the 'question of terms is far less clear'.[103] Dalton cabled Washington setting out ministers' views: 'If best American offer is large loan at 2% interest we would not accept it. We remain firm that we will not accept obligations which we do not see reasonable certainty of discharging.'[104]

Armed with the views of ministers, Halifax and Keynes called upon Vinson and Clayton on 9 October. Again Keynes asked for grant in aid or an interest-free loan and again the Americans said no. Vinson made the point that whilst the concessions being asked for were only 'peanuts to him as Secretary of the Treasury . . . he was solely moved by what was possible in the present mood of Congress and the public'. He added that 'the result of the London Conference had caused . . . a considerable recurrence of Isolationist sentiment'.[105] When pressed as to what they were prepared to offer, the Americans indicated that they would consider an interest-bearing loan of $5 billion repayable over 50 years with repayments beginning in five years and with flexibility on interest and capital payments in difficult periods. The rate of interest would be somewhere between 1% and 2%. The mission cabled London with this informal proposal.

Dalton's reply, which came on 13 October, was clear: 'we do not find a loan on these terms acceptable', he wrote. One of the reasons given was that it did not contain 'the sweet breath of justice'.[106] The telegram went on to discuss Britain's role in the war and to go over the old ground of retrospective Lend Lease. It instructed the mission to try again for interest-free terms. The gulf between London and Washington could not have been much greater. In a letter to Brand, Eady suggested that there was disappointment about the lack of grant in aid: 'partly because Maynard had made the whole conception so attractive in the paper he had produced and in his little oration', but also, Eady added rather interestingly, 'because there is some feeling that something like that is owed to us'.[107] Eady's sentiment was that 'we should not be called on to pay interest to enable the Americans to enter sterling markets'.[108] Keynes' earlier optimism, which had infected Dalton and others, was now beginning to seriously hamper negotiations. It was not the only factor to do so, however. There was a genuine belief in London that interest should not be payable. Dutifully Halifax and Keynes put the ministers' position to the Americans. They made no progress at all and reported that the atmosphere was 'gloomy and unconstructive'. The best chance the mission had to obtain $5 billion was being lost.

On 18 October, and in an effort to awaken London to the realities of the situation, Keynes, with the support of the other members of the delegation, sent to London what must be one of the most elegant telegrams ever sent by an official to his ministers. In explaining why he had failed to get a grant Keynes pointed out that in America, where there is 'a moral duty' to make money, some 'imitation' of a normal banking transaction is necessary. If the elements of a trade are present, the American way of life requires that at least the appearance of a trade should emerge. Thus precisely those elements which will spoil the flavour to us are necessary to make the result palatable here.' In reference to the US Administration versus Congress, he said 'we cannot demand what they tell us does not lie within their power to give'. The telegram was sent after consultation with Halifax and Brand. It was a plea to London to accept the American terms (i.e. $5 billion at 2%) or, in Keynes' analogy, to substitute the 'poetry' of grant in aid for the 'prose' of American commercialism.[109] Halifax, on reading the draft of the telegram, commented that 'it was quite brilliantly done with pleasant touches of wit redeeming the atmosphere of official telegrams'.[110]

Keynes went to the heart of the matter and posed the question: 'Can anyone honestly argue that the difference between this [broadly the above American proposal] and a loan which is interest-free in all circumstances is so material that even in the last resort we should prefer a breakdown of the present discussions with all that means to our standard of life, to our hopes of recovery, to our position in the world and to Anglo-American friendship?'[111]

Whilst telegrams shuffled between London and Washington, the embassy continued to work behind the scenes. During the first half of October, the embassy organised several further dinners for Senators and Congressmen. On 5 October, Halifax met with seniors such as Senators Saltonstall (Republican, Massachusetts) and Millikin (Republican, Colorado); a few days later he met with senior Congressmen including McCormack (Democrat, Massachusetts) the majority leader and Eaton (Republican, New Jersey). Others in the embassy played their part; for example, John Lockhart had a series of Congressmen to dinner to meet with Keynes. Keynes commented 'the ambassador has thought it prudent on this occasion, and I am sure he is right, to seek far more intimate contact than I have ever had before with members of Congress'.[112] As noted in chapter 1, Keynes estimated that he would meet a quarter of the Senate before he left America, as well as a number of the most influential Congressmen.[113]

It is interesting to observe that the message Halifax seemed to take from these meetings with Congressmen was more positive than the message he was getting from members of the US Administration: 'my feeling has always been... that if the administration went flat out for any scheme they would, in fact, get it through'. Halifax also said 'I do not believe Congress are going to be too excited about whether it is 2% or 1% or 0%; they are going to judge the broad issue of whether it is desirable to help us'.[114] By contrast, Vinson and Clayton were concerned about the attitude of Congress to any deal; a sentiment supported by Byrnes who told Halifax that 'he did not think the atmosphere on Capital Hill was going to be easy'.[115] A reading of Clayton's correspondence during the period demonstrates the Congressional pressure on the negotiators not to enter into any soft deal with the British.[116] What this demonstrates is the conflicting views that will exist in any negotiating situation and how important it is to have people on the ground. As Halifax observed: 'In all these talks there is a good deal of room for intuition rather than reason.'[117]

The embassy did not rely only on these sources for feedback. The BIS produced regular and frequent reports specifically on the press reaction to the prospects of a loan to Britain. These reports were not only sent to London but were also circulated to members of the British delegation so that appropriate rebuttals and corrections could be prepared if necessary.[118] The embassy also monitored public opinion; for example, in a Political Report sent to London in mid-October, it reported a Gallup poll on the prospect of a loan to Britain. In answer to the question 'would you approve or disapprove a loan of between £3 billion and £5 billion to help England get back on its feet?', 27% approved, 60% disapproved and 13% had no opinion.[119]

By mid-October, the Americans had pushed Keynes down the road of temptation. The task the mission now faced was to lead London down the same road. What should Halifax have done at this stage? The original strategy had failed. London did not appear to accept this; yet there was, at least at this stage, a sense that there was still an opportunity to secure $5 billion. Halifax had a number of options: he could have recommended that the talks be called off or at least suspended, he could have returned to London to speak directly to ministers or he could take the course he did take, which was to attempt to 'dehypnotise London' from afar whilst continuing with the talks.

It is unlikely that Halifax would have seriously considered calling off or suspending the talks. As noted above, Halifax maintained a certain optimism. This may have been based on his conversations with the President and almost certainly reflected his positive meetings with Congressmen. He may also have been aware that there were still, even in mid-October, elements in the US Treasury Department that were supportive of an interest-free loan.[120] Halifax may also have believed that his continuing conversations with regard to 'sweeteners' would encourage the American negotiators to be more generous and at the same time less concerned with the Congressional reaction to financial assistance to Britain. Halifax did not believe that the Department of State was applying undue pressure with regard to issues such as bases, telecommunications and civil aviation but rather that the department itself was responding to pressure and, as Halifax put it, 'they are appealing to us to find a helpful way out for both of us'.[121] Halifax was also certainly aware that a break in the talks could have had a serious impact upon Anglo-American relations and therefore he would have sought to avoid such a break if possible. Commenting upon the possibility that the talks be suspended for 12 months, Halifax noted that to think one could 'pick up things where we left off [is] I am convinced a profound illusion'.[122]

Another alternative, given the difficulties the talks had run into, was for Halifax to return to London and discuss the problems the mission was encountering directly with ministers and officials. There is no evidence that Halifax considered this. Perhaps this was for a number of reasons. By mid-October, Halifax was aware that Attlee was planning a visit to America in the near future to discuss nuclear weapons.[123] Halifax would have regarded this as an opportunity to discuss matters with Attlee and even for Attlee to discuss the issue with the President. Halifax also saw Attlee's visit as an opportunity to discuss matters with senior civil servants. He was quick to write to Attlee:

> In such an event [visit to America] it occurs to me to ask whether you might think it well to bring Bridges. Presence of the Secretary of the Cabinet for atom bomb talks would seem natural enough and it might be easy for Chancellor to send over Treasury representative. If this idea smiled on [by] Dalton and yourself, Keynes would welcome it.[124]

Keynes too, sensing an opportunity, wrote to Bridges:

> Next week will be critical in the financial negotiations. It will be valuable if proposed visit could come next week and that you should be in the party. Cabinet will have to make decisions shortly. It will be difficult or impossible for me to come back for consultation. It would therefore be of the utmost help if you could be in a position to size up the general atmosphere here and advise them in the light of it. I beg you to come. Indeed to come anyhow whether the proposed visit is put off or not.[125]

In the event Bridges did not come to Washington at that time and there is little evidence that Attlee's visit had much effect at all on the negotiations, either with the British or the Americans.

In addition to believing 'London' was coming to Washington, Halifax probably also had in mind that he always had the option to send representatives back, possibly Keynes or Brand. It transpired that Attlee's visit was delayed until 10 November 1945 and Halifax, on 28 October 1945, decided to send Hall Patch back, suggesting that 'he will be able to give you the general background of the present discussions'.[126] Hall Patch was also joined by Robbins, who returned to discuss progress with regard to the commercial talks. Finally, considering Halifax's high profile in America, his return to London would have an unpredictable effect on the momentum of the talks and was therefore risky. Halifax decided, probably for all of the above reasons, to persevere with the talks in Washington.

In the event, by mid-October, the opportunity to secure $5 billion was probably lost. Harry Dexter White (Director of Monetary Research US Treasury) had reworked the numbers and the Americans were now of the view that Britain only needed $3.5 billion plus whatever was needed to clean up Lend Lease. At a meeting on 18 October, this figure was offered at 2% repayable over 50 years with the Lend Lease portion at 2.375% repayable over 30 years.

Keynes cabled Dalton with the $3.5 billion proposal from the Americans together with some suggested counter-proposals. The impending budget of 23 October delayed the reply but when it came, it drove Keynes 'white with rage and [to] talking about resigning'. His colleagues initially feared that the latest proposal made a breakdown in negotiations simply a matter of time.[127] The cause of such drama was contained in telegrams from Dalton dated 27 October, the contents of which were based on a discussion of ministers on 26 October. There were two alternative proposals, A and B. Alternative A was a loan of $2.5 billion repayable over 50 years at 1% and an option of a further $2 billion interest-free to facilitate convertibility on current transactions within the sterling area. On this basis, the government would recommend to Parliament that Britain adhere to the Final Act of Bretton Woods and that she would be a sponsor to the International Trade Conference. If A was not acceptable to the Americans, then Alternative B was to borrow on commercial terms without commitments of any kind.

Keynes dismissed Alternative B outright: 'All of us here are convinced that this alternative has to be ruled out altogether as being quite beyond any practicable possibility.'[128] He demonstrated that the terms of a loan on commercial terms, even if it were available, would entail more onerous repayment provisions than had already been discussed and rejected, and that repayments would start in 1946, the very time when the British economy was least likely to be able to afford them. After hearing that B was a non-starter, Dalton cabled Washington imploring them to 'Try A for all you are worth'.[129] Notwithstanding this and knowing that interest-free money was simply not available,

Halifax and Keynes delayed presenting Alternative A to the Americans whilst they attempted to get London to shift ground. As noted above, it was on 28 October that Halifax decided to send Hall Patch back to London in an effort to remove some of the misunderstandings that were occurring between London and Washington and to impart some sense of reality. Halifax noted in his diary, 'one is discouraged by the gulf that prevails between the London and Washington atmospheres'.[130]

As a result of a continuing debate by way of telegrams, and no doubt through the influence of Robbins and Hall Patch, a revised set of proposals came through on 6 November. These were produced after a cabinet meeting where a vigorous debate took place, which Dalton described as 'heavy work'.[131] The proposals were that Alternative B could be dropped but that Alternative A as amended should be pressed. Crucially, however, it went on to say: 'If Alternative A is unobtainable our limit is an open credit for $4 billion at 2% on the amount of the credit in use, with an option on a further $1 billion at 2%.'[132] Dalton was now on the road to temptation.

In addition, London was now prepared to accept some form of waiver clause, albeit with certain conditions attached. Correspondence had been taking place on the suitability of a waiver clause over the previous weeks. London had resisted a waiver clause, seeing it as a mechanism for future interference by the Americans; it was now, however, beginning to recognise that it was a way of squaring the circle. Brand played a part in securing London's acceptance of a waiver clause. At the end of October Brand wrote to Eady:

> Having been closely in touch with American opinion throughout last war debt controversy and seen the serious consequences in the relations between the two countries . . . I cannot believe any trouble arising out of a waiver could possibly equal that which would be caused by another default.[133]

By early November, then, London had begun to move towards the Washington delegation's position, encouraged perhaps by the explanations of Hall Patch and Robbins and by the progress that was being made on the commercial talks. Ministers and officials in London were also perhaps mindful of the point made by Robbins at a meeting of ministers on 5 November where he had stressed the 'complete contrast between the Administration, anxious to be helpful to us, and the public and Congress, who were losing interest rapidly in the outside world'.[134]

The Americans rejected Alternative A as amended on 9 November. Keynes then began to present the new alternative, i.e. the acceptance of $4 billion credit, something which had it been presented in early October, would have met little resistance. However, 'the field', as Hall Patch commented, 'was not so clear as it was'.[135] The Americans were seeking further assurances. In the event of difficulties in meeting interest payments, they were now looking at deferment of interest rather than waiver. Additionally, American loan repayments were to rank ahead of other debts. The Americans and the British were unable to reach an agreement; the Americans, however, promised to come back with a proposal by 15 November. These setbacks drove Keynes to the edge. 'M[aynard] nervy and difficult to deal with. He is quite exhausted and the effects are not easy for the rest of us...everything is rather a nightmare', reported Frederic Harmer (Keynes' personal assistant during the loan negotiations).[136] Keynes, of course, was an ill man and this sort of stress could have driven him over the edge.

The American's revised proposals, circulated on the morning of 15 November, did nothing to improve Keynes's humour. They contained new points which the mission knew would be unacceptable in London and a number of 'silly and insulting' technicalities had been written into the draft. Keynes, upon reading the document, was 'white and shaken'. A meeting of the British representatives took place at the embassy, where Halifax 'took charge very firmly of the position'.[137] It was decided that they should refuse to discuss the draft and merely send it to London for instructions warning the Americans of the possible consequences. At the meeting of the Anglo-American Finance Committee that afternoon, Halifax opened for the British. After a suitable preamble, Halifax 'warned that if the draft embodies the final and considered view of the US Administration the United Kingdom Government would be forced to the conclusion that the present negotiations had failed'.[138] He continued that whilst talks might possibly resume in a year or so, in the meanwhile, approval of Bretton Woods and the proposals for commercial policy would be suspended. A note by Paul Bareau, a financial journalist attached to the Treasury, who was present at the meeting, illustrates the American reaction:

> The statement caused very visible shock to the Americans. Vinson immediately began to urge how completely at a loss he was to understand the ambassador's contention that parts of the American document did not even offer a basis for discussion. While Eccles was droning on... Vinson and Clayton had a whispered conversation at the end of which Vinson said that nothing which the ambassador had indicated suggested that we must face a breakdown. This document and the clauses which gave offence to us must be discussed over again. We must not remit the document to London... The ambassador picked up the ball admirably 'We are all friends in this room' he said 'and we all want to serve the same cause'.[139]

The stance taken by Halifax on 15 November was clear and decisive and probably had the effect of dissuading the Americans from pressing their hand too firmly. The manner in which he grasped the issue and dealt with it is all the more impressive given that this took place in the middle of Attlee's visit. Halifax had a number of events to attend to, including Attlee's discussions with Truman on atomic energy, the embassy's functions surrounding such a visit and Attlee's speech to Congress. The contrast between Keynes' state of mind and Halifax's at this stage of the negotiations is striking. Keynes wrote to Eady and Bridges: 'There can be no doubt that the position here is deteriorating... the subject has gone stale and critics and sceptics of all kinds... are recovering their courage.' Keynes added, 'personally I am now rather near the end of my physical reserves'.[140] Halifax complained that 'the Americans continue to be most trying and on many points utterly unreasonable'. Halifax's view was that many of the problems were being caused by people below the level of Vinson and Clayton, but he added: 'my own judgement stands that if we combine patience with resolute firmness on essential points, and if we do not die first, there are distinct possibilities of reaching a reasonably satisfactory solution'.[141]

Several meetings followed over the next few days and on 21 November, the mission cabled London with the revised position, which, although it still did not meet British requirements, was an improvement upon the offending draft of the 15th. After a meeting of ministers on 23 November, Attlee sent his response. Britain would accept a credit of not less than $4 billion, including Lend Lease at 2%, to be paid over 50 years and, in essence, the commercial policy proposals that had been agreed. Britain would not, however, agree to the following American proposals: the completion of negotiations with creditor countries by end of 1946, abrogation at the end of 1946 of her transitional rights under Bretton Woods and the formal ranking of the American debt ahead of all other external obligations.[142]

In the same telegram, Attlee informed Halifax that he was contemplating asking the President to intervene, and he asked Halifax for his views 'particularly on the proposed procedure'. The suggestion that the President be approached came out of the meeting of ministers on 23 November. The variety of views expressed indicated the disarray in London and the problems which Attlee faced. Dalton suggested that 'we had to take the risk of a break', while Cripps suggested that the matter be taken up at a higher level and that 'the Chancellor and the Foreign Secretary might go out and explore the position'. Bevin thought that either a break or an unsolicited ministerial approach would bring difficulties. The Secretary of State for India felt that 'our technique of negotiation had been at fault in that we had tried to hold on to untenable positions for too long'. Morrison thought that Keynes had not been given enough of a free hand and had been held up by London. He said: 'The basic fact was that we needed the money; we could not get it elsewhere; and we should be in very grave difficulties if we did not get it.'[143] The conclusion of the meeting, however, as summed up by Attlee, appeared to be that Attlee should telephone Truman.

Attlee then asked what effect such an approach would have on the negotiations, as 'we did not want to arouse the resentment of Vinson and Clayton'. Only then was the suggestion made 'that to meet this difficulty the Prime Minister should first send a telegram to the ambassador, setting out what he proposed to say to the President, asking for his comments and leaving it to the ambassador to settle what should be said to Vinson and Clayton'.[144] It is remarkable that the most senior group of ministers in the British government were contemplating approaching the President without seeking the ambassador's advice.

Attlee did, however, seek Halifax's advice. The ambassador's response was that he should first put forward the latest proposals[145] and let them sink in 'before you call in a higher opinion'. 'We should I think get as far as we can on the present basis before invoking the President.'[146] Halifax added, however, that the time may come when this would be desirable. Attlee agreed to leave it to the ambassador 'to determine when you want to call me in'.[147]

Attlee, then, readily acceded to Halifax's view notwithstanding the views of his ministers. It is an indication that Attlee at least understood the importance of people on the ground and that he still had faith in Halifax's judgement. It might also be noted that Attlee had recently returned from a visit to Washington where the performance of Halifax and the embassy had been impressive. Attlee's visit to Washington and the part the embassy played in it is discussed in the following chapter. It may also have been the case that Attlee was conscious of the fact that Dalton was not being quite as diligent as he might have been and that this was possibly a cause of the problems between London and Washington. When Eady visited Washington in February 1946 and he and Halifax reminisced about the negotiations, Halifax noted: 'Eady made it quite plain that Dalton had never taken the trouble to read many of our telegrams with the result that when things came out less well than they had hoped it was rather a shock.'[148]

Neither Keynes nor Halifax spotted the danger which lurked in the Attlee telegram of 24 November. The Prime Minister's refusal to commit to a date of end 1946 for completion of negotiations over sterling balances with creditor countries was taken to mean accumulated balances built up during the war. That is Britain could not commit, in advance, to have reached agreement on the treatment of the sterling balances. This had always been the case and the mission had always reserved Britain's position in this regard. The mission, however, had always taken it to have been agreed that from the end of 1946 onwards sterling receipts by these countries in respect of current transactions would be freely convertible. It was noted above that this was a concession Keynes made very early on in the negotiations and was a key requirement of the Americans. It was in this manner, i.e. assuming convertibility on current transactions, that Keynes presented his redraft of the Prime Minister's telegram to the Americans. Dalton, on discovering the way Keynes had presented the Prime Minister's telegram, claimed that in refusing to commit to a date of end 1946 for agreement on the treatment of sterling balances the Prime Minister was refusing to commit to any convertibility at the end of 1946. 'We do not wish this formal public promise to be made – a promise to "release all current earning throughout the whole of the sterling area from the end of 1946".'[149] At this stage, Keynes threatened to resign and was only dissuaded from doing so by Halifax.

A flurry of telegrams followed. The mission drafted a telegram emphasising the long history of the current earning convertibility commitment. London put up its own defence and regretted the misunderstanding but insisted that there would be no automatic convertibility at the end of 1946. The Cabinet met on 29 November and with dissention from Emanuel Shinwell and Aneurin Bevan agreed the 'final' terms. These terms had been cobbled together from the American texts and some comments from the mission, with some ideas from London thrown in. These were sent to the mission on the same day with instructions that they were: 'to give the text to the Americans as representing what we [ministers] would be prepared to accept'.[150]

The mission replied the next day:

> Your instruction...means if we are to be frank with the Americans, that the position [i.e. with respect to convertibility] as we and they have understood it hitherto is fundamentally altered...Our concern is with the future. We fear the effect on the negotiations of the steps we are instructed to take, and we do not believe that the policy suggested is one we can defend in argument...our unanimous conviction [is] that the course we are told to take must be disastrous.[151]

Attlee and Dalton offered an immediate response: 'It is now our firm opinion that you should put that text to the Americans as soon as possible as from His Majesty's Government with the supporting arguments which we have supplied you.'[152]

The mission was on the verge of mutiny; so Dalton sent Bridges to Washington. This led to yet another threat of resignation from Keynes and another talk by Halifax to talk him out of it. Time was now crucial. The agreement needed to be signed by 6 December if Parliament was to conclude its deliberations by the end of the year and thus also be able to ratify the Bretton Woods timetable. Bridges arrived in Washington on 1 December and he immediately went into a series of meetings with the Americans. As instructed, the Cabinet proposal was put to the Americans but it did not take Bridges too long to realise that it was unacceptable and, perhaps predictably, the result 'was according to one member of the British team "exactly as expected, humiliation".'[153]

Nevertheless, major issues were resolved. The amount was fixed, after the intervention of Truman, at $3.75 billion plus an agreed figure for Lend Lease of $650 million. Repayment would begin in five years, headline interest was 2% and the effective rate was 1.6%. The form and nature of the waiver was finally agreed. The sterling area exchange arrangements were to be completed one year after the effective date of the agreement. Two further meetings took place on 4 and 5 December where the mission, under instructions from London, sought to reintroduce the five-year transitional arrangements outside the sterling area that it had been entitled to under the Bretton Woods agreement but which had been conceded during these negotiations. The American response can be seen from a telegram Bridges sent to London: 'The US delegation made it perfectly clear that they would break off the negotiations rather than concede the point about the transitional period.'[154] Attlee sent Bridges a rather desperate cable: 'In my view if we tried to get Bretton Woods through Parliament without transitional period we should probably fail.'[155] Halifax, in an effort to save the agreement from further Cabinet interference, sent a rather dignified telegram to the Prime Minister and the Foreign Secretary:

I, of course, appreciate your difficulties and we have all done our level best to move the Americans to meet them. I am sorry we have failed. During this last sticky week I have been struck by the real friendliness and desire to get over or round difficulties that Americans have shown. But they are, of course, painfully conscious of their own.... I cannot think the practical disadvantage of accepting [the] American Draft comes anywhere near the grave mischief over many fields of Anglo-American relations that must be the inevitable and enduring consequences of rupture. Most earnestly I trust the Cabinet may take the same view.[156]

The transitional arrangements were not reinstated and the agreement was signed on 6 December.

It is always difficult to assess whether a negotiation has been a success or otherwise. One method is to compare the aspiration with what was actually achieved. On this basis, the negotiations did not go well. This method may, however, be inappropriate in this case given that the aspiration was largely in Keynes' head and, indeed, was one which the embassy said was unattainable from the beginning. As was concluded above, the aspiration only stood because of the charisma and brilliance of Keynes and because ministers and officials, distant from the American mood, firmly believed that Britain was somehow owed the terms which Keynes was espousing.

Another method of assessing the negotiation is to consider what other nations received. America handed out over $20 billion worth of aid after the war. At the time, Brand suggested that the terms Britain received were vastly better than any other country had got and probably better than any other country would get. Brand also indicated that the Americans were prepared, notwithstanding the fact that other countries had suffered greater devastation, to put Britain first.[157] But as Brand also pointed out, they were not prepared to give Britain the money free or on terms hopelessly different from those they intended to give to others.[158] In this sense, the negotiations, although not matching the aspiration, delivered for Britain a privileged position. It might be possible then, on this basis, to conclude that they were a success.

Finally it is also possible when considering the success or otherwise of the negotiations, to reflect upon the strategy and tactics the embassy employed.

One of the consequences of ignoring the embassy in the pre-negotiation period was that the negotiations floundered at the beginning, a position from which it is often difficult to recover. Given this was the case, the question is whether the embassy took the appropriate action after the talks had got into difficulties. There is strong evidence that it did. The central strategic point which the embassy grasped from the beginning, although some in London did not, was that it was the attitude of Congress that mattered. The embassy sought to monitor public opinion on the loan through the BIS, court members of Congress and, importantly, devise strategies designed to make the US Administration's proposals more palatable to Congress. This strategy would in turn be likely to encourage the Administration to offer better terms.

The embassy's tactics also appear to have been sound. For good reasons, Halifax did not recommend calling the talks off, nor did he recommend returning to London, yet when it mattered, for example on 15 November, he was capable of taking a tough line with the Americans and threatening such action. It is also the case that Halifax, in the main, performed well during the negotiations. He made very few gaffes, kept his head, developed a trust between himself and the opposing team and held his own rather fractious team together in difficult circumstances.

Negotiations are not, of course, only about what one gains or loses; they are also about the effect one can have upon the relationship with the person or organisation one is dealing with during the negotiating process itself. Although there were tense moments during the negotiations, there was also cordiality between the two sides. Halifax perhaps recognised that the larger goal was the long-term Anglo-American relationship. It is difficult not to conclude that the embassy's role in the negotiations was crucial and that in this context at least, the embassy played an important part in post-war Anglo-American relations.

The press release announcing that agreement had been reached ended with the words 'the realisation of these proposals will depend upon the support given them by the peoples and legislatures of the United States and the United Kingdom'.[159] That support was not wholehearted. The House of Commons, after only two days of debate and amidst considerable controversy, approved the Loan Agreement by a vote of 345 to 98 with the majority of the Conservatives abstaining. The American debate was to be more protracted. As Vinson indicated to Keynes, 'the fireworks here will extend over a longer period of time than over on your side'.[160]

The part the embassy played in the passage of the Financial Agreement through Congress was not as intense as its part in the actual negotiations with the Administration. It could not have been so, because of the taboo on an embassy being seen to partake in American political affairs. However, once the Financial Agreement was signed, the embassy lost no time in trying to understand what was required of it. In mid-December, Makins spoke with Clair Wilcox of the American Treasury Department to ascertain what the embassy might do with regard to the 'public relations aspect of the passage through Congress of the Loan Legislation'.[161] Wilcox suggested that the embassy be ready to answer questions, not make public speeches and that it should not put out any literature. Wilcox added that he hoped that 'we [the British] would carefully consider our public actions and statements on delicate matters during the critical period'.[162] Wilcox also indicated that members of the Administration would be making speeches, literature would be distributed and that the Administration was 'getting busy' with the business community, organised labour and the farm groups with a view to these influencing Congress indirectly.

By early January, however, the embassy was reporting that 'there was little evidence of the promised official propaganda campaign by the US Administration'. Further it reported that there were differences in the Administration as to what sort of campaign should be run; the Treasury preferred a sober unemotional campaign while the State Department wanted a 'raging and tearing' one. The same report, however, did say that the US Treasury had invited the UK Treasury Delegation to cooperate in providing the 'factual and dialectical' material required to counter any criticism made during the Congressional hearings and debate.[163] At least the embassy would have some direct influence on the material being presented to Congressmen.

Towards the end of January, the embassy was concerned with the progress of the proposed legislation and, indeed, with the general climate in the political establishment. Brand expressed this concern to the Administration.[164] There were good reasons, however, for the delay in presenting the proposed legislation to Congress. The Administration was redrafting the provisions of the bill dealing with the Financial Agreement so that the bill could be sent to the Banking and Currency Committees, which the Administration believed was 'a much better forum than any other'.[165] Clayton also indicated to Brand that he would now be taking a more active role and that 'he would devote practically all his energies to this matter, till it was through'.[166]

The political climate, however, was more of a concern. A Weekly Political Summary produced by the embassy at the beginning of February indicated that: 'Not since the time of Hoover has Congress been so completely out of White House control . . . The growing loss of presidential prestige in an election year is sending chills into the lowest echelons of the Democratic party.'[167] On 30 January, Halifax arranged for a group to meet at the embassy to discuss what help, if any, could be offered to improve the atmosphere in Congress with regard to the loan. He noted: 'we all had a feeling that the Administration was not doing an awful lot . . . and that the situation was slipping'.[168] So concerned was the embassy that Brand even wrote to Keynes to dissuade him from publishing an article on America's balance of payments in the *Economic Journal* until after Congress had reached a decision, lest it be used as ammunition to argue against the Financial Agreement in the Congressional debate. Keynes readily agreed to the suggestion.[169]

The spirits of the embassy staff were perhaps raised a little by the arrival in America, in mid-January, of both Herbert Morrison and Winston Churchill. Morrison was warmly welcomed as a visitor in both New York and Washington and according to the embassy 'his exposition of British problems and policies made a considerable impression'.[170] Churchill's arrival in the country was enthusiastically welcomed and prominently reported, as were his remarks on the Financial Agreement. Churchill supported the loan and this promulgation of support went some way towards dispelling the American misunderstanding of Churchill's position garnered from the Conservative abstentions following the Commons debate on the Financial Agreement in the previous December.

Truman sent the Financial Agreement to Congress on 30 January 1946. In a special message which accompanied it, Truman asked Congress to act promptly, saying that 'Britain needs this credit and she needs it now'.[171] The signals coming from Congress and elsewhere were not good, however. As indicated above, the presidential stock was low and the Democrats were jittery in an election year. In addition, whilst practically all the organised bodies such as the banking sector, Chamber of Commerce, the women's organisations and the AFL were in favour of the agreement, the majority of Americans were still against the loan.[172] A Gallup poll indicated that 60% of Americans were opposed to it.[173] Other factors conspired against Britain. There were some in America who were influenced by Britain's imperial past; the Irish and Jewish lobbies were a particularly potent force. In addition, in approving the dollar allocation for the International Monetary Fund and the International Bank for Reconstruction and Development 'men like Dean Acheson and Will Clayton . . . made extravagant claims about what the two new institutions could be expected to achieve: and they flatly denied the need for any other measure to finance the post-war reconstruction of Europe and Asia'.[174] Some in Congress had not forgotten this claim when asked to provide assistance to Britain.

The embassy's role was not, of course, restricted to exerting its influence in America. It also sought to persuade London to adopt certain actions or follow a particular course. Halifax, in conversation with a member of Congress, discovered that there was a feeling of disappointment in America that Britain had never thanked the United States for Lend Lease. Halifax then suggested to Attlee that both Houses of Parliament might pass a suitable motion to remedy the position. Halifax even went as far as drafting the wording of a proposed motion.[175] The proposal never materialised, however, because as Attlee indicated there could be 'no guarantee of substantial unity in Parliament'.[176]

This occasion also demonstrates the closeness of the embassy, or at least of Halifax, to the American establishment. Halifax suggested to Attlee that if Parliament delivered the required motion, then he [Halifax] could talk to the Speaker and Senate leaders to see if both Houses of Congress could record their pleasure at the proposed motion and record their thanks to Britain for her part in the war. Although this might seem far fetched and Halifax did acknowledge that he might be 'flying high', he did 'not entirely despair of getting it'.[177]

The embassy also needed to keep abreast of the various forces which were operating behind the Congressional scene. Brand, for example, was aware of the activities of a subcommittee of the Committee for Economic Development, which was formed by the Carnegie Peace Foundation. The subcommittee was set up for the purpose of advocating the Loan Agreement and consisted of labour leaders, heads of women's organisations, who were strong supporters of the loan, and other influential and prominent Americans. The Chairman of the subcommittee was Charles Dewey, an ex-Congressman from Illinois; he indicated to Brand that 'the opponents of the Loan Agreement were now concentrating, not on direct opposition, but on proving that the Agreement was all wrong because the UK could never carry out its terms'.[178] The opponents also suggested that Britain was indifferent to the loan, as evidenced by the Conservative Party's abstention during the House of Commons Loan Agreement debate and the assertion, although a distortion of the truth, that Churchill when he was in America 'never in any great speech referred to the loan or took the trouble to urge on [the] American public that it should be passed'.[179]

Dewey asked whether anything could be said in Parliament by either the Chancellor or another leading minister to 'spike their guns'. Brand gave a measured response when reporting these events to Eady: 'I do not rate the importance of the action proposed as likely to have any decisive results, but I believe such a speech, if couched in the right terms, might be very effective when the Agreement is before the House [of Representatives].'[180] The next day Brand cabled the Treasury with the suggestion that, as the Chancellor would have to refer to the Loan Agreement in his budget speech anyway, then perhaps he could confirm that Britain wanted the loan, that America was not a Shylock and that Britain would do her utmost to fulfil her obligations.[181] Dalton suggested that he was disinclined to make any reference to the Loan Agreement with Eady, adding 'we are all very doubtful whether anything we say here will really influence Congressional decision'.[182] Halifax then cabled Dalton directly and said that he believed that Dewey's suggestion was sound and he hoped that the Chancellor would be able to say something in his budget speech along the lines suggested.[183] Dalton in the end complied with the embassy's request and his budget speech included the following words:

> The proposed Anglo-American Loan Agreement is now before the American Congress; and it would not be proper for me to intervene in that debate. But it is right for me to emphasise now how greatly we need and how greatly we shall appreciate, the proposed measure of assistance.[184]

The above event is a good example of the embassy being close to the ground, keeping in touch with events and offering London feedback. It is also evidence of the embassy's persuasiveness when dealing with ministers; there were other occasions, however, when London could not be moved.

One such occasion was the proposal by Brand and Halifax, although based upon a suggestion by Clayton, that the Irish Taoiseach, Eamon de Valera, be approached and asked to 'make a public declaration to the effect that he looks upon the [Financial] agreement as a valuable contribution to world prosperity'.[185] The proposal was not well received by London. After the idea was finally quashed, Dalton was moved to write 'this saves me from having to consider any further the humiliating suggestion brought forward by Brand, that H.M.G. should ask De Valera to make a public statement in favour of our getting the loan'.[186] Given Anglo-Irish history, this was not an unreasonable remark from Dalton.

An important event which took place during the passage of the Financial Agreement through Congress was the visit by Churchill to America in January to March 1946.

Churchill undertook a number of engagements in America, which ranged from collecting honorary degrees and delivering speeches, including his now famous Fulton speech, to meeting with influential Americans including Congressman Colmer (Democrat, Mississippi) who, as indicated above, was the Chairman of the House Post-war Economic Planning Committee.[187] Two events, however, were specifically relevant to the embassy and the passage of the Financial Agreement through Congress.

The first was a meeting organised at the suggestion of Halifax between Byrnes, Baruch and Churchill, which took place on 16 February 1946. (Churchill also met with Baruch subsequently to discuss the Financial Agreement.) Baruch was known to be against a large loan to Britain and had indicated that he would testify before the Congressional hearings against such a loan. Halifax thought that Churchill might be able to dissuade Baruch from taking such a course. Churchill also met with Brand before his second meeting with Baruch specifically to be 'coached up on the loan...against his next talk with Baruch'.[188] It transpired that Baruch did, after his meetings with Churchill, decide not to testify. It is not known for certain that Churchill's action led to this outcome. There could be other factors. It is possible that, as was noted above, Brand was persuasive when he met with Baruch the previous autumn. Baruch may also have been influenced by the decision of the Administration to appoint him as the US representative on the International Commission on Atomic Energy.[189] There is, however, at least an argument for suggesting that Churchill was a significant factor in Baruch's change of heart.[190]

The second event was a dinner organised by and held at the embassy, which was attended by leading Congressmen and Churchill and took place on 10 March 1946. The embassy in organising the dinner would have been conscious of at least two concerns Congressmen had with regard to the provision of a credit to Britain. The first was the fact that the Conservatives had abstained in the Financial Agreement debate in the House of Commons. Churchill himself was told of Congressional concern at the Conservatives' abstention by Vinson at a dinner at the embassy on 7 March. The second reason was a wariness of doing business with a 'socialist government'. Churchill, to a certain extent, addressed both of these issues. An account of the dinner prepared by Judson, the embassy's Congressional liaison officer, indicates that Churchill was supportive of the loan and that his objections to it were largely of a technical nature. Further, in relation to concerns with regard to British socialism, Churchill pointed out that 'most of the leaders of the present Government had been members of the Wartime Coalition Government; were men of experience and understanding and were certainly not rash doctrinaire socialists'.[191]

Whether Churchill's intervention was successful is again difficult to determine. Judson concludes that the Congressmen were reserved and that 'the mood was one of friendliness and sympathy, though not necessarily support'.[192] Out of those who were present one voted against the loan, two were paired, abstained or were absent,[193] and five voted in favour with the Speaker not voting. However, a review of the track record of the voting pattern of those present sheds little light on whether Churchill changed any opinions. Only two of the eight had consistent track records in terms of voting for or against foreign aid and economic issue bills, one consistently voted for, the other consistently voted against and neither of these two changed their view. The others had no discernible voting record in relation to such bills and therefore it was difficult to determine whether they had changed their stance or not.[194]

It is difficult to be conclusive with regard to Churchill's intervention either with the Congressmen or Baruch. The important point, however, from our perspective is that the embassy was prepared and able to harness the asset of Churchill's visit to America for the specific purpose of attempting to enhance the chances of the Financial Agreement passing through Congress. Whilst there are instances where Churchill made comments in support of the loan[195] there is no evidence to suggest that Churchill would have met Baruch and the Congressmen without the embassy's intervention.[196] The embassy knew, however, that 'Americans really listen to Mr Churchill'.[197]

Open hearings on the Loan Agreement eventually began before the Senate on 5 March 1945, making 'a dull but not unsatisfactory start'. In a stroke of good fortune for Britain Senator Wagner (Democrat, New York), the Chairman of the committee was unwell and therefore the Majority Leader Senator Barkley (Democrat, Kentucky), who was to become Truman's running mate in the 1948 presidential election and who was a firm supporter of Britain, chaired the committee. As the embassy indicated Senator Wagner may have some difficulty reconciling support for the loan with his Zionist loyalties.[198]

The Administration in the form of Vinson and Clayton presented their case. Vinson, echoing the negotiations, stressed to the committee that 'the credit is not a gift; that it is a loan which England is to repay;

that it is to be repaid with interest'.[199] The expected opposition from a number of opponents evaporated. The embassy reported that Joseph Kennedy, a former ambassador to Britain and something of an isolationist, had been driven into the British corner by the 'Red Menace' and possibly by Cardinal Spellman's account of the Vatican's views on the world situation. Leo Crowley, one of America's leading Catholics, also decided not to appear at the hearings in opposition to the loan.[200] The hearings lasted only two weeks and on 10 April, by a vote of 14 to 5, the Banking and Currency Committee reported favourable to the Senate.

The Senate debate opened on 17 April and was dogged by a variety of manoeuvres designed to defeat the loan. The opponents of the loan concentrated their efforts on the introduction of a number of amendments to the bill. The most threatening of these was an amendment introduced by Senator McFarland (Democrat, Arizona). It provided that 'as a quid pro quo for the loan to Britain, the United States should permanently acquire the leased Atlantic bases'.[201] The amendment only failed by 40 to 45 votes. A change of only three votes therefore could have led to the defeat of the Financial Agreement. The resolution to approve the loan, however, was, 'largely thanks to the skilful Parliamentary tactics of...Senator Barkley', passed on 10 May by a majority of 46 to 34. Thirty democrats and 16 Republicans voted in favour and 16 Democrats and 18 Republicans voted against.[202]

The ambassador's gratitude for Barkley's management of the bill was such that Halifax made a point of visiting Dean Acheson's house, where Barkley was dining on the evening of 10 May, so that he could 'shake Barkley by the hand and congratulate him on his handling of the loan in the Senate'.[203] The Senate and, in particular, the McFarland amendment was probably the bill's toughest test. Employing racing parlance, the embassy reported that 'it may be said that the British Loan is now safely past Beecher's Brook but has still a hard course ahead of it including the water jump i.e. The House'.[204]

The bill was then sent to the House of Representatives where, after three weeks of hearings, the Banking and Currency Committee reported the bill favourably to the House. The Administration then lobbied hard on the bill's behalf. Truman wrote to Spence (Democrat,

Kentucky), Chairman of the House Banking and Currency Committee, urging support for the bill. The extent to which the Administration took the embassy into its confidence might be gauged by the fact that Bernstein, an assistant to Vinson, showed Inverchapel (who had replaced Halifax in mid-May) a draft of Truman's letter to Spence. Inverchapel was shown the draft before the President had seen it, let alone approved it. Inverchapel was told that the idea for the letter was Vinson's and the intention was for Spence to read the letter on the floor of the House when he opened the debate.[205] On 13 July 1946, and after dozens of amendments all of which were voted down, the House approved the Loan Agreement by 219 votes to 155 votes. One hundred and fifty-seven Democrats and 61 Republicans voted in favour of the Loan Agreement and 32 Democrats and 122 Republicans voted against.[206]

The embassy, through its Congressional liaison officer Judson, closely monitored the passage of the Loan Agreement through Congress. Judson produced regular reports which contained the views of leading Congressmen, the tactics being employed by the Administration and those of the opposition and details of any obstacles to the bill's progress through Congress.[207] These reports were circulated within the embassy to the ambassador, Balfour, Magowan, Chancery and the UK Treasury Delegation including, of course, Brand.

Judson's role was not an entirely passive one. He was in touch with the Democratic whip's office, and was aware of the various arguments being presented in order to defeat the Financial Agreement. One such argument was the assertion that the loan under consideration would not be repaid, any more than World War I debts were repaid. The World War I debt situation was not quite as straightforward as not having repaid the debt; there were other mitigating factors and, indeed, some of the debt and interest was repaid.[208] Judson, together with Brand, prepared a list of facts relating to the debt for use by the Democratic whip, which Judson was assured they would 'make excellent use of'.[209] Further, Judson also managed to 'get into the Congressional Record a really satisfactory account of the World War I debt situation' and to put a statement regarding the debt 'quietly' into the hands of 'thirty or forty carefully selected members of the House'.[210]

Judson was also, through his connections in Congress and by 'persistent but unobtrusive backstage manoeuvring', able to organise meetings between certain members of the embassy staff and selected Congressmen. One such meeting was that arranged between Brand and four members of the House Banking and Currency Committee, the most prominent being Jesse Wolcott (Republican, Michigan), the ranking Minority member of the House Banking and Currency Committee, and the 'most influential man in the House in matters of international finance'.[211] Brand, in reporting the meeting to Eady, indicated that there was a 'long discussion about the whole affair'. Interestingly, however, although the Congressmen indicated their support for the Financial Agreement saying they thought it was the right and statesmanlike thing to do, Brand concluded that three of the four might not vote for as they were more persuaded by the response of their constituents than by the arguments.[212] The fact remains, however, that through the efforts of the embassy, in the form of Judson, Brand was able to present arguments in favour of the Loan Agreement directly to four important members of the Legislature. There are several other examples of meetings between various members of the embassy and Congressmen.

One of the final and somewhat unorthodox actions the embassy took in relation to the passage of the Loan Agreement was the summary approval by Inverchapel personally of a visa for a Mr Lennox, someone connected with Sol Bloom. Bloom (Democrat, New York) was a leading Representative and Chairman of the House Foreign Affairs Committee; he was incidentally one of the Congressmen who attended the dinner with Churchill in March. He was known to be averse to the loan and the Administration was concerned that he would make a speech against it on the floor of the House. Acheson approached Inverchapel and asked if he could see his way to removing 'the personal grievance which this sensitive Congressman harbours against His Majesty's Government for the prolonged failure to return any reply to the visa application of Lennox'. Inverchapel, using his 'emergency discretion', granted the visa.[213] Sol Bloom voted for the Loan Agreement.[214]

On 15 July, the day the Financial Agreement was signed by Truman, Inverchapel wrote to Bevin:

> I was invited by the President to attend the signing with Mr Balfour and the Economic and Financial ministers. I found a large gathering at the White House including the Chief Justice, the Secretary of State, the Secretary of the Treasury, the Speaker of the House of Representatives, the Majority and Minority leaders of both Houses of Congress, the Chairman of the Banking and Currency and Foreign Relations Committees of the Senate and the House, Mr Acheson and Mr Clayton, the Chairman of the Export-Import Bank, the Chairman of the Federal Reserve Board and other officials.[215]

The letter to Bevin conjures up a powerful image, with the ambassador and his colleagues standing side by side with the leaders of the Administration, the Legislature and the Judiciary. It is perhaps a vivid demonstration of the importance of the embassy in both the American political environment and the British political system. Later that day, the Economic and Finance ministers from the embassy called on the Under-Secretary of State. They were formally told that the effective date of the Financial Agreement was to be 15 July 1946. A letter was also received from the Secretary of the Treasury informing them that money could be drawn under it from 15 July 1946 until 31 December 1951. The US Treasury was then informed that the British government wanted to draw $300 million of the credit forthwith.[216]

The effectiveness of the embassy's role in encouraging the passage of the Financial Agreement legislation through Congress is difficult to evaluate. Diplomacy is not unlike advertising. In advertising you know that for every pound you spend only a half of it (say) will yield a successful result; the problem is you do not know which half. With diplomacy too, it is impossible to say with any certainty which aspect of the work yielded a positive result. Did, for example, the embassy do anything to encourage three more Senators to vote against the McFarland amendment than voted for it? If so, was it comments made at a dinner given by the ambassador, was it the placing of an argument in the Congressional

Record, was it the content of a speech made in the House of Commons and reported in America? Quite possibly it was none of these. All of these examples of the embassy action are, of course, possibilities but one cannot say which is the more effective or, indeed, if they were counterproductive. Without wishing to labour the comparison, diplomacy is also like advertising in that it is cumulative. Relationships are built up over many years and it is not possible to say whether it was a recent or an historic encounter with a member of the embassy, if indeed, it was any encounter at all, that persuaded a Congressman to support or not to support Britain at a particular time.

Perhaps the way to judge the role of the embassy is to look at its closeness to both the Administration and the Legislature. Ultimately, if one wants to influence people, one has to be trusted by them. It appears that the embassy was in this rather privileged position, both in relation to the Administration, and indeed certain elements of the Legislature. The Administration were prepared to share their plans, with regard to pushing the legislation through Congress, with the embassy, offer advice to the embassy in terms of what action the embassy should and should not take and to share confidential information.

It is also the case that some members of the Legislature were prepared to meet with embassy staff in order to discuss the Financial Agreement. Although the meeting between Churchill and the most senior members of the Legislature was exceptional because of Churchill's stature, there were other meetings between members of the embassy and the legislature. The embassy's Congressional liaison officer clearly had the ear of certain members of Congress and, in particular, the Democratic whip's offices, thus enabling the embassy to get the full picture as events were evolving. As importantly, it appears to have done so without falling foul of the rules or being seen to be influencing the process.

The embassy, in part because it was trusted, had a very good sense of what was going on. It was thus able to report to London appropriately and, where possible and when necessary, take action to enhance the chances of the Financial Agreement succeeding by, amongst other things, countering fallacious arguments and supplying appropriate information. The intensity of the embassy's involvement in the passing of the legislation was not as great as that in the negotiations. There was some involvement, however, and it is difficult not to conclude that the embassy played a positive part.

The Financial Agreement delivered to Britain a line of credit amounting to some $3.75 billion. Whilst the terms were a disappointment to Britain, it was nevertheless a source of dollars which Britain desperately needed access to. The embassy played a crucial role in securing this credit for Britain. It offered sound advice on the negotiating strategy to be employed, identified and courted key members of the American negotiating team, headed the negotiations in Washington, including determining the tactics, and played a significant part in bringing together Congressmen and those who might influence them to support the credit.

Before moving on to discuss atomic energy collaboration, however, one further issue needs to be considered. Why was the embassy's advice ignored in the pre-negotiation stage, and was the ignoring of the embassy's advice systematic? As was shown above, in the period prior to the negotiations the embassy offered clear advice to officials and ministers on the proposed negotiating stance to be taken. The embassy understood that a grant in aid or even an interest-free loan would not be available and further that the arguments upon which such a request was to be based, for example relative war efforts, would not go down well in America. Why then did ministers and officials ignore the embassy's advice? There are, perhaps, two reasons; the first was the persuasiveness of Keynes, the second was the genuine and perhaps stubborn belief by ministers and officials alike that Britain deserved the package that Keynes was promising.

Keynes was a charismatic figure, a renowned economist and widely seen as a genius. He had spent over a year of the war in America and had been involved in all the significant economic discussions with the American Treasury Department. He was saying something ministers desperately wanted to hear. Brand would have been no match for Keynes around the Cabinet table late in the evening on 23 August. The second reason why, on this particular occasion, ministers were prepared to ignore the embassy's advice was that there was 'some feeling that something like that [grant in aid] was owed to us [Britain]'.[217]

This view was not only based upon Britain's war contribution but also on the feeling that commercial principles, i.e. interest, should not be charged on loans designed to free up the sterling area.[218] These were, then, special circumstances. The emotion of coping with Britain's economic weakness as she emerged from war and the presentation of the case by a man as great as Keynes was too much for the embassy to counter. Aside from the rather special circumstances surrounding this particular case, however, there is little evidence that in other instances the embassy was not taken notice of. Therefore the conclusion drawn, at least at this stage, is that ignoring the embassy's advice was not a systematic problem.

What is clear, however, is that the embassy got it right. This notion further supports the importance of the embassy in understanding and advising on Anglo-American relations. It also draws our attention to the distinction between the amateur and the professional. Keynes knew America fairly well. Because he had spent a long period of time in America he might have felt that he understood the American mood. This, however, was no substitute for the combined knowledge of the embassy staff. One only has to glance at Halifax's diaries to see the intensity and breadth of the contact he had with Americans. In addition to his regular meetings with informed Department of State officials and other members of the Administration, he had continual contact, whether formally or informally, with members of the legislature and a range of other organisations, which were influential in America. This pattern would have been repeated albeit at different levels by all the diplomats attached to the embassy. In addition, the embassy was receiving feedback from the Consular offices and other organisations attached to the embassy such as the BIS. The feedback from all of these sources built up into a formidable body of knowledge. Further, the building of this knowledge was continuous and cumulative, so that it took account of historic information giving it perspective and yet, at the same time, gave a very current view of events and thinking in America. In addition to the individual talent or judgement of the diplomat, it is access to this pool of knowledge which adds to his effectiveness and makes him a professional. To underestimate this is likely to lead to problems.

It is worth reflecting on what people at the time thought of the embassy's importance. Attlee was prepared to defer to Halifax when deciding whether to appeal to Truman; an independent-minded Chancellor, Hugh Dalton, was prepared to alter his budget speech on the advice of the embassy; and two members of the embassy, Halifax and Brand, were invited to attend a meeting of senior Cabinet ministers in August 1945 to debate the tactics to be employed. These things may not amount to much in themselves but they are clues to the embassy's importance.

This chapter has demonstrated that the embassy was an effective force, whether in terms of providing commentary on the American political landscape, utilising its extensive contact base, or in offering sound judgement. These characteristics are considered further in the next chapter when Anglo-American atomic energy collaboration is discussed.

CHAPTER 3

ATOMIC ENERGY
COLLABORATION, 1945–1946

The elements of public life which gave vigour to isolationism are
now being transmuted into the active exponents of a somewhat
truculent new brand of 'America first'.[1]

For many in Britain, the continuation of a strong Anglo-American
relationship was the foundation stone of both Britain's post-war security and her continuing status as a major power. A proxy for this relationship was continued collaboration on atomic energy, important not
just for the benefits that might be derived but as evidence itself of
the Anglo-American relationship. As Churchill pointed out, it was an
issue which 'touches the life of the State'.[2]

The embassy picked up early warning signs that the atomic energy
issue was becoming politicised. But Britain, at the end of the war,
had every expectation that collaboration with America would continue. The successful use of the atomic bomb against the Japanese and
their subsequent surrender, however, precipitated a re-evaluation of
the Anglo-American atomic relationship. This led, in the immediate
post-war period, to a breakdown in atomic energy collaboration. To
witness the breakdown in atomic energy collaboration was, for some,
to witness the breakdown of the Anglo-American relationship itself.[3]

The shift from a wartime to a peacetime basis also introduced
a variety of new factors which had to be considered in the task of

readjustment. These included: firstly, Britain's desire to embark upon an atomic production programme of her own in the United Kingdom, a programme that would require supplies of raw materials and access to industrial knowhow. Secondly, there was the realisation of the impact of atomic weapons development on international relations and the feeling of an urgent need to obtain security through international control. And thirdly, the contemplation of American legislation aimed at the domestic control and development of atomic energy.[4]

On becoming Prime Minister in 1945, Attlee almost immediately set up an Advisory Committee on Atomic Energy. One of its terms of reference was to advise the government as to what steps should be taken for the development of atomic energy either for military or industrial purposes.[5] Attlee appointed Sir John Anderson, who had been the minister responsible for atomic energy affairs in Churchill's government, as the Chairman of the Committee.[6] Whilst the Advisory Committee, and, indeed, Attlee had a strong interest in atomic energy, the reality of the situation was that much of the negotiation and discussion with regard to the future of atomic energy collaboration took place in Washington. This placed the British embassy in Washington at the centre of the post-war atomic energy debate. Prior to a discussion of the embassy's role, however, it is necessary to consider how the framework for wartime atomic energy collaboration evolved and the structure that was in place as the war ended.

The Maud Committee, which consisted of eminent scientists, was set up in April 1940 with the aim of investigating the feasibility of an atomic bomb. The committee worked fast and it reported in the summer of 1941. It demonstrated 'lucidly and with great cogency how and why an atomic bomb was possible'.[7] American progress on understanding the practical application of atomic energy was, up until this point, unimpressive. It was their reading of the UK's Maud report and the work that it reported upon that led the American government to take the production of an atomic bomb more seriously.[8] It led directly to the setting up of the American atomic project.[9] The Americans, with the impetus provided by Pearl Harbor and with their considerable resources, forged ahead on their own.

Whilst a certain amount of interchange of atomic information was taking place between Britain and America, the British, by the middle of 1942, were encountering difficulties and they began to see the opening up of a technology gap between themselves and the Americans. Realising that the atomic bomb would be a crucial card in a post-war world and understanding the commercial possibilities, the British sought to introduce themselves into the American project on equal terms. The British wanted a full exchange of information and the development of a joint project. The Americans in the form of Dr Vannevar Bush, Director of the Office of Scientific Research and Development, James Conant, Chairman of the National Defence Research Committee and General Groves, Director of the Manhattan Project, were reluctant. Whilst they 'considered the exchange of scientific and technical information justified only when it advanced the war effort, they could see little but trouble in a joint project'.[10]

The interchange of information on atomic energy had by March 1943 effectively broken down. This led Churchill to intervene and characteristically he badgered the President until the position was changed. Roosevelt overruled Bush and Conant and instructed them to renew full interchange. Sir John Anderson and Bush worked out a mutually acceptable modus operandi and submitted it to their respective leaders. These provisions, together with four political points, became the *Articles of Agreement Governing Collaboration between the Authorities of the USA and the UK in the Matter of Tube Alloys*,[11] a document otherwise known as the Quebec Agreement. This agreement, signed on 19 August 1943, was designed to resolve the conflicts that had been brewing over the previous year.

The agreement set up the Combined Policy Committee (CPC), which was responsible for ensuring 'full and effective collaboration between the two countries' and dictated that 'There shall be complete interchange of information and ideas on all sections of the project'.[12] The Quebec Agreement succeeded in producing the basis of a working relationship during the war. It was, however, a wartime agreement and its validity in the post-war period was questionable.[13]

Uranium ore was crucial to the production of atomic energy. General Groves recognised that America had enough of the ore for its immediate expected needs, but he was not so sanguine about the long-term prospects for the supply of raw materials. Significant quantities of the ore were to be found in the Belgian Congo and the Americans realised that the best hope of obtaining a commitment for the ore was through the British, who had close connections with the Belgian government in exile. This need for British help led to the signing of the *Declaration of Trust* on 13 June 1944. This agreement between the Americans and the British set up the Combined Development Trust (CDT), whose objective was to 'gain control of and develop the production of the uranium and thorium supplies situate in certain areas other than the areas under the jurisdiction of the Two Governments'. The Trust was to 'carry out its functions under the direction and guidance of the Combined Policy Committee'. In the post-war period, British access to uranium deposits, particularly those in South Africa, and an entitlement to her share of uranium ore under the trust agreement were practically the only significant cards the British held.[14]

The final piece in the jigsaw of agreements drawn up during the war was the Hyde Park Aide-Memoire, signed on 19 September 1944. This document, drawn up after a conversation between Roosevelt and Churchill, was less than 150 words long but dealt with three significant issues. It identified Japan as the first target for the bomb, confirmed that the bomb was to 'continue to be regarded as [of] the utmost secrecy'[15] and confirmed the continuation of post-war Anglo-American cooperation on atomic energy. The aide-memoire contained the following sentence: 'Full collaboration between the United States and the British Government in developing Tube Alloys for military and commercial purposes should continue after the defeat of Japan unless and until terminated by joint agreement.'[16] This unambiguous statement gave Britain considerable hope and every expectation that collaboration would continue after the war.

The Washington embassy, however, detected early signs that this assumption might be challenged. Sir Ronald Campbell, a minister at the embassy and one of the British representatives on the CPC, noted as early as February 1945 that the issue of atomic energy was 'acquiring a more and more political aspect'.[17] American officials were becoming increasingly concerned at the prospect of an eventual Congressional

enquiry into the Manhattan project and that Congress would question the levels of expenditure incurred and the return America had
got for her investment. The Americans bore the bulk of the cost of
the atomic project, the British contribution being essentially limited
to the provision of scientists. The British, however, continued to claim
the status of equal partners in the project. American officials were
unsure of Congress's response to this situation. It led Campbell to conclude that 'there can be no doubt at all that if at any moment there
was a disagreement which produced a deadlock, the Americans would
be ready to ignore the present partnership agreement and proceed
upon their own account'.[18] This was, perhaps, the first sign that continued collaboration could not be relied upon. Further evidence of this
politicisation came when Halifax reported that the 'Americans [had]
brought the State Department in the persons of Mr Stettinius...fully
into the TA picture'.[19] The American atomic project initially came
under the jurisdiction of the War Department and the Secretary of
War was the Chairman of the CPC until December 1945 when he was
replaced by the Secretary of State.[20]

At the same time as American officials were expressing concern
over the increasingly political nature of the atomic issue, they were
also suggesting that 'the CPC was in danger of becoming a body so
incapable itself of taking decisions as to be more or less useless in its
current form'.[21] Concern was expressed by Vannevar Bush that British
members of the CPC were incapable of making decisions on any matter without reference to London. This fact, as well as the politicisation
of the atomic issue, led Halifax to suggest that he himself, rather than
anyone else, should replace Campbell on the CPC. Campbell had been
recalled to London to take up the post of Assistant Under-Secretary
of State at the Foreign Office. Halifax told Anderson in January 1945
that the 'first essential must be to maintain American confidence'.[22]
Given Halifax's status in America in 1945 his joining the CPC would
have given Americans that confidence. It would also put Britain's most
senior diplomat at the heart of the atomic energy discussions.[23]

It was also agreed that Makins, who was working temporarily at
the embassy at the time, should remain there and become Halifax's
assistant in atomic energy matters and, in due course, become the Joint

Secretary of the CPC.[24] Originally Anderson had wanted to appoint an official from the Ministry of Aircraft Production instead of Makins but, as Ronald Campbell pointed out, the preparatory work of the CPC and, in particular, the discussions with Harvey Bundy, the American Joint Secretary on the Committee, would 'become more and more diplomatic in character'. He added that 'the sort of person needed for the work is one with a diplomatic training and background'.[25]

The position in early 1945 was, therefore, that the embassy had identified a potential threat to the assumption that collaboration would continue after the war. This threat was communicated to London and taken on board. Anderson wrote: 'I fully realise the importance of not giving a handle to those elements in Congress and elsewhere who may be hostile towards the policy of collaboration embodied in the Quebec agreement.'[26] The embassy not only identified the threat and kept London informed, it also instituted changes designed to meet the challenge and strengthen the British representation on the CPC. By early 1945, the British had a formidable team in the form of Halifax and Makins working on their behalf on atomic energy issues in Washington. Makins indicated that working with Halifax on atomic energy collaboration was his principal function in 1945.[27]

Both Truman and Attlee were profoundly affected by the devastation caused at Hiroshima and Nagasaki. Truman wrote:

Ever since Hiroshima I had never stopped thinking about the frightful implications of the atomic bomb. We knew that this revolutionary scientific creation could destroy civilisation unless put under control and placed at the service of mankind.[28]

In a telegram to Truman written shortly after the first bomb, Attlee said:

The attack on Hiroshima has now demonstrated to the world that a new factor pregnant with immense possibilities for good and evil has come into existence... There is widespread anxiety as to whether the new power will be used to serve or to destroy civilisation.[29]

In the midst of these sentiments, however, both leaders had an eye on the national interest. Attlee wrote to Truman again on 16 August indicating that he was 'strongly of the opinion that means should be sought to enable... collaboration and exchange of information to be continued'. Attlee added, 'my proposal is that you and I should issue directives authorising this collaboration'.[30] Ironically, the day before this, Truman wrote to the Secretaries of State, War and Navy, as well as the Joint Chiefs of Staff, directing the appropriate government departments 'to take such steps as are necessary to prevent the release of any information in regard to the development, design or production of the atom bomb... except with the specific approval of the President'.[31]

Aware of Attlee's desire to progress Britain's atomic energy interests, Makins sent a note to London setting out his thoughts on the subject. The note was discussed at the Cabinet's Advisory Committee on Atomic Energy on 24 September. Makins suggested that with the ending of the war and with the change of organisation and personnel on the American side, relations with the Americans were entering a critical stage.

Echoing earlier messages from the embassy, Makins warned:

Although full recognition was given in the United States to the British contribution, American public opinion is inclined to look on the bomb as an American possession and Congressional opinion will certainly incline to the view that it should remain one.

It is important to act quickly before the American views have crystallised and while the machinery of the Combined Policy Committee and of the Trust is still in active operation. President Truman... said that he will make a decision about atomic energy... in the interests of the United States and its foreign policy. We can only influence that decision by putting in our ideas at once.[32]

This was a prescient remark by Makins. At a meeting of the Secretaries of the State, War and Navy a few weeks later, Byrnes indicated in the context of a forthcoming CPC meeting that 'he would plead with the President not to push the question of consultation'. In addition, Forrestal, Secretary of the Navy, 'expressed his fears that the British might wish to consider the question of the future of the bomb *de novo* and that he would be inclined to the view that it would be better to consider the Committee [CPC] defunct'.[33] Makins was quick to recognise the proprietorial attitude certain Americans were developing towards atomic energy.

In addition to the foregoing generalities, Makins also produced a list of points upon which a decision was required 'as soon as possible if we are to have a serious chance of maintaining our position as an effective partner with the United States'.[34] Makins' list of points included deciding what form atomic control in Britain would take, estimating the amount of raw material Britain would need for the future and clarifying the position the Commonwealth might play in Britain's nuclear programme. At this point, Makins was verging on setting the agenda for London. At the very least Makins was inculcating London with the sense of urgency it now required if it was to secure continued collaboration.

The relevance of some of Makins' comments may be gleaned by reading the minutes of the CPC meeting held on 13 October 1945. At that meeting, Halifax informed those present that Britain proposed to set up a Research Establishment to deal with all aspects of atomic energy, including a 'pile' to provide material for research and development. As Makins had predicted, the question was immediately asked whether this would result in a modification of the raw material allocation, which had hitherto been approved by the CPC. Sir James Chadwick was forced to acknowledge that the British government had not yet decided its general policy with regard to material. This is another example of how effective the embassy was at predicting potential issues which the Americans might raise.[35]

The question therefore arises: why, if the embassy was so efficient at raising these issues, was London so slow to respond? A glance at the workload might provide a clue. In the few months between the formation of the new post-war government in July 1945 and the end of that year, the Advisory Committee on Atomic Energy met ten times and considered over 65 memoranda on the subject of atomic energy. These ranged from *International Control of the Use of Atomic Energy* by Niels Bohr to *The Position of the Commonwealth in Relation to the Development of Atomic Energy* by Roger Makins.[36] Ministers as well as officials were busy. Gen 75, the committee of senior ministers formed to consider atomic energy issues, met on nine occasions in the same period and considered over 20 memoranda, several of them prepared by the Prime Minister himself.[37] The topic of atomic energy was, of course, just one of the important issues the new government had to address; there were literally dozens of others, some of which are addressed in this book. The point to be made, however, is that whilst an embassy can be efficient in providing a government with pertinent and relevant information, the effectiveness of the embassy and the information it provides is constrained by the extent to which the politicians and officials in London are able to respond to and use the information they receive.

On 25 September, the day after the Advisory Committee met in London to discuss Makins' note, Halifax met with the President. It was the ambassador's first meeting with the President since he met him in Plymouth Sound aboard the *HMS Renown* during Truman's return from Potsdam in early August. Halifax recorded in his diary that the President was very friendly and talked quite freely, with the atomic bomb very much on his mind.[38] Halifax's conversation with the President covered the Loan Agreement talks, the foreign ministers' conference then taking place in London and atomic energy. Truman discussed the sharing of the atomic secret and the position of the Soviets. Halifax indicated that these subjects were very much on Attlee's mind as well, which elicited from Truman the comment that he would very much like to talk to the Prime Minister about them.

Halifax then moved the conversation on to ask whether Truman had had an opportunity to reply to Attlee's letter of 16 August, asking for continued collaboration. Truman replied that this was 'all part of the same question and he thought it of great importance that collaboration between us should continue'.[39] This was perhaps the crucial point. Whilst Truman was indicating that collaboration should continue he was also saying that it was part of the larger question of the overall control of atomic energy and the debate on the sharing of the atomic secret. It seems that, at this stage, the people below Truman with whom Makins was talking had stronger, or at least more advanced, views than Truman himself did. This would not be out of character for Truman, who had a habit of listening to those around him and then taking a decision himself. The day after the Cabinet Advisory Committee considered Makins' paper and on the same day that Halifax met the President, Attlee wrote again to Truman. Attlee, after analysing the threats and problems posed by atomic power, suggested a meeting to 'discuss this momentous problem together'.[40]

On 3 October, Truman sent a message to Congress recommending the establishment of a US Atomic Energy Commission. For Britain, the message contained two crucial points. Firstly, it confirmed that the issue of domestic control and security arrangements for atomic energy was to be the subject of legislation and that the atomic energy issue was now therefore in the hands of Congress. Secondly, Truman confirmed that he intended to 'initiate discussions first with our associates in this discovery, Great Britain and Canada, and then with other nations in an effort to effect agreement on the conditions under which cooperation might replace rivalry in the field of atomic power'.[41] Attlee was to have his meeting with the President on the issue of atomic energy. After further badgering by Attlee, a conference to discuss atomic energy, to be held in Washington, between Truman, Attlee and Mackenzie King, the Canadian Prime Minister, was scheduled for 11 November 1945.

The embassy played a significant background role in setting up this meeting. As noted above, when meeting with Truman on 25 September, Halifax was instrumental in eliciting a response from Truman that a meeting between the President and Attlee would be desirable. Halifax met the President again on 20 October. At that time the announcement of, and the date for, a meeting of the three leaders had not been announced. Truman, concerned with the effect that a meeting of the three leaders might have upon the Soviets, asked whether Attlee could visit Canada and 'drop down' to Washington on some pretext. Halifax diplomatically pointed out that it would be impossible to conceal a meeting between the Prime Minister and the President and that such subterfuge could only result in incurring all the 'mistrust from public opinion in the United States and United Kingdom' that false pretexts inevitably aroused. Halifax also pointed out to the President that his message to Congress had already put the Soviets on notice that such a meeting was to take place. Halifax reported that the President felt the force of his argument and asked Halifax to discuss the matter with Byrnes.[42] Halifax met with Byrnes on 24 October and Byrnes told him that once the terms of the Palestinian enquiry had been agreed and Truman had received a response from a message he had sent to Stalin, then it would be possible to make an announcement regarding Attlee's visit. Byrnes suggested that the above two issues would be cleared by 1 November, after which an announcement could be made.[43] Attlee's proposed visit to Washington was, in fact, announced on 31 October.

The embassy participated in the Washington Conference; both Halifax and Makins were members of the United Kingdom delegation, which was formed for the purpose of handling the Washington negotiations. Other members of the delegation were Sir John Anderson, Field Marshal Sir Henry Maitland Wilson, Major General E.I. Jacob, (Offices of the Cabinet and Minister of Defence,) the Right Honourable Malcolm MacDonald (High Commissioner in Canada), Neville Butler and Sir John Cockcroft. The delegation was chaired by Attlee.[44] The embassy also played a part in the various preparations for the conference. Halifax wrote to Attlee, suggesting pointers for the speeches he was to make in Washington. These included making reference to the Labour government not being Communist; 'neither you nor your colleagues violent revolutionaries: no guillotine yet in Trafalgar Square'. Halifax also suggested that Attlee might point out that 'it was His Majesty's Government and not Laski who were responsible for British policy'.[45] The Reports Division of the embassy also began the preparation of a new regular report entitled 'Report on Congressional and Public Opinion in the USA on the Use and Control of Atomic Energy'. The report, which was normally issued on a bi-weekly basis, ran to over 50 issues.

The embassy was less successful, however, at persuading the Americans to focus on preparations for the conference. On 3 November, Halifax sent a telegram to Attlee indicating that he was trying to discover what the Americans had in mind with regard to procedure and what team they might field. Halifax was forced to conclude that

'I have the impression that in this case, as in so many others their organisation will be loose and their ideas untidy'.[46] Three days later, Makins told Halifax that, when he asked Dean Acheson what the Americans had in mind for the conduct of the negotiations, Acheson had replied that 'he had not the slightest idea' since no one had spoken to him or consulted him on the subject.[47] This response was symptomatic of the State Department's, or rather Byrnes's, lack of interest in the issue at the time. In fact, it was the War Department that put together information for the conference and set the agenda.[48]

Halifax, by paying attention to the pre-conference preparations, was instrumental in securing a place at the negotiating table for John Anderson. At a dinner given by Halifax on 7 November, Judge Rosenman, one of Truman's special advisers, informed Halifax that the President intended to hold the first day's formal meeting on the atomic energy discussions aboard the Secretary of the Navy's yacht *Sequoia*. Rosenman further indicated that the President wanted Halifax to attend and that only Byrnes would attend from the American side. Halifax was aware that Truman did not want to include Anderson in the party. After Attlee had arrived in Washington on 10 November, Halifax telephoned T.L. Rowan, the Prime Minister's Secretary, and told him that he needed to arrange things so Anderson could attend. A formal dinner for the three leaders had been organised at the White House for that evening. At a meeting with Attlee immediately prior to the dinner, Halifax discovered from Rowan that the President had declined to have Anderson on the yacht and that the Prime Minister felt he could do no more.

At the formal dinner, however, Halifax was seated next to the President and in appropriate diplomatic language told the President that it was a mistake not to include Anderson in the meeting on the yacht the next day. He argued that 'it would inevitably affect Winston's attitude if he ever heard about it and after all John Anderson had come three thousand miles, etc, etc'.[49] Truman changed his mind and Anderson was included. Halifax had secured a seat at the negotiating table for, perhaps, Britain's most knowledgeable politician on atomic issues. It is traditional when discussing Halifax to disclose his closeness to Roosevelt. What this and other encounters with Truman demonstrate is that Halifax managed to develop a close relationship with Truman as well.

Of the two issues that the British wished to see discussed at the conference, i.e. the international control of atomic energy and continued Anglo-American atomic collaboration, the embassy was more influential in the latter. It was the former issue, however, that took up most of the time and which also led to the Washington Declaration.[50] The Declaration, which was made by Truman, Attlee and Mackenzie King, recommended that a commission be set up under the United Nations with the objective of finding ways to control the use of atomic energy.[51] The proposal was based on a plan prepared by Vannevar Bush.[52] It was not enthusiastically received by the British. They objected to the piecemeal release of scientific information and they did not like the American proposal for control and inspection necessary to police any international agreement. However, after several days of debate, it was the American view that prevailed and 'the final product was more a matter of British resignation than compromise'.[53]

On the second issue, continued Anglo-American collaboration, the embassy played a more influential role. When Truman met Halifax on 25 September, he indicated that he wanted continued collaboration with Britain; Truman reconfirmed this at the conference.[54] The position on the ground, however, was not quite consistent with this. In a memorandum prepared by Butler on 4 November, he pointed out that in the only recent meeting of the Combined Policy Committee 'the Americans were not particularly forthcoming'. He continued: 'Sir J. Chadwick reports that since the end of hostilities we have been getting no information out of them under it [i.e. the Quebec agreement].'[55] It is possible that the dragging of American feet was a response to Truman's memo, dated 15 August, instructing government departments not to divulge information on the atom bomb without his specific authority.[56] It is also the case, however, that the members of the team responsible for the atomic project during the war who were reluctant to share information then, still retained that point of view. On 31 October, Butler recorded a conversation with the American ambassador, J.G. Winant, in which he was told 'very confidentially that General Groves wanted to keep the inner secrets from us'.[57]

It was against this background that the British hoped to reignite atomic energy collaboration. The matter was raised at the Washington Conference but, according to Makins, the 'talks on international control were so "long and arduous" that there was no time for the leaders to consider drawing up an agreement to continue their countries' cooperation'.[58] Consequently the task of agreeing a basis for future collaboration was delegated to a group of aides: Anderson and Makins for the British and Groves and Patterson (US Secretary of War) for the Americans. The main discussion of this group centred on collaboration with regard to raw material supplies which the Americans needed and the complete exchange of information which the British wanted.[59]

These second-level meetings took place towards the end of the conference on 15 and 16 November and under considerable time pressure. The meetings resulted in two documents. The first, a short document, was the Washington Memorandum, addressed to the CPC, signed by the President and the two prime ministers, expressing their desire for continued full and effective cooperation in the field of atomic energy. It also stated that they agreed to the continuation of the CPC and the Combined Development Trust and it asked the CPC to consider and recommend appropriate arrangements to bring this about.[60] The second document was the Anderson Groves Memorandum, a document signed by Groves and Anderson and addressed to the Chairman of the CPC, which gave guidance on the points to be considered by the CPC in the preparation of a new document to replace the Quebec Agreement.[61] The memorandum also expressed views on the revisions to be made to the Combined Development Trust.[62]

Makins was present at the meetings which led to the production of the above two documents, although it was John Anderson who led the discussions. Makins, however, claimed that it was his intervention which led directly to the production of the Washington Memorandum. 'In desperation I [Makins] intervened strongly and produced [three sentences] providing for the continuation of collaboration in the uses of atomic energy.'[63] If this was true it was an impressive intervention from the embassy minister. The American version of events was, however, different. Their record indicates that it was Groves and Harrison who suggested that there should be a short directive, i.e. the Washington Memorandum, signed by the President and the two prime ministers, and a longer statement, the Anderson Groves Memorandum. Their record states that 'Mr Rickett and Mr Makins did not dissent from this view', although it does acknowledge that the Washington Memorandum was prepared by the British.[64] Given that the source of Makins' quotation is his draft memoirs, which were produced 40 years after the event and are inconsistent with other records, there must be some doubt as to whether or not Makins did intervene in such a decisive manner.

Perhaps the most significant intervention during these meetings came not from Makins, but from General Groves during the negotiation of the Anderson Groves Memorandum. It was Groves who persuaded Anderson to accept the words 'in the field of basic research' after the words 'full and effective cooperation'. Groves managed to persuade the British that if 'full and effective cooperation' was used before the wording providing for the exchange of technical information, etc., then it would cause great difficulties if the wording ever came before the eyes of the Senate.[65] The Anderson Groves Memorandum provided for ad hoc arrangements with regard to collaboration in respect of the design, development and construction of nuclear plants. This was the area of most importance to the British. Only Denis Ricketts (an Assistant Secretary in the Cabinet Office and Secretary to the Advisory Committee on Atomic Energy) put up the 'bitterest of opposition' to Anderson's concession; apparently Makins was silent on the matter.[66] Truman would later use this clause as justification for ending collaboration with Britain.

The Washington Conference resulted in three documents: the Declaration, which was published, the Washington Memorandum and the Anderson Groves Memorandum, which were not published. Attlee returned to London believing that he had secured a start to the process of the international control of atomic energy and that he had entered a new era of atomic energy collaboration with America. Events did not quite turn out in the way Attlee hoped, however.

The Combined Policy Committee held its first meeting after the Washington Conference on 4 December 1945.[67] After consideration and discussion of the Washington Memorandum and the Anderson

Groves Memorandum, Halifax proposed that a subcommittee be set up to produce a replacement document for the Quebec Agreement. A subcommittee consisting of Makins, Groves and Lester Pearson (the Canadian ambassador) was appointed.[68]

Groves pushed for an early meeting of the subcommittee and a meeting was held on 14 December. Makins reported that 'it went unexpectedly well, and there was not, as I at one time feared, any apparent difference of intention between us'.[69] There were several further meetings of the subcommittee and by the end of January Makins was reporting that the negotiation of the new agreement was going along fairly smoothly.[70] However, Makins also warned London that 'there is a good deal of disarray in the American camp on the whole question of atomic energy and unless we get these agreements through very soon we may miss the market altogether'.[71]

The subcommittee had, by early February 1946, produced a draft report for the CPC. The report produced three documents: a replacement for the Quebec Agreement, a revised version of the agreement regulating the Combined Development Trust and an exchange of letters specifically releasing Britain from the provisions of the fourth clause of the Quebec Agreement.[72] In seeking approval for these documents, Makins counselled London not to seek too many amendments to the drafts he was sending them. He sensed that the American attitude to atomic collaboration was changing and believed that if an agreement was to be reached it needed to be reached quickly.[73]

The three documents produced by the subcommittee, which together set out the basis for future Anglo-American collaboration on atomic energy, were presented to the CPC on 15 February 1945. There was no dissenting voice in the report presented with it; i.e. Groves acquiesced in its submission. However, two days before the CPC met, Groves sent a memorandum to Byrnes the only effect of which was to undermine the subcommittee's work. The memorandum stated:

> The scope of the new arrangements [i.e. the subcommittee's proposals] extends far beyond that ever contemplated by the Quebec agreement . . . The military, political, legal and international implications require the closest consideration by the highest

authorities of the possible consequences which may result from
this alliance if it is consummated in its present form . . . The proposed form of cooperation in the field of atomic energy could
well be considered as tantamount to a military alliance.

The memorandum denied that Britain had played an important part
in the development of the atomic bomb and then listed arguments as
to why there should be no agreement with the British.[74]

At the meeting of the CPC on 15 February, Byrnes, now suitably
briefed, 'took cover' behind Article 102 of the United Nations Charter.
This article provided that all international agreements had to be reg-
istered with the United Nations and therefore made public. Because of
this provision, the committee decided that each of the three governments should reconsider the form of the agreements proposed by the
subcommittee and consider the desirability of making them public.[75]
The effect of this, of course, was to shelve continued atomic energy
collaboration. If the Americans were seeking to avoid continued collaboration then the 'discovery of Article 102 seemed a blessing and
deliverance'.[76]

Halifax, who had clearly been outmanoeuvred, protested and
reminded the meeting of the Washington Memorandum signed by the
President and British Prime Minister on 16 November providing for
'full and effective' cooperation. He 'observed that this was now the document which was intended to guide the Combined Policy Committee'.
Further, Halifax 'emphasised that H.M. Government plans [i.e. the
building of an atomic plant] had been based on the assumption of
full further cooperation . . . and that H.M. Government would now be
placed in a quite impossible position'.[77] Byrnes was unmoved but said
he would talk to the President.

Only two weeks before the CPC meeting, Makins had written to
London saying that 'since this draft is based on a proposal by Groves
he will be committed to make it work. Furthermore, it is altogether
probable that unless there is some basic change of US policy, a unanimous recommendation of the subcommittee is likely to go through
the Combined Policy Committee without difficulty.'[78] Was there a
change in American policy or had Makins been duped? It is difficult

to discern a fundamental change in American policy. There were events, however, which may have made the Americans more reticent to conclude a deal with the British. The Gouzenkou spy case was about to break,[79] the momentum behind the McMahon Act was building in Congress, the atomic issue was now well and truly politicised,[80] and a secret agreement made between Roosevelt and the Soviets over the Kurile Islands had recently been disclosed.[81] All these factors could have made the Administration nervous about entering into a secret agreement with the British. The other alternative is that Groves had been playing the British along with a view to increasing the amount of raw material coming into America and persuading the British to include the recently discovered South African supplies within the provisions of the Combined Development Trust. Makins, however, was alive to this possibility and was already aware that Groves' main objective was securing raw material supplies.[82]

It seems more likely that the changing sentiment in America, coupled with the move of the atomic issue from the War Department to the State Department, afforded Groves the opportunity to head off a policy that he had always been reluctant to pursue. As explained above, it appears that Makins recognised the threat from changing sentiment in America. In addition, he understood the consequences of moving the atomic issue into the State Department. Makins reported in January 1946 that 'the whole trend of Byrnesian foreign policy is away from exclusive Anglo American arrangements'.[83] However, Makins does not seem to have realised that Groves would use the changing climate to subvert the work of the subcommittee and the earlier work upon which its work was based.

Halifax's response to the meeting of the CPC on 15 February was perhaps a little naive. He ascribed the behaviour to the potential political problems the Administration would have with Congress and undertakings Truman had given to the McMahon Committee. Halifax's initial conclusion was: 'I doubt whether Byrnes or Patterson have yet given serious thought to the problem, but I think they will do their best, if and when they do, to cooperate in finding a solution.'[84]

After the disappointment of the February meeting Attlee, 'reluctant to throw away the results so far achieved', wrote to Halifax acknowledging that, due to Article 102 and the undesirability of a secret agreement, no agreement was possible. However, as an alternative Attlee suggested that the minutes of the Combined Policy Committee record the intentions contained in the documents drawn up by the Makins-Groves-Pearson subcommittee.[85] He indicated that, as a second best, this would have to do.

After some difficulty, a further meeting of the CPC was organised for 15 April and Attlee's proposal, which had been previously circulated, was discussed. The Americans indicated that this device did not solve the problem and would not accept it.[86] Halifax then asked for the American proposals. They said they had none. Byrnes then said that the CPC 'had not the authority to decide the matter' and that it must be referred to the three leaders.[87] Halifax immediately advised Attlee to send a message to Truman setting out the circumstances and the British grievance.

Halifax's response to this meeting was also accommodating. Halifax suggests that 'we did not securely understand what the President and the Prime Minister meant by a short general statement [i.e. the Washington Memorandum] that they signed'. Halifax indicated that he was not surprised since he recognised how the situation, presumably referring to Congress and the setting up of the United Nations Commission, had changed in the last few months. Halifax then suggested that cooperation between the British and Americans was more difficult now than it might have been a few months previously. Halifax concludes his diary entry with 'But London will not readily understand any of this and will be gravely disturbed and, if I mistake not, pretty resentful.'[88]

Halifax was right. London was resentful and Attlee wrote to Truman on 16 April expressing disappointment at the turn of discussion at the meeting of the CPC. He indicated that the documents signed at the November conference 'cannot mean less than full interchange of information and a fair distribution of material'. Attlee urged the President 'most strongly that the Combined Policy Committee should make a further attempt to work out a satisfactory basis of cooperation'.[89] Truman, after having taken advice from Byrnes and Patterson, replied on 20 April. The essential point that Truman made is that whilst the Washington Memorandum signed by Truman and Attlee on 16 November refers to 'full and effective cooperation in the field of atomic energy', clause 5 of the Groves Anderson Memorandum, drawn up a few hours later, states specifically that:

> There shall be full and effective cooperation in the field of basic scientific research . . . In the field of development design and construction, and operation of plants such cooperation . . . shall be regulated by such ad hoc arrangements as may be approved from time to time by the Combined Policy Committee as mutually advantageous.

The Groves intervention referred to above had provided Truman with the ammunition he needed. Truman further argued that if he thought that signing the Washington Memorandum on 16 November would have obligated America to supply information leading to the construction of another atomic energy plant he would not have signed it.[90]

Whilst it was true that Truman had a point, the 'reply caused great resentment in Britain. To British Government leaders and officials it seemed to be a denial of the phrase "full and effective" cooperation agreed to in Washington and included in the Hyde Park aide memoir.'[91] Dean Acheson (Under-Secretary of State), who attended both the February and April CPC meetings, provided a succinct summary of the position in his memoirs: 'Our Government, having made an agreement [i.e. the Quebec Agreement] from which it had gained immeasurably, was not keeping its word and performing its obligations.'[92] This position by Acheson is supported by a remark he made to Makins where he was apologetic about the American performance and indicated that he understood that the American action represented a volte face on their part.[93]

The meeting of the CPC on 15 April also discussed the raw material allocations. The raw material, for example uranium ore, was required for the American and, yet to be built, British nuclear plants. At this time, it was also anticipated that there would be a shortage of the ore by the end of 1947. The allocation of raw materials was the one card left in British hands. Halifax and Makins had recognised from the previous discussions that Groves had as one objective 'to get as much raw material [as possible] into the United States while the going is good'.[94] They realised that now was a good time for the British to put in for a substantial allocation of raw material, as was permitted under the Combined Development Trust. The effect of the British proposal would be to divert a proportion of the raw material supplies from America to Britain. Groves objected to the proposals and indicated that materials should be allocated on the basis of need. Groves's proposal was that virtually all the raw material should be allocated to the Americans. Little progress was made on this issue at the meeting and the matter was delegated to a group consisting of Acheson, Bush, Groves, Chadwick and Makins.

In order to expedite matters, Halifax and Makins arranged to meet Acheson on 1 May 1946. Halifax indicated that in the absence of any progress and on his authority Chadwick and Makins had met Groves earlier and had put forward a compromise from the proposal the British had presented to the CPC on 15 April. The effect of this was to give the Americans more raw material, but not as much as they wanted or claimed they needed. Acheson, who was somewhat embarrassed, said that Groves had rejected the compromise on the grounds that acceptance would lead to the curtailment of the operation of the American plants and that material should not be supplied for the construction of a plant in the UK. Halifax rejected these arguments. He said that 'the first represented an outrageous claim to the whole of the Trust material; the second raised a question of the national defence and security of the UK of which I thought HMG must be the final judge'. Halifax ended the meeting indicating that the British government was not prepared to let matters drift and that 'HMG were seriously disturbed about the failure to agree on cooperation'.[95]

After further discussions, a compromise was reached which Acheson communicated to the American members of the CPC on 7 May. All raw materials received in America as of 31 March 1946 would be allocated to America, for the remainder of the year the allocation was to be split equally: 1,350 tons to America and 1,350 tons to Britain.[96] Future allocations would be decided at a later date. Halifax wrote to Anderson on 12 May indicating that Acheson had fought 'hard and sincerely' for the compromise arrangement and strongly recommended that Anderson accept it. The embassy had persuaded Acheson of their case and, as a result, Acheson persuaded others on the American side. This was a significant diplomatic success for the embassy and was achieved because of the mutual respect that existed between certain embassy officials, in this case Makins and Halifax, and certain State Department officials, particularly Acheson. In the end, the compromise proved beneficial to the British because it secured uranium supplies which were far more useful to the British than technical information.[97] Acceptance of the compromise may have been aided by a comment made by Halifax to Acheson. 'He [Halifax] had warned Mr Acheson that if General Groves view was allowed to prevail the US Govt. was likely to see us denouncing in some way the Belgium agreement and denying America access to raw materials within the Commonwealth and Empire.'[98] Such action would have resulted in the Americans having to shut down at least part of their nuclear operations. Whilst the above deliberations were going on, another event was taking place in Congress which was to seal the fate of collaboration at that time. Truman's message to Congress on 3 October initiated the legislative process that led to the control of atomic energy in America. Initially it was seen by Truman as a measure to regulate domestic control of atomic energy; soon, however, it became an effective mechanism for controlling the relationship of America with other countries.

The first bill to be introduced for the domestic control of atomic energy was the May–Johnson bill. Whilst this bill did little to regulate the exchange of information between countries, it was disliked by scientists because it gave too much control to the military. It was succeeded by the McMahon bill. This bill originally emphasised the international control of atomic energy and placed very little restriction on the flow of information between countries. During the passage of the bill, however, Congress became more paranoid about keeping the atomic bomb secret, and this sentiment was fanned by the Canadian spy case referred to above.

Consequently, when the bill reappeared in the open in April 1946, it indicated that one of its prime objectives was the 'common defence and security' of the United States. In addition: 'A new clause . . . introduced a new concept of "restricted data" which covered all data about the manufacture or utilisation of atomic weapons, the production of fissionable material or its use in the production of power.'[99] The US Atomic Energy Commission, which was to be set up under this bill, was to control the dissemination of this data and do so in a manner which ensured the security of the United States. These security measures were expanded as the bill was debated in Congress. In the end, the interchange of information with any other country became virtually impossible and so the door that had already become closed to Anglo-American cooperation was now locked. The McMahon Act, or more formally the Atomic Energy Act, was passed by both houses on 26 July 1946 and was signed by Truman on 1 August.

One question that might be asked is what action the embassy took to influence this bill as it passed through Congress. The answer seems to be not very much. 'In March 1946, when admittedly the draft bill was fairly innocuous, the British Embassy in Washington had written to London that there was no need to worry about it.'[100] The embassy indicated that the Americans had not agreed the way forward and that there would be many changes before the bill received Congressional approval. The embassy also sent a revised bill to London on 13 April but with no comment. Chadwick, however, seemed alive to the problems. In a letter to Anderson dated 17 April 1946 he wrote:

> the bill [i.e. the new draft of the McMahon bill] seems to almost exclude the possibility of collaboration with us except by the express approval of Senate or Congress; ... to prevent the transmission of information we require and to which, I think, we are entitled; [and] to prevent our acquiring material from the US.[101]

Anderson minuted on this letter 'this is very serious & shd be considered at once by the Depts concerned'. He continued: 'It is odd that we have apparently had nothing from the ambassador.'[102]

Gowing indicates that Chadwick wanted to talk privately to Senator McMahon, but the embassy in Washington was conscious that lobbying Congress was a notoriously risky tactic and advised that any such action by Britain would not affect the bill since the Senate Committee was 'quite unamenable to official promptings'.[103]

It has also been suggested that, had the Congress been aware of the various agreements entered into during the war, the outcome might have been different. Indeed, years later, 'McMahon told British ministers that, had he been properly briefed about the history of US atomic cooperation with Britain and Canada, his bill would probably not have needed to have been passed on such restrictive lines'.[104] This, however, is an easy remark to make several years after the event. Whilst the Senate might not have known all of the details of Anglo-American wartime agreements, it seems implausible that they were not aware of the statement issued by Attlee and Churchill on 6 August. This statement set out in considerable detail the nature of Anglo-American cooperation during the war and even referred to the CPC.[105]

Makins says:

> Such was the strength of opinion at the time in favour of guarding the American 'secret' that nothing could have made any difference, and suggestions to the contrary made in conversations some years afterwards by Senator McMahon . . . do not carry much weight.[106]

It seems that the embassy felt that lobbying Congress on this particular bill would have been unproductive. There is no doubt that the embassy had the ability to lobby Senator McMahon (Democrat, Connecticut). Halifax had dined with the Senator on at least three occasions in 1945.[107] Also, McMahon was described as 'a friendly and pleasant person with warm feelings towards Great Britain and an excellent voting record on Foreign Affairs'.[108] In response to a suggestion by Anderson that Attlee should attempt to get Truman to intervene, Makins' response was clear: 'There is no chance of intervention by the executive to delay the passage of legislation or to introduce amendments'.[109]

By the spring of 1946, the negotiations on continued Anglo-American cooperation had broken down. In an attempt to influence Truman before the passing of the McMahon Act, Attlee wrote to him again on 6 June 1946 stressing Britain and America's 'special relationship' in the atomic energy field. The telegram ended with a request for 'full information to which we believe we are entitled, both by the documents and by the history of our common efforts in the past'.[110] Truman did not reply to this letter until December and then in a very cursory manner. The Anglo-American relationship, which exhibited such warmth during the war, had now cooled considerably.

The embassy, then, played a significant part in the atomic energy discussions, which took place in 1945–1946. It is important, however, not to exaggerate its role or to lose sight of the fact that it failed to identify the biggest single threat to continued collaboration, i.e. General Groves. The embassy, however, was quick to spot the politicisation of the issue and to communicate that fact to London. It was also effective in repositioning itself to deal with these changed circumstances. Halifax, who was close to Truman, played an important part in improving the opportunities available to the British at the Washington Conference. Securing a place at the negotiations for John Anderson is something which Halifax, not the Prime Minister, managed to achieve. It is a telling example of how important diplomats on the ground can be, even when their political masters are present.

During the Washington, Conference both Halifax and Makins were members of the British delegation and both participated in the various discussions at the conference. The embassy's part, however, was subordinate to those of Attlee and Anderson. It has been suggested that Makins had a 'major influence on the formulation and execution of British policy'.[111] If he did, it was not at this time. The key document produced at the conference, from an atomic energy collaboration point of view, was the Anderson Groves Memorandum and Anderson took the lead in this. Even when Anderson made the mistake of accepting the words 'in the field of basic research' after the phrase 'full and effective cooperation', the only objector was Denise Ricketts and not Makins. It is also suggested that Makins was responsible for the production of the Washington Memorandum. This suggestion is based on a memoir by Makins written some 40 years after the event and is not consistent with the American record.

After the conference, it was Halifax and Makins who had the job of formalising the understandings which had been reached. Groves, however, was not prepared to concede anything to the British. Throughout the winter and spring of 1945–1946, he cleverly orchestrated events and those with influence around him, in particular Byrnes, and put an end to atomic energy collaboration. The embassy did not seem to spot this manoeuvre by Groves; indeed, Makins reported Groves' intentions rather favourably. This, together with some of Halifax's accommodating remarks about the American's behaviour, raises the question of whether the embassy was too trusting. It is perhaps apposite to quote a paragraph from one of the more recent accounts of Anglo-American atomic relations.

> The British approached these discussions with a naiveté that would have been appropriate to a world governed by the chivalric code of a bygone age but not to the diplomatic arena of the twentieth century, where the primacy of national security and national interest took precedence over questions of principle. It was a naiveté based on the understanding that a gentleman could be taken at his word. . . . time and time again over the next few years the British would place their trust in the vague words of the Americans and be disappointed. They even attempted to rationalise the Americans' behaviour.[112]

This assessment is, perhaps, too harsh but it has a ring of truth to it. One of the concerns which the Foreign Office has with all diplomats is that they can become too close to, or too trusting of, the officials and/ or politicians in the country to which they are posted.[113]

It is, nevertheless, true that Halifax had a tough edge and, indeed, diplomatic skill. Securing the raw material allocation was one of the few successes the embassy had in the negotiations on the atomic energy issue. The British realised that their access to raw material gave them leverage and, perhaps for the first time, played their hand in this regard to something like its full strength. Once it was realised what the Americans were up to, Halifax, with the approval of London, was prepared to threaten to stop all shipments of uranium ore to America in order to force a compromise on the issue of raw material allocation and to use the offices of Acheson, who was known to be supportive of the British position, to achieve it.[114]

The loss of Anglo-American collaboration in the atomic energy field was a blow for Britain, not simply because of the loss of 'know how' but because of the loss of status it implied. It is difficult to see what action the embassy could have taken to counter this loss. Clearly there were a number of issues which contributed. The officials, Groves in particular, were against continued collaboration, Byrnes was not particularly pro-British, and the issue became politicised, thus involving Congress. Underlying all of these considerations, however, was the changing mood of America in the post-war period – something about which an embassy could do very little on its own. As Halifax indicated in a telegram to Bevin dated 12 December 1945, 'the elements of public life which gave vigour to isolationism are now being transmuted into the active exponents of a somewhat truculent new brand of "America first".'[115] There is then something of a mixed conclusion as to the role of the embassy in the atomic energy discussions of 1945–1946. The embassy was effective in its anticipation of the changing mood and trends in America with regard to atomic energy but ineffective in seeking to head off the threat from General Grove and others.

Ironically, there was to be a revival in Anglo-American collaboration towards the end of 1947. This revival led to the Modus Vivendi agreement. By then, however, the world was a different place. The embassy's role in that agreement is discussed in chapter 5.

CHAPTER 4

PALESTINE

The fact has to be faced that there is no common ground between the Arabs and the Jews. They differ in religion and in language; their cultural and social life, their ways of thought and conduct, are as difficult to reconcile as are their national aspirations. These last are the greatest bars to peace. Both communities lay claim to Palestine; the one on the ground of a millennium of occupation, the other on the ground of historic association and of an undertaking given to it in the First World War. The antithesis is thus complete.[1]

The irreconcilable nature of the Palestinian problem, so aptly described in Halifax's memorandum, above, has remained at the forefront of international politics since World War II. The era when it caused the most friction in Anglo-American relations, however, was the period from July 1945 to May 1948. Consequently, it was an issue that impacted upon the ambassadorships of both Halifax and Inverchapel. Halifax, who left Washington in May 1946, dealt with the issue at the end of his tenure. It was a period when Britain was in desperate need of a loan from America and the embassy needed to be highly sensitive to the effect of Britain's actions, particularly in relation to Palestine, upon Congress. Sensitivity was also required during Inverchapel's tenure; but perhaps less so. The Loan Agreement was approved by Congress in July 1946 and during the rest of Inverchapel's tenure, May 1946 to May 1948, the perception of the threat posed by the Soviets increased and the perceived utility of Britain as a strong ally of the Americans also increased.

In assessing the role of the embassy, it is important to be aware of two factors which were to influence it. Firstly, Truman took a different line on the Palestinian issue from the Department of State; consequently the President took his own initiatives, often by-passing the department. This tended to change the dynamic of diplomacy. If the Department of State was in the dark, the embassy probably was too. Connected with this issue was the fact that much of the impetus for Truman's actions came from Zionists inside the White House. These people, for example David Niles, tended to work in the background and were outside normal diplomatic circles. This also affected the diplomatic process.

Secondly, unlike the Financial Agreement negotiations, where the diplomats were a part of the face-to-face negotiations, and the atomic energy discussions where the diplomats sat on the relevant committees where events were discussed and settled, the embassy was not, in the main, directly involved in face-to-face discussions. This was because Palestine was a third party issue rather than one solely between the two countries. As a result, the role of the embassy tended to be more focused upon formal communication between the two countries and presentations of the American mood to London. Notwithstanding this, the embassy did make a contribution to policy formation on the Palestinian issue.

Although Bevin and the military regarded the Middle East as the most important region in the world in relation to the defence of Britain, their ambitions for, and credibility in, the region were frustrated by their inability to solve the Palestinian problem. This inability rested in part on the intractable nature of the problem but was also due to the lack of resources available to Britain in the post-war period. Bevin and, indeed, Halifax believed that involving America in the problem would lead to its solution. This did not prove to be the case and the differences between Britain and America in relation to the Palestinian issue were the cause of some of the most acrimonious exchanges between the two countries in the post-war period. These differences were driven not so much by strategic reasons as domestic ones. As Balfour, minister at the embassy, pointed out 'American foreign policy is always liable [to become] the shuttlecock of domestic controversy'.[2]

Prior to considering the role of the embassy, however, it is necessary to consider the background events and the different attitudes with which Britain and America approached the Palestinian problem.

In 1917, the Lloyd George government promised the Jewish people the establishment of a National Home in Palestine. The Balfour Declaration, as it was called, was made at a time when the outcome of World War I was not certain and Britain sought help from whichever quarter it could be found. It was felt, by some, that a sop to the Jews would aid the war effort. After the war, the Mandate for Palestine was assigned to Britain and the terms of the Mandate were approved by the Council of the League of Nations in July 1922. The Mandate governed the policy of successive British governments for 20 years. It embodied the Balfour Declaration and, in addition to the obligation to protect holy sites, imposed three further obligations on the Mandatory. Firstly, 'To place the country under such political, administrative and economic conditions as will secure the establishment in Palestine of a Jewish national home'; secondly, 'To safeguard the civil and religious rights of all the inhabitants of Palestine'; and thirdly, 'to place the country under such...conditions as will secure the development of self governing institutions'.[3]

As a series of white papers on the subject pointed out the Mandate was, in places, ambiguous and contained a number of uncertainties. These contributed to the unrest and hostility that developed between the Arabs and the Jews. The Arabs were fundamentally opposed to Jewish immigration and 'communal violence between resident Arabs and Jewish immigrants mounted...during the twenties and thirties'.[4] Hitler's persecution of the Jews in Europe led to an increase in immigration into Palestine and this only exacerbated the problem. In 1922, there were 650,000 Arabs in Palestine and only 84,000 Jews; by 1936, however, the Jewish population had swollen to 400,000. Whilst the Arab population had also increased it was not by the same rate and the percentage of the population that was Jewish rose from 11% in 1922 to 31% in 1936.[5]

The increase in immigration led to an Arab rebellion, which started in 1936, and to escalating violence directed against the Jews.

In response, Prime Minister Stanley Baldwin set up a royal commission, chaired by Earl Peel, to enquire into the working of the British Mandate. The commission's report, issued in July 1937, concluded that the two communities could not be expected to live together and that the British had committed themselves to incompatible policies in the same country. The report also contained the first formal recommendation that Palestine be partitioned into two separate states: one Arab, the other Jewish. The report, which only led to further violence, did not find favour with the majority of Arabs and Jews; both had expected to become sovereign in Palestine. Its recommendations were never implemented by the British.

The menace of war focused the British on the strategic position of the Middle East. Oil would be important, as would the strategic routes through the region. These issues, together with the fact that the empire contained millions of Muslims, inclined the British to the Arab point of view. In a white paper issued in 1939, Britain produced her last words on Palestine before the war. The white paper dealt with three issues: the Constitution, immigration and land.

In discussing the Constitution, the white paper indicated a desire to see an independent state 'in which Arabs and Jews share in government in such a way as to ensure that the essential interests of each community are safeguarded'. The paper also said, however, that the British government 'now declare unequivocally that it is not part of their policy that Palestine should become a Jewish state'. Immigration was to be controlled, being limited to 75,000 immigrants over the next five years, with Arab consent required thereafter for further immigration. Land purchases by Jews were also to be restricted.[6]

Neither the Jews nor the Arabs liked the 1939 white paper. Its principal effect, however, was to cause the Zionists to change tactics: instead of concentrating on the Mandatory power, they focused on the United States. The Biltmore programme, proposed by the Zionists in New York in 1942, called for the establishment of a 'Jewish State in Palestine that would stretch from the River Jordan to the Mediterranean'.[7] The powerful Jewish community in America adopted the Biltmore programme and so enshrined the necessity for a Jewish state into the arena of American politics. This change of tactics on the part of the Zionists was to prove extraordinarily successful; at the same time, it was to be the cause of considerable friction in Anglo-American relations. The Arabs, too, became politically active and in an effort to increase the cohesiveness of the Arab cause the Arab League was founded in March 1945. The Arab lobby, however, was never a powerful force in America.

In 1945, Attlee inherited a tangled morass of obligations, discontent on all sides and a Jewish terrorist organisation that had grown strong during the war. He also inherited a President conscious of the need to build a winning coalition at the next presidential election, due in 1948, and a Zionist lobby in America whose influence and moral authority had greatly increased due to the Holocaust.

In the immediate post-war period, Britain and America viewed the Palestinian situation from different perspectives. The British approach was conditioned by a number of factors. Firstly, there was the belief, held by the Chiefs of Staff at least, that a presence in the Middle East was essential to British security. The inability of the British to conclude satisfactory agreements with either Iran or Egypt raised the importance of Palestine. Secondly, the Labour Party which, of course, formed the post-war government, had consistently supported the Zionist cause. The Labour Party first made a pledge to support a Jewish homeland in December 1917 and it repeated this pledge at ten other Party conferences, the last in May 1945.[8] Thirdly, the Foreign Office was pro-Arab and worked on Bevin as soon as he arrived. According to Kenneth Harris, 'Within a few days of being at the Foreign Office, Bevin went to Attlee and said "Clem, about Palestine. According to my lads in the office we've got it wrong. We've got to think again".'[9] The Foreign Office with its pro-Arab stance was influential not only in its effect upon Bevin but also in the subsequent negotiations on Palestine.

Finally, and perhaps the biggest factor, however, was the financial position of Britain. This position has been well documented elsewhere; the effect of it, however, was two-fold. Firstly, Britain simply did not have the resources to impose any solution that she may have negotiated or favoured. Given the intractable nature of the problem, the military resources required to continue to police Palestine would have been too much for Britain. Attlee knew this and it undoubtedly affected his thinking. Secondly, and irrespective of the Palestinian problem, Britain had committed herself to receiving a loan from America to shore up her balance sheet. This loan was not finally approved by Congress until July 1946. Britain, as she was often reminded by James Byrnes and others, in approaching the issue needed to tread carefully in the light of the support for the Zionist cause both inside and outside Congress.

America did not have the historical association with the Middle East that Britain had. Its interest in the region was galvanised during the war, however. Roosevelt interrupted his return trip from the Yalta Conference to meet King Ibn Saud of Saudi Arabia, where America was developing valuable oil concessions. During the meeting, the President assured King Ibn Saud that 'he would make no move hostile to the Arab people and would not assist the Jews against the Arabs in Palestine'. Roosevelt also assured the king, as he had other govern-ments in the region, that 'there should be no decision respecting the basic situation in Palestine without full consultation with both Arabs and Jews'.[10] At the same time, as issuing placatory statements to the Arabs, however, Roosevelt had a tendency to make pro-Zionist state-ments, particularly after meetings with prominent members of the Zionist lobby.

These two approaches, moreover, became embedded in the atti-tudes of the different organs of state. The Department of State tended to be pro-Arab, believing that this was where America's interests lay; the White House, at least under Truman, tended to be pro-Zionist, believing that this was where the incumbents and his party's elec-toral interests lay. The root cause of this dichotomy was the power of the Jewish lobby. This power resided in both the numbers of Jews in America and in their access to the White House.

Nationally the Jews represented 3% of the vote but because they were more active politically than other sectors of the population they cast an estimated 4% of the votes in presidential elections.[11] In addi-tion, the American Jewish voters were concentrated in the metropoli-tan areas; for example, they represented 20% of the population in New York City. Clark Clifford, one of Truman's closest advisers, pointed out to Truman that since 1876 no one, except Woodrow Wilson in 1916, had won the presidency without taking New York, which accounted for 47 out of the 266 delegates needed to win the presidential election.[12] Jewish finance was also critical to Truman. Truman was not a wealthy man and the Democrats did not receive large industrial donations. Truman depended upon personal donations to fund his election campaigns and many of these came from the Jewish community. Contributions to campaigns gave Jews considerable access to Congressmen and Senators throughout America.[13]

The Jewish lobby also had pro-Zionists in the White House who had direct access to the President. These included people such as Clark Clifford (Special Counsel to the President), who was mentioned above, Samuel Rosenman (Special Counsel to Roosevelt and Truman) and David Niles (Administrative Assistant in the White House).[14] The last of these stands out as particularly influential in terms of the President's policy on Palestine. Niles worked for Roosevelt in the area of liaison with minorities, particularly Jews. Truman kept him on and 'it is clear that Niles played a vital behind the scenes role in helping Truman avoid the pitfalls in the bewilderingly fragmented world of Jewish affairs'.[15] The role of Niles should not be underestimated; he fixed committee appointments, intercepted and dealt with Department of State pro-Arab memoranda aimed at the President, effected introductions of important Zionists into the White House and was instrumental in influencing a number of critical votes in the Congress and the UN. Loy Henderson (Director of the Office of Near Eastern and African Affairs), the chief protagonist of the Arab cause in the Department of State, said that Niles 'was the most powerful and diligent advocate of the Zionist cause'.[16]

Levelled against the Zionist lobby was the Department of State. Within days of taking office, Truman received a memorandum from Secretary of State Stettinius warning him that 'efforts will be made by some of the Zionist leaders to obtain from you...commitments in favour of the Zionist program which is pressing for unlimited Jewish immigration into Palestine and the establishment of a Jewish state'. The memorandum then went on to point out that 'as we have interests in that area [Near East and Palestine] which are vital to the United States, we feel that this whole subject is one that should be handled with the greatest care and with a view to the long range interests of this country'.[17] The memorandum was followed by many others, which sought to remind Truman of America's interests in the region and the commitments that America had given to the Arabs.[18] The Department of State continued to counter, wherever possible, the Zionist pressures on the President. The department, however, struggled to persuade Truman of its perception of America's best interests.

The above discussion tends to polarise the American approach to the Palestinian problem. There was, however, another factor at work in America and that was the genuine sympathy for the plight of the Jews in Europe during the war.[19] The Holocaust had a profound effect on the world, including on America and its leaders. There were many in America who could not see why the suffering that the Jews had endured was being exacerbated by the British with their continued insistence on restricting immigration, thus committing thousands of Jews to remain in the displaced persons camps. The Jewish lobby may have amplified this sentiment and played upon it but the sentiment was real none the less.

To what extent did the embassy understand the approach taken by the Americans and the tension that existed between the White House and the Department of State on the issue of Palestine? In June 1945, Ronald Campbell, who had recently moved back from Washington to the Foreign Office, wrote to Halifax indicating that the Jewish immigration quota into Palestine was due to expire in November 1945. It was thought desirable that any incoming government should reach a decision on the future of Palestine a couple of months before the quota was exhausted. Campbell enclosed a memorandum setting out a number of policy options and asked the embassy to 'let us have an appreciation of the probable reactions of the Department of State and of American opinion generally'.[20] Campbell added that such an appreciation would be of great help to the new government when taking its eventual decision. This is a clear and interesting example of the British government asking the embassy for its views on a specific topic prior to putting a policy together.

Halifax reported back on 1 July 1945 in a long letter to the Foreign Office.[21] He made a number of interesting points. The Jews in America numbered five million, half of all Jews left in the world, and 'many of them occupy prominent positions round the White House, in the Administration and in the press'. Halifax, echoing Clark Clifford's report to Truman, also pointed out that the Jewish vote could swing New York in election years. Halifax concluded therefore that the Jews could exercise 'considerable pressure on the Administration, in Congress and on public opinion'. However, he also noted that they are not by themselves 'as powerful as they are vocal'. The Jewish lobby needed to carry non-Jewish opinion with them if they were to be successful. Halifax then made the point that non-Jewish opinion was not particularly interested in Palestine other than on the issue of immigration. In liberal quarters, there was a feeling that if the British had allowed more immigration before the war then more Jews would have escaped Nazi persecution. Halifax also added, however, that the average citizen did not want Jews in America and salved their conscience by advocating immigration into Palestine. The consequence of this was that the Jewish lobby could carry both 'liberal humanitarians and many anti Jews'. Whilst indicating that the Arab vote in America was not significant, Halifax did point out that 'the State Department itself is more favourable to the Arab than to the Zionist cause'.

The embassy at this stage, then, understood the complexities underlying the power of the Jewish lobby and, importantly, the limitations to that power. It understood that the issue in America was immigration into Palestine more than anything else. The embassy also understood that there were influential Jews in the US government; indeed, that there were several in the White House. Whether at this stage the embassy had understood the extent of this influence on the President is difficult to say but it is an issue which is considered further below. It is, of course, one thing to identify a potential threat, but quite another to counter it. Also, the embassy had grasped the point that the Department of State was pro-Arab. Again it is difficult to know whether, at this stage, the embassy understood the full extent of the divergence of opinion that existed between the Department of State and the White House but it certainly understood the implications of the Jewish lobby for a politician.

Halifax also addressed the relative positions of Britain and America. He concluded that America was in an illogical but comfortable position. America could not be ignored on the issue of Palestine because half of the world's Jews lived in America and most of the money pouring into Palestine came from America; yet, on the other hand, America did not bear any of the responsibility. Halifax suggested that 'for the Americans to be able thus to criticise and influence without responsibility is the most favourable and agreeable situation for them and, I must suppose, the exact converse for us'.

Halifax warned that the Americans viewed Palestine as a British colonial possession. He made the point that if any proposed solution to the problem led to disorder which, in turn, was quelled by British troops then 'public opinion might become violently inflamed against His Majesty's Government'. In any event in the absence of the 'miracle' of a solution acceptable to both sides, there would be criticism of the British government. It was possibly this conclusion that led Halifax to question whether it was right for Britain to continue to shoulder the burden of Palestine alone. Halifax ended his note with 'it is to our advantage to encourage the United States to cooperate with us in any attempt to solve the Palestinian and connected problems'. Halifax, then, was an early advocate of bringing in America in order to find a solution to the Palestinian problem.

Shortly after this, Truman raised the issue of Palestine at Potsdam. He wrote to Churchill expressing the 'great interest in America in the Palestine problem' and their concern with the drastic restrictions on Jewish immigration imposed by the 1939 White Paper. Truman expressed the hope that 'the British Government may find it possible without delay to take steps to lift the restrictions...on Jewish immigration into Palestine'.[22] Truman also asked for British ideas on a solution to the Palestine problem so that they could, in the near future, discuss them. This was yet another ball for Attlee to pick up and, after consulting Bevin, he wrote to Truman on 31 July 1945 indicating that he needed time to consider the matter but that it would be given his 'early and careful consideration'.[23]

Prior to the Potsdam Conference, possibly in a move to circumvent the Department of State, Truman sent Earl G. Harrison (Dean of

Pennsylvania Law School)[24] to investigate the plight of the refugees in Europe; in particular, 'the problems and needs of the Jewish refugees among the displaced persons'.[25] His report, delivered in August 1945 was, according to Truman, a moving document.[26] The report, which painted a grim picture of conditions in the displaced persons' camp, was to become the ammunition attached to a letter sent to Attlee on 31 August 1945.[27] The letter suggested facilitating the immigration of a further 100,000 Jews into Palestine from Europe – a request consistent with a petition to the British government from the Jewish Agency. The letter ended with 'if it is to be effective, such action should not be long delayed'.[28]

On learning that Truman was due to make a public statement on the issue and publish the Harrison report, Attlee cabled Truman on 14 September stating that 'any such action could do grievous harm to relations between our two countries'.[29] The First Secretary at the embassy responsible for Near Eastern and Jewish Affairs was A.H. Tandy. He indicated to Halifax that the publication of the Harrison Report was anticipated by the Zionists to be a major event and Tandy suggested that action be taken at the highest level to impress upon the American Government the seriousness of the President's proposed move.[30]

The next day Attlee sent a further extended telegram. He explained that in relation to Palestine the Arabs were to be considered as well as the Jews and that both America and Britain had given them a commitment that they would be consulted before there was any change in the basic position in Palestine. 'It would be very unwise to break these solemn pledges and so set aflame the whole Middle East.' Attlee continued by pointing out to Truman that 'the responsibility of preserving order with all the consequences involved rests entirely on this country'.[31]

In response, Truman indicated that he would wait for Byrnes to return from the conference of foreign ministers being held in London before he took any further action.[32] Notwithstanding this, Attlee learnt that at a press conference held on 29 September 1945 Truman had published a summary of their correspondence and had indicated, falsely, that he had not had a reply to his request to admit 100,000 Jews into

Palestine. Bevin protested to Byrnes only to be told that the promise to take no action had been broken because of pressure from Democratic Party managers. The mayoral election in New York, a city where over a fifth of the electorate was Jewish, was about to take place.[33]

These events encapsulate the essence of the friction that the Palestine issue caused in Anglo-American relations. America, at least in the person of Truman, was advocating a policy of mass immigration but with little regard to the problems that an influx of Jews may cause. America was at the same time distancing itself from any effective action in arriving at a solution or providing the resources to police one. It was, as Halifax had pointed out, a comfortable position to be in.

Truman was taking a lead on the Palestinian issue and in so doing was, to a certain extent, bypassing the Department of State. Evidence for this can be gleaned from an interdepartmental memorandum lamenting the fact that Truman had 'addressed a secret communication' to Attlee asking for the immigration of 100,000 refugees and enclosing a copy of the Harrison report.[34] The interesting point here is not that the civil servants were irked by being kept out of the loop (although they were), but that the dynamic of the diplomatic process was altered. If the Department of State was not fully informed, it was unlikely that the embassy was either. Isaiah Berlin commented that the executive officials in the British embassy derived much of their information about American attitudes from their opposite numbers in the Department of State.[35] The embassy had over many years established a network of connections at every level between its staff and corresponding staff at the Department of State. For example, Tandy would liaise with Loy Henderson, the Director of the Near Eastern and African Affairs Section in the Department of State. The purpose was to exchange information, brief each other and so on. However, when normal channels broke down, the effectiveness of the embassy was diminished.

Tangential to this point is the motivation of the President and the influences upon him. As Halifax reported, the Jewish lobby both inside and outside the White House was extremely active. The embassy was aware of the most significant activists in the Jewish lobby, and in particular those who supported the cause of Zionism. These people and their relationship with the embassy are discussed further in a later section. But was the embassy aware of the Zionists close to the President, in particular those who advised him in the White House? Two individuals stand out – Samuel Rosenman and David Niles.

Clearly the embassy was aware of Rosenman. It was noted in the previous chapter that Halifax met with him and discussed the President's aspirations for the conduct of the Washington Conference on atomic energy. Such contact, however, would not have been on a systematic and regular basis as it was with the members of the Department of State. Therefore, countering any advice Rosenman might give the President, even if the embassy knew about it, could only be done in ad hoc manner. Rosenman was advising Truman on the Palestine issue. As one might expect, his advice was supportive of the Jewish cause; it was, however, rather biased. For example, Truman sought his advice on whether or not there was an inconsistency between the statements he, Truman, had made and those of President Roosevelt. Rosenman concluded that 'I do not think that opening the doors to Palestine is in any sense an act which is a "move hostile to the Arab people". Nor does it in my opinion contravene the conversation of President Roosevelt.'[36] Clearly the embassy's effectiveness is limited when the President is being advised outside of the normal Department of State structure. But at least the embassy had an opportunity to counter advice if it knew it was being given and who was giving it.

A more serious matter is a situation whereby the President is making policy outside the Department of State and at the same time is being advised by an individual or individuals whom the embassy are not even in contact with or possibly, not even aware of. It appears that this may have been the case with David Niles. The extent of Niles' influence was discussed above and instances of this influence are discussed below. The question is, to what extent was the embassy aware of Niles' influence and, if it was, is there any evidence that it attempted to counter it?

It appears that the Foreign Office became aware of Niles in early May 1948, the point at which Truman was considering recognising Israel. Michael Wright, who at that time was Assistant Under-Secretary of State at the Foreign Office and was also Superintending Under-Secretary of the Eastern Department, sent a telegram to Hadow, a Counsellor at the embassy,[37] asking 'Who is Niles and what is his origin and present position?'[38] Within hours Hadow replied: 'David Niles is a Zionist who is Truman's confidential Adviser on Jews...He is credited with considerable power over the President.'[39] It appears that at that time the embassy knew of Niles or, at the very least, was able to find out about him very quickly.

It appears that the embassy actually knew of Niles as far back as 1945. Shortly after the above exchange of telegrams, Hadow wrote to Wright enclosing a letter, sent by Gore-Booth (a First Secretary at the embassy in 1945) to the Foreign Office. The letter was dated 1 August 1945.[40] Gore-Booth's letter confirmed Niles' reappointment as an Administrative Assistant at the White House and provided background information on Niles. The letter did not specifically mention that Niles would be working on Jewish affairs; rather it said that Niles was 'trouble shooting for the President' and that he was largely concerned with 'liaison work with labour and with the liberal element among the supporters of the Administration'.[41]

Other than the 1948 file discussed above, it has not been possible to find any other reference to Niles in the Foreign Office files reviewed. Nor is Niles mentioned in the embassy publication *Leading Personalities in the United States*, which contains details of some 300 individuals spread across the Administration, Congress and the Judiciary. Niles had been part of the White House Administration since 1933, yet there is no mention of him in the index of *Washington Despatches 1941–1945* (Isaiah Berlin's Weekly Political Reports from the embassy) and only one reference to him in *Confidential Despatches* (the ambassadors' quarterly political reviews 1939–1945); and this reference is in the context of Niles being a New Dealer.[42]

It is probably the case that, whilst the embassy was aware of his re-appointment in August 1945, Niles was not considered to be particularly influential or important in the context of Anglo-American relations. It seems, therefore, that he was not courted by the embassy and hence the embassy would not have been able to counter any arguments which he may have been presenting to Truman or, indeed, have been able to influence him at all. If the embassy was not aware of the extent of a person's influence on the President, then in a situation like Palestine, where the President was deciding policy, it could not be effective, at least in this regard.

There is one final point to be made before moving on to discuss the embassy's part in the Anglo-American enquiry. Bullock, in his biography of Bevin, wrote: 'Looking back one is driven to ask whether it would not have been better if the Labour government had listened to Truman's advice – or better still acted on its own initiative – and offered up to 100000 places as a once-for-all gesture.'[43] What Bullock does not mention is that it was precisely this advice that Halifax offered to the Foreign Office in his letter of 1 July 1945. Halifax wrote:

> It occurs to me that there is a possible variant of the short term courses, which is not discussed [in the draft Foreign Office policy document]; namely that instead of considering a continuation of Jewish immigration at the rate of 1500 per month, His Majesty's Government might propose, with Arab consent, the admission to Palestine as a special humanitarian action of a total of, say, 100000 Jews who wish to leave Europe as a sequel to their sufferings under the Nazis.

Halifax acknowledged that there might be difficulties with the Arabs but concludes, with typical understatement, that 'it might have merit from the point of view of American opinion'.[44] That Halifax made this suggestion demonstrates his considerable grasp of what was going on in the American political machine.

In early October 1945, Halifax wrote to Bevin and Attlee warning that 'the tempo of agitation over Palestine is rising here'. In the same letter, Halifax pointed out that the President was under strong political pressure and that, for example, he had allowed statements to go out from the White House, which indicated that Roosevelt had given no undertaking regarding Palestine to Ibn Saud. This was the statement that Rosenman had advised the President to make.[45] Halifax was also concerned that the release of the Harrison report and the comments by Truman had sparked off another 'Zionist pressure campaign'.[46] He was aware of the effect Palestine could have on other issues being dealt with by the embassy. Halifax had originally felt it best not to counter propaganda put out by the Zionists but later suggested that if mis-statements 'take a firm root in the minds of Congress and the public they will not only be most harmful in themselves but may to a lesser or greater degree affect the atmosphere surrounding the Lend Lease talks'.[47]

Halifax, pushing at an open door,[48] continued an earlier theme suggesting that an approach to America would 'at least to some extent get us out of the uncomfortable position in which the Americans can criticise us quite irresponsibly from the sidelines'.[49] Bevin and Attlee responded. Bevin, who was not well versed in Middle Eastern affairs, was astute enough to realise that the matter of Palestine was urgent and that the issue had repercussions for both the Middle East and America.[50] Consequently, although irritated by Truman's behaviour and no doubt influenced by the embassy in Washington, he realised that 'American pressure could not be ignored, and that in the interests of good relations with the USA which were crucial for the British, they would have to come up with a new initiative'.[51]

In October 1945, Bevin wrote to Halifax asking for his view on a proposal, to be put to the Americans, which suggested the setting up of an Anglo-American Committee of Enquiry to examine the position of the Jews in Europe and to suggest ways of improving it.[52] Halifax was obviously supportive and, although wary of the Zionist response, suggested that 'If the US Government accepts your proposal they will be committed to search for a solution. If they reject it . . . our position will none the less be greatly strengthened.'[53]

On 19 October, Halifax sent a long memorandum to the State Department inviting America to participate in the Anglo-American Committee and setting out its proposed purpose and terms of reference.[54] Halifax and Byrnes also had several meetings to discuss the issue. Halifax informed Byrnes that the Palestinian issue was 'embittering relations between the two countries'; hence the invitation to take part in the enquiry.[55] The initial response to the proposal was not enthusiastic. Byrnes, who appeared to be concerned with the proposal's effect on the forthcoming New York election, also expressed concern with the terms of reference, complaining that 'as set out [they] do not even mention Palestine'. In addition, he felt that the committee of enquiry might be seen as a delaying tactic aimed at leaving the immigration rate as it was.[56]

A reading of the documents reporting the above meetings discloses two other interesting points. At the end of one meeting, Byrnes said to Halifax 'let me fix my ideas and send them over to you and you can send them over to him (Bevin)'. Halifax's immediate response was 'Would you like me to send one of my fellows down to sit with one of your boys?' It was then agreed that someone from the embassy would meet with Loy Henderson that day in order to draft some proposals. This is a good demonstration of how close the embassy and the Department of State were and how easy it was for them to work together. In the Palestinian context, this may not have amounted to much but the general point stands. Another interesting point is that Halifax told Byrnes that he had been instructed to see both Byrnes and the President. He asked Byrnes, 'should I see him [the President] or not?' Byrnes suggested there was no need and that he, i.e. Byrnes, would discuss it with the President anyway. It is odd that Halifax, if he had the chance to do so, did not meet with the President on this matter. The reason he gave for not doing so was that he hesitated to bother anyone so busy. This may be true or it could be that Halifax's suggestion that he meet with the President was simply a negotiating ploy with Byrnes. It was nevertheless the one issue, given what has been said about White House versus Department of State politics, where it was crucial to get a first-hand impression of what the President was thinking. Besides, as shown in the last chapter, Halifax was close to the President and therefore he might have had an effect.

After considerable wrangling between Byrnes, no doubt deferring to Truman, and Halifax, under guidance from Bevin, the terms of reference were finally agreed.

It is interesting to note the extent to which the British had moved. The original concept from the British point of view was to 'examine the position of the Jews in British and American occupied Europe as it exists today'.[57] The focus of the committee's work became to 'examine political, economic and social conditions in Palestine as they bear upon the problem of Jewish immigration and settlement therein'.[58] Moreover, and against Bevin's wishes, a timetable was imposed. In the end, it was decided that the committee should report within 120 days. A question arises as to the effectiveness of Halifax in negotiating these terms of reference. Clearly they had moved against the British. But could Halifax have averted this? Was Halifax not tough enough, or did he in fact do rather well in the light of the pressure being brought to bear in relation to other matters, e.g. the Loan Agreement?

An example of this pressure is contained in a record of a conversation between Byrnes and Halifax dated 19 November 1945. In this conversation, Byrnes was attempting to impose a time limit on the Anglo-American committee's deliberations, which the British did not want. Byrnes informed Halifax that a bill was about to be introduced in the Senate restating the American position on Palestine. He added that 'this bill would cause a lot of anti British comments on the floor of the Senate'. Byrnes continued, 'the only thing that will stop the introduction of the bill, in his opinion, is the announcement of a time limit for completion of the work of the Commission'.[59]

In addition to this sort of pressure, Halifax was also up against the President. Halifax recorded in his diary that 'the President has run back on the terms of reference about Palestine that I had agreed with Jimmy Byrnes last night'.[60] Halifax also, of course, had to contend with the Zionists in the White House. Truman passed the British memorandum of 19 October to Rosenman and asked for comments. Rosenman's response was unequivocal: 'I think it is a complete run out on the Mandate, as well as on the Democratic platform. I certainly do not think you ought to agree to it or have anything to do with it.'[61]

It is impossible to say whether Halifax was responsible or not for the dilution in the terms of reference for the Anglo-American enquiry. But what is clear is that he was not negotiating under ideal conditions from the British point of view; further he was frustrated by the Americans:

> One is irritated with the Americans behaving as if political agitation of the Jews here was equivalent in importance to the actual staring of off riots, shootings and dead bodies in Palestine. Meanwhile, the democratic candidate whose fortunes they have been assiduously nursing has romped home in New York as everybody said he would.[62]

Halifax did, however, manage to involve America in the Palestinian problem, which, at the time, was the objective of the British government. It was, moreover, an objective based on an original idea by Halifax.

During the discussion on the terms of the Anglo-American enquiry, the situation in Palestine deteriorated. During October, there were a series of coordinated raids on British installations in Palestine and illegal immigration continued. The strength of the Jewish paramilitary formations in Palestine were estimated as follows: Haganah, the body controlled by the Jewish Agency itself, 60,000–80,000, the more extreme Irgun Zvai Levmi 6,000–7,000 and the terrorist Stern Group some hundreds.[63] Whilst Chaim Weizmann and his colleagues denied responsibility and even knowledge of the terrorist acts, messages intercepted by the British demonstrated otherwise.[64]

It was amongst this turmoil and disappointment that the Anglo-American Committee, which consisted of six American and six British members operating under a rotating Chairmanship, commenced its deliberations in Washington in January 1946.[65] The strength of the White House lobby is evident from the composition of the Committee on the American side, which was 'uncompromisingly and uncritically pro Zionist'.[66] One name stands out – Bartley Crum, who was a prominent west coast Jew and critic of Britain and an associate of both Niles and Rosenman. On 7 December, Halifax informed the Foreign Office of the original composition of the Committee. It included Max Gardner, a former Governor of North Carolina, Byrnes' home State.[67] On 13 December, Rosenman wrote to Crum, saying 'I am very distressed not only about your absence from the Commission but also about the presence of a couple of names on the Commission. I still cannot learn why your name was dropped from the list except that I know it was done by someone in the State Department.'[68] Rosenman's view prevailed and by the time the committee met Crum had been substituted for Max Gardener. It was a significant intervention by the White House Zionists and one which was very difficult for an embassy to counter. It is another example of how normal channels of communication in diplomacy could be rendered effectively useless on certain occasions.

As indicated above, the Committee began its deliberations in Washington. This was not always going to be the case. In fact,

Sir John Singleton, the British Chairman of the Committee, was against the Committee commencing its work in America.[69] It took the embassy mediating between Singleton and Joseph Hutcheson, the American Chairman, to persuade Singleton otherwise. There were some extremely vocal groups in America who would need to be heard by the Committee and it was felt by the embassy that there was a great deal to be said 'for getting the American hearings out of the way at the beginning and in having the Committee removed from the American atmosphere for the remainder and particularly for the final phases of its work'.[70] After the hearings, A.H. Tandy was able to report 'it was obviously a wise second thought which induced the decision to open the enquiry in Washington'.[71] The embassy did not believe that the Zionists had presented their case well. Halifax commented that the 'Zionists have been overplaying their hand both in their testimony before committee and in other fields'.[72]

At this time, the embassy itself was not immune from Zionist agitation. Halifax was presented with a petition by Rabbi Baruch Korff signed by 20 Senators calling for the immediate admission of 100,000 Jews from Europe into Palestine.[73] Halifax perhaps allowed his irritation to get the better of him by telling Korff that the British people were fed up with abuse from people like him when they had themselves been through 'hell to destroy the evil thing that had so persecuted the Jews'. Halifax noted in his diary 'With all my feelings of compassion for Jews I find it impossible to suppress my irritation with the agitators'.[74] Perhaps Halifax's instincts were right, however. In February 1946, Korff approached Dr Edward Acheson, Dean Acheson's brother, and offered him money to work on his campaign to defeat the British Loan. The propaganda coup if they had secured the services of Acheson's brother is obvious. The money for the campaign was put up by the American Zionist Group, the Zionist Emergency Committee and the American Committee for a Free Palestine. Korff said that 'the basic strategy is to use their opposition to the loan to get concessions from the British with respect to Palestine'.[75] In fact Dr Acheson played no part in the campaign but it is a good example of what the embassy was up against.

The embassy and the Consulates were also subject to various protests. A constant stream of letters and telegrams of protest were sent to the embassy. The tone of the campaign began to change, however, from mere protest to tactics calculated to cause annoyance and irritation. The embassy and Consulates were inundated with enquiries and telephone calls covering such details as customs duties into Palestine, mails for displaced persons in Europe and so on.[76] Later, particularly after Bevin's Labour Party Conference speech (discussed below), the threat increased. There were several Jewish threats of bomb attacks against the Consulate-General and other British offices in New York. The threat was taken so seriously by the police that the Consulate's offices were searched by the bomb squad and a plain clothes detective was stationed outside the offices.[77] Every attempt was made by the embassy to combat anti-British feeling generated by the Palestinian issue; this included issuing guidance notes, giving talks and correspondence.[78] In addition, a widespread publicity campaign was conducted by the embassy and the Foreign Office to counter anti-British propaganda.[79]

The above action did not deter the embassy from dealing with the Jewish community. Halifax had several dealings with prominent Jews and Zionists and would have known some of the protagonists well. For example, Halifax took Weizmann to meet Truman at the White House. Halifax reported that Weizmann did not get much out of the President and that Halifax felt sorry for him.[80] Halifax also met with anti-Zionists – for example, men such as Lessing Rosenwald – who was a prominent member of the American Council for Judaism.

From Washington, the Anglo-American Committee moved to London and then to Germany to examine, at first hand, the conditions of the displaced persons. The Committee had its headquarters in Berlin but was denied access to any eastern zones or territories. After Berlin, the Committee moved to the Middle East, initially to Cairo and then to Palestine. In accordance with agreed procedure, the Committee reported at the end of April 1946. It made ten recommendations,[81] the most eye-catching of which was the immediate granting of 100,000 immigration certificates and the lifting of the land purchase restrictions for Jews contained in the 1939 White Paper. The majority of the other recommendations were not so favourable to the Jews. 'In the end, the committee arrived at no positive answer to the Palestine riddle: it rejected partition and recommended that the Mandate be continued pending the execution of a trusteeship agreement under the United Nations. This not merely left the situation where it was. It made it worse.'[82]

Judge Hutcheson, the American Committee Chairman, flew to Washington to present the report to Truman on 22 April 1946. Bevin, wary of Truman's track record, sent a message to Truman via Halifax expressing 'the earnest hope that no action be taken by the United States Government on the report of the Palestine Committee of Inquiry without prior consultation with him'.[83] The report was published on 30 April 1946 and, without consulting Britain, Truman issued a statement approving the committee's unanimous endorsement of the immediate admission of 100,000 Jews into Palestine and reserved judgement on the long-range proposals. As Dean Acheson (Under-Secretary of State) put it, in somewhat of an understatement, 'Mr Attlee was annoyed by Mr Truman's taking the plum out of the pudding'.[84] In fact, Attlee and Bevin were furious; their mood was not helped by the fact that news of the President's statement reached London just after a Jewish attack on a car park in Tel Aviv, which resulted in the deaths of seven British servicemen.

Initially the Cabinet had agreed not to comment upon the report until the reaction of Arabs and others had been ascertained. Attlee, however, after reading Truman's statement, decided that he needed to make an announcement. In a Commons statement, Attlee firstly indicated that he wanted to be clear that Britain was not to shoulder the sole responsibility for the implied commitments in the report and wanted to ascertain the extent to which the US government was prepared to share the burden and secondly, with regard the proposal for 100,000 immigrants, he said that it 'would not be possible for the Government of Palestine to admit so large a body of immigrants unless and until these formations [i.e. illegal terrorists] have been disbanded and their arms surrendered'.[85] As Acheson put it in his memoirs, 'the United States and the United Kingdom were further apart than ever'.[86]

What lay behind the President's action? According to Bullock, the American Zionists were about to denounce the report out of hand because it did not endorse a Jewish state. They were persuaded, however, by two pro-Zionist members of the committee, Macdonald and Crum, that this would only anger the President and that the best course would be to accept the 100,000 proposal and defer comment on the other proposals. It was Niles who drafted a statement to this effect and put it before Truman, who signed it 'out of hand'.[87] It appears that the embassy had no knowledge of what was going on in the White House. Halifax even wrote to the Foreign Office two days before the release of the report advising on the best method of making a statement with regard to the British policy, which was to accompany the report when released. A radio broadcast to the American public by Bevin or Attlee was suggested.[88] There was no suggestion of any need to counter a statement to be made by Truman.

The publication of the Report by the Anglo-American Committee coincided with Halifax's final days in Washington. Halifax's last working day was Friday 11 May 1946; the following Tuesday he sailed for Britain aboard the *Queen Mary*. One of his last telegrams to the Foreign Office concerned Palestine. Once again, Halifax was in the vanguard of policy formation. Halifax pointed out that there was little prospect of America committing either money or troops to implement the proposals contained in the Committee's report. Attlee had already made it clear that Britain would not shoulder the responsibility alone. The conclusion Halifax drew was that Britain should bring the matter before the United Nations General Assembly. Halifax understood the possible objections to this proposal, i.e. the UN had no armed forces and a reference might encourage the Soviets to meddle. He did nevertheless conclude that 'reference of the matter to the United Nations Assembly would merely anticipate a step which in any event is only a matter of time'.[89] Against the Foreign Office minute indicating what Halifax had proposed Bevin scribbled 'No'.[90] The reference to the United Nations would not come at this time.

Halifax was replaced by Lord Inverchapel in May 1946. Inverchapel was a completely different character to his predecessor. Although Halifax became irritated with Jewish activists, there is no evidence that he was anti-Semitic. But nor was he particularly interested in the subject of Zionism.[91] Inverchapel was different. He was a pro-Zionist of long standing and an acquaintance of Chaim Weizmann since 1919, and had once even been offered a job by the Zionists.[92] Inverchapel was never reticent in putting the Zionist point of view. Within a month of taking office, he wrote to Bevin reporting a conversation with Dr Nahum Goldmann (a prominent member of the Zionist movement in America). Inverchapel lamented the fact that neither Bevin nor Attlee had allowed the moderate Zionists such as Weizmann and Shertok to meet with them. Inverchapel added that Weizmann was in London the following month and urged Bevin to meet with him, ending his letter by saying that Weizmann was a 'very old friend of mine and a wise and decent man'.[93]

Inverchapel's pro-Zionist stance caused concern both within the Foreign Office, and the Department of State. A few months after taking office Inverchapel met with a delegation from the American Jewish Labour Council, an extremist Zionist organisation.[94] It led to a rebuke from Sir Orme Sargent, Permanent Under-Secretary of State at the Foreign Office:

> I do not wish to suggest that you should make yourself less accessible to representatives of American public opinion; I am sure that your policy in this respect plays handsome dividends. But we are rather apprehensive lest the success of the Jewish Labour Council in making personal contact with you may encourage other groups of an extreme Zionist and anti British character to try to score the same point.[95]

The correspondence between Inverchapel and Sargent on this matter continued until the end of the year.[96] It was, perhaps, an early sign that the Foreign Office was not happy with Inverchapel's performance in America.

Inverchapel's pro-Zionist stance also caused problems in the Department of State:

> Lord Inverchapel...was an agreeable companion but unsatisfactory as a diplomatic colleague. Unquestionably eccentric, he liked to appear even more eccentric than he was, producing an ultimate impression odd enough to be puzzling. He also professed strong Zionist sympathies, certainly not shared by Attlee or Bevin. This deepened the conversational puzzle of knowing

what he meant, whose views he was representing, and how what one said in reply appeared in his telegrams to London.[97]

The above remark by Dean Acheson mixes up Inverchapel's eccentricity with his pro-Zionism. Nevertheless, Acheson was clearly wary of Inverchapel and this issue is discussed further below.

The enormity of the task facing both the British and American governments can be gauged by the responses of both the Arabs and the Jews to the requests for their views and comments on the recommendations of the Anglo-American Committee report. The Arabs 'rejected it completely', stating that the 'Arabs of Palestine are the sole people to decide on their fate and they reject any foreign intervention in the country'.[98] The Jewish response was not much more encouraging. The Jewish Agency indicated that it was 'bitterly opposed to parts of the report denying basic Zionist political aims'.[99]

On 12 June 1946, Truman, in a fresh attempt to find a way forward, announced the formation of a Cabinet Committee with alternates to consider the Palestinian issue and related problems. The committee consisted of the Secretaries of State, War and Treasury; the work was to be carried out by their alternates Henry Grady (Chairman), Goldthwaite Dorr and Herbert Gaston.[100] The committee would travel to London to discuss the Palestine issue with British representatives. On the same day as Truman announced the Cabinet Committee, Bevin, in a speech to the Labour Party conference at Bournemouth, suggested that the reason the Americans were pushing so hard for Jewish immigration into Palestine was because they did not want 'to have too many of them in New York'. In the same speech, Bevin suggested that immigration of 100,000 Jews would require an extra division in Palestine and expenditure of £22 million, which the exchequer did not have.[101]

Inverchapel reported the American reaction to Bevin's speech, which had inevitably caused uproar. Inverchapel indicated that the speech became the main theme at a New York rally, attended by 12,000 people, which had been organised to protest at the lack of immigration into Palestine. Speakers at the rally, including Rabbis Wise and Silver, Bartley Crum and Senator Johnson (Democrat, Colorado), demanded that the US government withhold the British loan unless Bevin repudiated the speech. Inverchapel thought that the more serious point was that the speech was being taken as evidence that the British government had already made up its mind not to admit the 100,000 and that it never intended to implement the recommendations of the Anglo-American Committee. Inverchapel commented that 'your criticism of New York has, of course, not only hit the nail on the head but driven it woundingly deep'. Inverchapel followed his commentary with advice and urged Bevin to publicly welcome the formation of the President's committee on Palestine and give official recognition to the team of experts when they arrived in London.[102] Bevin took the embassy's advice.

Bevin's explanation to Inverchapel was that the speech was 'made in reply to a debate at a party conference, and was largely impromptu'. Bevin suggested that the embassy circulate the speech widely, including to the whole of Congress, in order to put the offending remarks into context.[103] Inverchapel duly circulated the speech together with guidance notes.[104] He refrained, however, from circulating it to Congress. Inverchapel reported that the BIS had succeeded in getting the speech put in the *New York Times* and therefore saw no merit in circulating it to the whole of Congress.[105]

The embassy also offered some practical advice in an attempt to counter the damage done in America. Inverchapel suggested that in response to a planted Parliamentary question, it be made 'crystal clear' that Bevin's speech did not mean that the government 'had prejudiced the entry of 100000'. Inverchapel even suggested that in Bevin's absence in Paris the 'statement might most effectively come from the Prime Minister, particularly as the President himself handles this matter here and his personal prestige is to some extent involved'.[106] Bevin wrote in the telegram 'I am not sure that this is wise...I am against getting upset with Jewish agitation. We have made our position clear.' Bevin, whether deliberately or not, missed the point. The question was not Jewish agitation but the perception of Britain in America and the effect such remarks had. Although this case is an extreme example, it does highlight another role for the embassy, i.e. the need to be aware of, and react to, controversial statements made by ministers outside of America.

In July 1946, Inverchapel wrote to Bevin and informed him that 'you have not got yourself across the American footlights in such a way as to be able to sway opinion here on major questions'. Inverchapel suggested that whilst Bevin was seen as a 'big and important' figure that 'bigness' had been 'blurred and bothered' by events. Inverchapel emphasised the power of Congress and strongly suggested that Bevin come to Washington, perhaps after a visit to the United Nations, and 'sweep a joint session of Congress off its feet with a thumping speech', adding 'it is really important'.[107] Interestingly, Bevin wrote on this letter 'keep private will write'.

Bevin's response must have deflated the ambassador: 'I frankly don't believe that addressing Congress will make any difference in their attitude towards this country – Churchill has done it, Attlee has repeated it, but notwithstanding all they have said it makes no difference.' Bevin indicated that he would not want Byrnes to address Parliament and concluded with 'In the carrying out of foreign policy I do not believe this method of exhibitionism has any effect at all'.[108] It was a somewhat puzzling and cutting response to someone who Bevin had appointed as the ambassador only a few months before.

Truman's Cabinet Committee arrived in London in mid-July and immediately met with British representatives. The joint body produced recommendations remarkably quickly. The recommendations, which collectively became known as the Morrison Grady Plan, were leaked to the press on 25 July 1946. The Morrison Grady Plan moved away from the Anglo-American Committee's concept of a binational state and towards provincial autonomy. The plan was to institute a federal system.

Truman was initially inclined to support the plan but when this became known, the Zionist lobby was rallied in an effort to change the President's mind.

Senator Robert Taft (Republican, Ohio) egged on by Rabbi Silver (President of the Zionist Organisation of America, and a resident of Cleveland who had worked with Taft on Zionist issues in the 1944 election) attacked the plan. Former members of the Anglo-American Committee attacked the plan, calling it a betrayal of the Jews. One of them, James Macdonald, went to the White House with Senators

Wagner and Mead (both Democratic Senators for New York) to protest. At a Cabinet meeting of 31 July 1946, Henry Wallace (Secretary
of Commerce) warned Truman that the 'Morrison Grady plan was
"loaded with political dynamite"'. Perhaps the final straw came
when Paul Fitzpatrick, Chairman of the New York State Democratic
Committee, told Truman: 'If this plan goes into effect it would be
useless for the Democrats to nominate a state ticket for the election
this fall.'[109]

It appears that the embassy was fairly well informed when channels
of communication were conducted along formal lines. Acheson called
on Inverchapel immediately after the Cabinet meeting to inform him
that the President would be unable to support the Morrison Grady
proposals. Acheson informed Inverchapel that the President was 'much
distressed' at being unable to meet Britain's wishes but the plan had
'met the strongest opposition in Cabinet', which had been fully shared
by the leaders of the Democratic Party in Congress'.[110]

Inverchapel cabled London with his comments:

> This deplorable display of weakness is, I fear, solely attribut-
> able to reasons of domestic politics which, it will be recalled,
> caused the Administration last year to defer the announcement
> about the establishment of the Anglo American Committee
> until after the New York elections...The Director of the Near
> Eastern Division [Henderson] admitted as much in a talk with
> me this evening. But for the attitude of the Zionists...there was
> nothing in the joint recommendations that would not have been
> acceptable to the United States Government.[111]

After the American Cabinet meeting, Truman decided to arrange
for the Grady Committee to meet with the American members of
the Anglo-American Committee to see if a solution could be found.
Whilst the embassy was aware that this meeting was taking place, it
was not, at the time, au fait with what was going on in terms of White
House politics. It took over a month for the embassy to find out what
was really going on. Cyril Cane, the Consul General in San Francisco,
met with his 'old personal friend of more than twenty years standing'

Henry Grady. Grady's account confirmed that Truman was in favour of the plan but wanted support. Truman called in Hutcheson, Chairman of the Anglo-American Committee, in the hope that he would come out in favour of it. Unfortunately, however, he was reluctant to see any changes made to his own plan. The other members of the committee 'of whom Crum is the most sinister and unprincipled, backed Hutcheson to the limit'. Grady was convinced that most of the leaks to the press were from Crum and that he twisted all the facts. 'He [Crum] did his level best to discredit Grady's committee and the British.'[112]

Balfour, in forwarding Cane's letter to the Foreign Office, commented that it was 'an interesting account of the inside history of the Cabinet discussions here, it looks as if the argument had been even closer than we had thought, which makes the President's final decision the more irritating'.[113] Cane's letter broadly confirms other accounts of Truman's change of heart on the Grady Plan.[114] It does, however, place more weight on the effect of Hutcheson's views rather than merely those of the Zionists.

The letter also demonstrates the reach of the embassy through its Consular network. At the same time, however, it calls into question its effectiveness. Knowing this information after the event has only limited utility. If Grady was a long-standing friend of Canes why wasn't that contact put to better effect? The embassy knew Hutcheson fairly well. If Truman's decision was close then to have known of Hutcheson's position at the time would have enabled the embassy to approach him and possibly have an effect. Whether earlier contact with Grady would have made a difference is something one cannot know but the episode does demonstrate the need for the embassy to keep abreast of the contacts within its Consular network. Merely having a network was not in itself sufficient.

Throughout the period, the embassy endeavoured to keep itself informed as to the arguments which might be used, in America, to support Britain's Palestinian position. Balfour wrote to Baxter, head of the Eastern Department in the Foreign Office, suggesting that there were still 'sections of the Administration' who understood Britain's dilemma in Palestine and that the embassy 'ought to be in a position to keep these people discreetly aware of the factors which determine

His Majesty's Government's policy'. Balfour then suggested that the embassy could not do this unless it was 'au courant' with these factors. Specifically, Balfour suggested two issues where the embassy needed more information. The first was with regard to the strategic importance of Palestine, and the second was Britain's policy if the London Conference (discussed below) failed. Balfour added that 'any background Chiefs of Staff and Cabinet papers on these subjects would be of the greatest assistance'.[115]

No doubt Balfour was genuine in his request for further information and it is indeed an example of the lengths the embassy went to in order to keep itself informed. There is, however, another side to this request. Donald Maclean, in a minute written for his colleagues, confirms that he had inspected all these background papers in particular 'British Strategic Requirements in the Middle East'. Maclean's minute contains details of Britain's position in the event of war with Russia including comments made at the Defence Committee of the Cabinet in relation to any offensive which might be launched against Russia from the Middle East. With a touch of irony perhaps, Maclean noted in his minute: 'Our main objective in getting a sight of this paper was to ensure that we had some accurate idea of the strategic importance of Palestine at the back of our minds when talking to US officials, and reliable journalists.'[116] Although this reference to Maclean is something of an aside, it does underlie the importance of and level of information which the embassy had access to. This, in itself, emphasises the importance of the embassy to the conduct of foreign policy.

Truman cabled Attlee on 12 August 1946 informing him that he could not support the Morrison Grady proposals.[117] Britain responded to America's rejection of the proposals by calling for a conference in London to discuss them. It also indicated, however, that other proposals could be discussed. The conference opened in London on 9 September 1946 but no representatives from either the Jewish side or the Arab Palestinian side attended. There were, however, delegates from Egypt, Syria, Iraq and the Arab League. The Arab delegates simply rejected the plan, believing that in the end it would lead to a Jewish state.

Bevin persevered, however, and opened up parallel talks with the Jewish Agency. There was a suggestion of a bi-national state with a period of transition of perhaps several years. Weizmann himself said 'statehood could not be reached in one day'.[118] There were signs that the Jewish agency might be prepared to compromise and even attend the conference. Partly in order to allow more time for these talks to bear fruit but also to allow the Arab delegates, who were also representing their governments at the UN in New York, to leave London, the conference was adjourned until 16 December 1946.

It was at this moment that Truman acted in a manner that precipitated one of the lowest points of Anglo-American relations during the Attlee era.

On 3 October, Truman cabled Attlee expressing regret that the London Conference had been postponed and the hope that the immigration of 100,000 Jews could begin in the interim. Truman also attached a statement he intended to release the next day, i.e. on the 'eve of the most solemn day in the Jewish calendar', Yom Kippur.[119]

The long statement contained the whole background to American involvement in the Palestinian problem since the war. It was, in effect, a list of all the actions Truman had taken in support of the Jewish cause. It also referred to a proposal the Jewish Agency had made, i.e. 'the creation of a viable Jewish state in control of its own immigration and economic policies in an adequate area of Palestine instead of in the whole of Palestine'. Truman continued with 'it is my belief that a solution along these lines would command the support of public opinion in the United States'.[120]

Attlee immediately replied to Truman's telegram: 'You are I am sure aware that we are in consultation with members of the Jewish Agency at the present time. I would therefore earnestly request you to postpone making your statement at least for the time necessary for me to communicate with Mr Bevin.'[121] The embassy also protested but was simply told by Acheson that the President had 'reluctantly yielded to intense pressure from elements within the Democratic party and from the Jewish groups in and about New York ... which had "blown up" when the news had come that the conference in London had been adjourned until December 16th'.[122] A cabal of Paul Fitzpatrick (Democratic State Committee New York), Robert Hannegan (Postmaster General) and Bartley Crum convinced the President to make a statement on Palestine, saying that 'a statement by him would clear the atmosphere as far as American Jewry were concerned'.[123] The Zionists had yet again proved successful at persuading the President to make foreign policy statements on his own initiative and outside of the normal channels. The embassy was powerless to react.

Truman then refused to comply with Attlee's request and the statement went ahead. Attlee's response was acidic:

> I have received with great regret your letter refusing even a few hours' grace to the Prime Minister of the country which has the actual responsibility for the government of Palestine in order that he might acquaint you with the actual situation and the probable results of your action. These may well include the frustration of the patient efforts to achieve a settlement and the loss of still more lives in Palestine.
>
> I am astonished that you did not wait to acquaint yourself with the reasons for the suspension of the conference with the Arabs. You do not seem to have been informed that far from negotiations having been broken off, conversations with leading Zionists with a view to entering the conference were proceeding with good prospects of success.
>
> I shall await with interest to learn what were the imperative reasons which compelled this precipitancy.[124]

Truman did respond on 10 October in a lengthy telegram that said nothing new. The embassy reported the American reaction to Truman's statement. Some papers suggested that the statement 'betokened an almost open break between the two countries'. The majority of the press took a more modest view, concluding that most of it had been said before and that electioneering was at the bottom of it. The embassy did report, however, a rather important point that is sometimes lost when discussing this issue, i.e. 'that in spite of these domestic political factors the President feels genuinely and strongly about Palestine'.[125] This was a factor that the Foreign Office and perhaps Bevin did not pay enough attention to when formulating policy. It is possible that if Halifax's advice of July 1945 had been taken (i.e. to admit 100,000 Jews into Palestine), then Truman may have behaved differently.

During November and December 1946, Bevin was in New York attending a meeting of the conference. Inverchapel, who thought that the British government was badly mishandling the Palestinian issue, saw it as an opportunity to introduce some of the leading American Zionists to Bevin.[126] Inverchapel persuaded Bevin to meet Rabbi Silver, President of the Zionist Organisation of America, and other influential Jews and Zionists.[127] Inverchapel explained that Silver was attending the World Zionist Conference in Basle on 9 December 1946 and that Silver was likely to be influential. It was at this conference in Basle that the Zionists would debate and decide whether or not to attend Bevin's London Conference. Further, although Silver was the leader of an extremist group, Inverchapel stated that he had met with Silver in Washington and had succeeded in moderating his outlook.[128]

After the above meeting, Silver wrote to Inverchapel: 'I know of your own deep and sympathetic interest in the matter and we are all very grateful.'[129] Inverchapel's pro-Zionist instincts were noted above. Whilst the meetings in New York were taking place, Inverchapel went to Washington to find out from Dean Acheson what the Department of State's and the President's view was of partition. This is something that elements of the Jewish Agency supported but Bevin did not. There are suggestions by Donald Gillies (Inverchapel's biographer) that Inverchapel's pro-Zionist instincts may have led to him pursuing private initiatives with Acheson rather than the instructions of his government.

Gillies tells us:

> It seems likely that Inverchapel's own preference, like Weizmann's, was for partition, that he wished to extract an American pledge of support for this policy, and so convince Bevin that partition was the solution to aim for. In that sense Inverchapel was following an independent diplomatic initiative by which he certainly hoped to aid Bevin, but only by having Bevin fall in with Inverchapel's own preferred position.[130]

A comparison of the record of Inverchapel's remarks made at the time to Acheson,[131] and the records of the various meetings between Inverchapel, Bevin and the Zionists, demonstrate that Inverchapel was not pursuing a private initiative.[132] That is, Inverchapel was recounting the conversations which took place in New York impartially to Acheson. In a record of the various meetings which Bevin sent to Attlee, Bevin stated that 'Lord Inverchapel has pressed me to accept the policy of partition and to tell this to the Jewish leaders at an early date'. Bevin continued, 'as a result of this discussion I pointed out that even on this the Americans had not expressed any view and I advised him to find out from the State Department as ambassador and not committing me what their attitude really was'.[133] It does not, therefore, seem as if Inverchapel was pursuing private initiatives. His position was clear to Bevin and it is clear that he was acting under Bevin's instructions.

Acheson was nevertheless wary of Inverchapel and therefore somewhat reluctant. 'What Lord Inverchapel wanted to know was whether he would be justified in encouraging Bevin to believe that the United States would support partition. The supposed facts from which this enquiry sprang rested so exclusively on [Inverchapel's] hearsay evidence that prudence in reply seems indicated.'[134] It is possible that this remark, from Acheson's memoirs, was responsible for Gillies' assertion. Gillies provides no reference himself.

What this episode demonstrates, in addition to the fact that Inverchapel was acting under instructions and not freelancing, is that when a diplomat has strong views then his request for information on a particular subject or clarification of another person's position on that subject can be affected. Acheson was wary of Inverchapel because of the views he was known to hold and therefore he was somewhat cautious in clarifying the American position.

The London Conference finally resumed in January 1947. It was Britain's last attempt to find a British solution to the Palestinian problem. It failed. The Jews, 'rendered intractable by Truman's support'[135] and unmoved by their meetings with Bevin and Inverchapel in New York, did not attend and in discussions outside the conference clung to the idea of partition. The Arabs, this time also represented by delegates from Palestine, never relinquished their claim for an independent Palestine, which 'meant in effect a permanent Arab majority'.[136]

Britain was left with three options: to impose the Jewish proposal of partition, to permit the Arab concept of an independent Arab state but with minority protection for the Jews or to surrender the Mandate. None of these options was palatable to the Cabinet. Britain took the only effective action left and on 18 February 1947 Bevin announced to the Commons that the issue was to be referred to the UN, something, of course, which Halifax had predicted nine months before.

A week later in a speech to the House of Commons, Bevin aired his frustrations in public. He accused Truman of playing politics on the Palestinian issue. He went into some detail regarding the circumstances of Truman's Yom Kippur statement and commented, 'in international affairs I cannot settle things if my problem is made the subject of local elections'. These words caused considerable bad feelings in Washington. The embassy reported that Bevin's speech was attacked by 'Americans of almost all shades of opinion', who saw it as 'a personal attack on the head of State'.[137] Truman indicated later 'it was a very undiplomatic – almost hostile – statement for the Foreign Secretary of the British Government to make about the President of the United States'.[138] Whilst Bevin understood the importance of good Anglo-American relations, his rhetoric was perhaps a mark of his anger and frustration at the position the Americans had taken on the Palestinian issue.

In February 1947, Britain approached Trygve Lie, the UN Secretary General, to request that the UN consider the Palestinian problem. A special session of the General Assembly met on 28 April 1947 and approved the appointment of an ad hoc committee. The United Nations Special Committee on Palestine (UNSCOP) was set up on 15 May 1947. It was composed of 11 'minor neutral' states and was instructed to report back by 1 September 1947.

The UNSCOP committee produced its report in August 1947. It was a majority report and advocated partition. There was to be a Jewish state and an Arab state but with Jerusalem under direct UN rule. Bevin was against partition, believing it to be unfair to the Arabs. Bevin also felt that a Jewish state in the Middle East would be a constant source of friction. Britain, at the time, was in the midst of a severe financial crisis and simply could not spare the resources needed to keep the peace in the region. At a meeting on 20 September 1947, the Cabinet accepted the views of both Bevin and Attlee that Britain must abandon the Mandate and withdraw from Palestine. The UN assembly, with minor nations being put under pressure from America, voted in favour of partition on 29 September 1947. Britain abstained. On 3 December, Britain announced to the UN that it would deem its Mandate to be at an end as of 15 May 1948.

The role of Britain's Washington embassy in the Palestinian issue diminished considerably after the referral of the issue to the UN. The action had moved to New York and became the prime responsibility of Sir Alexander Cadogan, Britain's Permanent Representative at the UN. It also ceased to be an issue which was solely concerned with bilateral Anglo-American relations; the issue was now clearly in an international arena. The embassy, however, never ceased to comment on the Palestinian question and Balfour wrote a long memorandum on the subject in May 1948. His conclusion was perceptive and balanced:

> We should, perhaps, temper our natural irritation at the irrespon-
> sible and vacillating attitude of many highly placed Americans
> with some recognition of the fact that, after a generation during
> which they could afford the luxury of backseat driving, these
> people have suddenly found themselves called upon to play a
> leading part in dealing with a problem so complex that even
> we ourselves, with our lengthy Middle Eastern experience, have
> been forced to admit our inability to arrive at its solution.[139]

Truman was elected President for the first time in November 1948. Ironically, however, he was the first President since Wilson and only the second since 1876 to be elected without taking New York.

Two themes emerge when considering the embassy's role in bilateral Anglo-American relations surrounding the Palestinian issue. The first is the extent to which an embassy can offer perceptive and pertinent commentary on policy; the second is the extent to which the effectiveness of the embassy is impaired when normal channels of communication break down. These two themes somewhat mirror the embassy's performance. The embassy appeared to be ahead of the game in terms of policy formation but almost constantly behind it in terms of appreciating and reacting to American policy initiatives.

Halifax's letter of 1 July 1945, itself a reaction to British policy proposals, contained what appear to have been the first policy proposals to bring the Americans into the Palestinian question. It was based upon a detailed understanding of the forces of Zionism in America and the inevitability of America's involvement in the question. It is debatable, of course, whether or not it was a good thing that America became involved, but as Halifax suggested, it was difficult to envisage a solution without American involvement. Halifax also understood that immigration was the key to addressing the concerns in America and, if he had been listened to in July 1945, it is possible that Truman's behaviour might have been different. There were other instances where the embassy took the lead in policy suggestions, for example Halifax's suggestion of an early reference to the UN. Such a reference might have saved Britain considerable anguish. The British Chancellor Hugh Dalton commented in February 1947: 'It is impossible to deny...that Bevin has wasted more than a year – and in that year has wasted much goodwill and created quite intolerable conditions for British troops and others in Palestine – by waiting until now to send this wretched problem to the United Nations.'[140]

There is, looking back, a definite sense that the embassy, at least under Halifax's tenure, had a significant grasp of, and was proactive in, the formation of the main policy issues. Halifax's tenure might be contrasted with Inverchapel's, where there was no significant commentary on policy, although, to be fair, the broad lines of policy (American involvement and the issue of mass immigration) had already been decided by that time. Inverchapel, who was not a supporter of the UK government's approach, did nevertheless encourage Bevin to communicate more with the Zionists. Bevin's neglect in this regard was possibly one of his biggest weaknesses in the context of the Palestinian question.

That the embassy was able to contribute to the formation of policy is perhaps not the most striking theme to emerge; it was, after all, the most knowledgeable body on the subject of Palestine and its impact on Anglo-American relations. The more striking theme is the extent to which the embassy's effectiveness was impaired by the fact that the President and those close to him in the White House were pursuing policy initiatives independently of the Department of State. There was a sharp contrast between the closeness of the embassy to members of the department and on the other hand of the embassy to certain people in the White House. One of the objectives of diplomacy is to seek to influence policy formation in the host country. In the case of America, this was most often achieved by communicating with members of the State Department, people with whom contacts had been built up over many years. An embassy's power to influence can be rendered useless if policy formation is taking place outside normal channels. It is difficult to determine whether the embassy could have countered this factor. In the case of David Niles, for example, the embassy was aware of his existence but underrated his influence and therefore, as far as is known, made little effort to court him. Niles was probably something of an exception and it is difficult to blame the embassy for clinging to a structure that had served it well for many years. On the other hand, it is worth recalling the words of Nicholas Henderson, even though he did not become the ambassador in Washington until 1979:

> The American Constitution makes no mention of foreign policy at all. All one can say with certainty is that the power is divided between the Congress and the Administration; and that within the Administration itself the decision-making process is diffused between the White House and the State Department . . . a diplomat in Washington will not carry out his duties satisfactorily if he focuses too much of his time and attention on confidential meetings with the State Department.[141]

CHAPTER 5

THE MARSHALL PLAN

History tends now and then to leap forward with a bound. We are now in the air as it were in the midst of that bound.[1]

'Turning point' is perhaps an overworked phrase in historical writing. It is, however, one that is difficult not to apply to the Marshall Plan. The approval of the Marshall Plan by the US Congress was the point at which both the Administration and the Legislature came together and decisively turned away from isolationism. The British embassy in Washington played a role in the Marshall Plan in a variety of ways. The embassy was instrumental in affording the Foreign Office and Bevin (the Foreign Secretary) prior warning of General Marshall's offer of aid to Europe. This prior warning gave Britain a significant advantage by enabling her to be in the vanguard of the European response. The embassy was also instrumental in easing the passage of Marshall Aid through the Administration and Congress. It played a key role in the Pentagon and the Modus Vivendi talks, both of which were important in securing support from various interest groups within the US Administration and the Legislature. In addition to these specific roles, the embassy played a part in the Administration's attempt to build a coalition of support for its proposals across the American political system. This chapter considers one of the principal drivers behind the Marshall Plan; that is, Britain's financial weakness. This weakness was most dramatically demonstrated by Britain's withdrawal of financial and military aid to Greece and by the country's failure to honour its convertibility obligations under the Financial Agreement. The embassy's role in these two events is also discussed. First, however, it is necessary to consider the evolution of the Marshall Plan and the background out of which it developed.

The Financial Agreement between the UK and US governments, signed in December 1945, was, as indicated in chapter 2, a disappointment at the time it was signed. There were many who had reservations with the terms and conditions of the loan and, indeed, the adequacy of it. These included Treasury officials, Robert Brand and Dalton himself. Although Keynes did not agree, there were many who felt that there would be a shortage of dollars in the post-war world. This in turn would make some of the terms of the loan (e.g. convertibility and non discrimination) unworkable. As also noted in chapter 2, however, Labour ministers, in optimistic mood, and believing they had little alternative, accepted the loan and its conditions.

Initially this optimism was well founded. The British economy performed ahead of expectations. Demobilisation and the reconversion of industry went well. The proportion of the nation's manpower in the armed forces or directly engaged in supplying them fell from 42% to 10% by the end of 1946.[2] Labour relations were good with fewer industrial disputes in Britain than elsewhere and, whilst the employed population fell by 2 million between June 45 and the end of 1946, in part because women left industry, the total employed population was over one million greater than it had been in June 1939.[3] The export and import figures also made good reading. In the fourth quarter of 1946, exports by volume were at 111% of the 1938 level whilst imports were only 72% of those in 1938. In fact, the balance of payments deficit for 1946 turned out to be just £344 million, half of the £750 million expected during the Financial Agreement negotiations.[4] In the foreword to the *Economic Survey for 1947*, Attlee stated that 'the accomplishments of the country during the first eighteen months of peace [were] achievements of which we can justly feel proud'.[5]

Whilst ministers were making these statements there were clear signs that the drain on dollars was greater than expected. Although the deficit for 1946 was only £344 million, the loan had been drawn down by over £600 million. This problem was the result of Britain, in common with the rest of Europe, needing large imports of foodstuffs and raw materials from the Western Hemisphere, principally America. In fact 42% of Britain's imports were from the New World but only 14% of its exports went there.[6] In normal conditions, the resultant deficit in dollars could be funded by Britain's surplus of exports over imports to the Eastern Hemisphere. Unfortunately the countries in the East with which Britain had a surplus had no gold or dollars to settle with.

The dollar drain escalated rapidly. In the final months of 1946, the dollar deficit was running at $50 million a month; by March 1947 it had risen to $200 million a month.[7] This deficit continued to grow and was to lead to the convertibility crisis in the summer of 1947 (discussed below). There were a number of causes for the swift use of the dollar loan. One was the rapid escalation of US prices. Dalton estimated that US price increases had the effect of reducing the loan by a billion dollars.[8] Another factor was government policy, in particular its failure to manage the dollar trade deficit. The Labour government sponsored large volumes of capital investment in areas such as housing, and approved substantial expenditure on food subsidies and social services. This led to excessive demand for imports and left inadequate resources for the export industries. A further factor was the level of military payments abroad. In 1946, these were £374 million, a figure which exceeded the overall balance of payments deficit.[9] Britain made significant payments in respect of Germany, where there was no prospect of a peace treaty, and continued with its commitments in overseas areas such as Palestine, the Far East and Greece.

By early 1947, the promise shown in 1946 had began to evaporate. Britain's reserves were deteriorating rapidly and the country was facing the prospect of defaulting on the terms of the loan she had accepted from her principal ally barely a year earlier. Britain was demonstrating signs of imperial fatigue; she needed to look west to the one country in the world capable of offering her financial assistance.

In contrast to the British economy, the American economy, which was estimated to be five times the size of Britain's and twice that of the Soviet Union, was booming. The threat of recession that had loomed only a year earlier had passed. 'Farm income, business profits and dollar volume of industrial production, all stood at new peaks, as did the income of individuals and consumer spending.'[10] The possible dislocation that might be caused by the reconversion of the economy to a peacetime setting had not occurred. President Truman, who wanted a balanced budget, presided over the rapid demobilisation of the military. These newly released resources were used to further increase the productivity of the economy.

Against this overall rosy picture, however, there were some niggling issues which came to dominate the 1946 Congressional elections held on 5 November. There were meat and housing shortages, a variety of wartime controls remained in place and labour became disenchanted with the Truman Administration and the level of inflation. The stature of Truman himself was called into question. In a little over a year, 'his popularity, as measured by a Gallup poll, plunged from 87% to 32%'.[11]

The election results were devastating for the Democrats. The Republicans won control of both Houses for the first time since 1928. In the House of Representatives, they had 246 to 188 and in the Senate they secured 51 against the Democrat total of 45.[12] The task which Truman faced, in what many thought were the last two years of his Presidency, in implementing both domestic and foreign policy initiatives was made considerably harder given the complexion of the eightieth Congress. Truman's first 18 months in office not only saw him lose control of Congress but they also marked the hardening of his attitude towards the Soviet Union.

Whilst the Far East, particularly the weakness of the Chinese Nationalists, was a source of concern for the US Administration, but the more serious threat to national security was increasingly seen to be the Soviets. At the Potsdam Conference in July 1945, Truman quipped 'I can deal with Stalin. He is honest – but smart as hell.'[13] Within a few months, the mood had changed and there was a toughening of attitudes towards the Soviets. In the period after Potsdam, a number of issues caused friction between the former allies. These included the failure of the conference to reach agreement over Germany, Stalin's speech in February 1946 where he 'affirmed the doctrine of irreconcilable conflict between socialism and capitalist imperialism',[14] the inability to reach an accord on atomic energy and the threat of Soviet expansion in Turkey and Iran. The embassy reported that 'as a result of the concatenation of recent events...Americans have been stung into consciousness that an ideological gulf exists between the United States and the Soviet Union'.[15] The Administration dropped the assumption it had been operating under (i.e. that the principal objective of the Soviets was to guarantee their own security) and substituted another, which was that the Soviets were seeking to increase their sphere of influence wherever they saw an opportunity.

By the end of 1946, the Truman Administration had determined to pursue a policy of deterrence and containment. That policy could take the form of building up America's military, offering military expertise to threatened nations or giving economic assistance to needy peoples.[16] These were not mutually exclusive options; they did, however, all require money and that money was controlled by Congress. The Democrats then lost control of Congress at the very time when their attitude towards the Soviets hardened. Whilst there were prominent Republicans who broadly supported the Administration's foreign policy stance, Senator Arthur Vandenberg (Republican, Michigan), Chairman of the Senate Foreign Affairs Committee, being a notable example, it was nevertheless true that extracting funds from Congress for the purpose of offering overseas assistance was, at that point, a daunting prospect.

Truman, perhaps recognising this, replaced James Byrnes with George Marshall as Secretary of State in January 1947.[17] It was an inspired choice. Not only had the General 'received invaluable training in the conduct of foreign relations when he accompanied President Roosevelt to Casablanca, Teheran, Cairo, Quebec and Yalta',[18] but he was highly regarded by Congress. In a rare display of unanimity, the Senate Foreign Relations Committee 'took only twelve minutes on 8 January to decide that General Marshall was the right man to succeed Mr Byrnes'.[19] Truman, then, started 1947 with a strong economy and a new Secretary of State. He was faced, however, with a Republican Congress and a policy of containment which required funds to pursue it.

It was against this background that on the afternoon of Friday 21 February 1947 the British ambassador in Washington Lord Inverchapel's private secretary sought to arrange an immediate appointment with George Marshall. Marshall, however, had left to go to Princeton where he was to make his first speech as the Secretary of State. Dean Acheson was alerted to the embassy's request and, having ascertained the subject matter to be discussed, arranged for H.M. Sichel (First Secretary at the British embassy) to meet with Loy Henderson (Director of the Office of Near Eastern and African Affairs). At the meeting, Sichel handed Henderson two notes: one relating to Greece and the other to Turkey. The notes referred to previous conversations between Secretary of State Byrnes and British ministers in which the Secretary had indicated a willingness on America's part to offer aid to Greece and Turkey. The notes outlined the problems faced by Greece and Turkey and the lengths Britain had gone to in an attempt to solve them. The notes stated that Britain would not be in a position, due to her own financial circumstances, to continue financial assistance after 31 March 1947 and ended with a request that a joint policy, agreed by Britain and America, might be developed (albeit that the policy would need to be financed by the Americans).[20] On Monday, 24 February, the notes were formally presented by Inverchapel to the Secretary of State.

Britain's indication of her withdrawal of assistance to Greece and Turkey could not have come as a complete surprise to the Americans. The US Administration was well aware that the British had been showing signs of strain in their international commitments. In the same month (February 1947), Britain referred the Palestinian issue to the UN, negotiations with Egypt broke down and that dispute too was sent to the UN, and Attlee announced that Britain would withdraw from India by the middle of 1948. Britain's financial weakness and the country's need for financial aid was no secret.

As the notes pointed out, there had been several conversations between Britain and America on the importance of the region to America and the need for America to provide aid to Greece and Turkey. Bevin spoke to Byrnes about the need for aid as early as the Meeting of the conference, which took place in Paris between April and July 1946.[21] In October 1946, Byrnes, in a conversation with Albert V. Alexander, the British Minister of Defence, indicated that the Americans 'were prepared to do everything they possibly could to help the two countries [Greece and Turkey] economically'.[22]

The embassy also had several conversations on the topic. On 28 October, Donald Maclean met Loy Henderson, and broached the subject of assistance to Greece and Turkey. Henderson indicated that he had just come from a meeting with Byrnes where that very subject had been discussed; he confirmed that Greece and Turkey were of strategic importance to America and asked if they could have Britain's assessment of the military situation there and of Britain's estimate of any future military assistance which might be required. Henderson confirmed that an economic mission was being sent to Greece to assess the situation, saying '[it] was obvious that financial assistance would be required but it was not clear how the USG could provide this'. Then, almost as a prelude to the Truman Doctrine, Henderson added 'one alternative was to get the Congress to vote a grant in aid which the political side of the State Department favoured'. Maclean concluded his minute with 'Generally speaking the State Department would welcome any suggestions we might have to make about economic assistance to Greece and Turkey ... The above confirms that Mr Byrnes's observations to Mr Alexander were not a mere flash in the pan.'[23] Two days later, on 30 October, Loy Henderson met again with the embassy and confirmed that a discussion with Byrnes had again emphasised that 'Turkey and Greece were of strategic importance to the United States'.[24]

In addition to discussions between Britain and America, there were also conversations between the Greeks and the Americans. At the behest of the UK, Constantine Tsaldaris (the Greek Deputy Prime Minister and Minister for Foreign Affairs) visited Washington in December 1946 and met with Truman, Byrnes, Acheson and Vandenberg, among other officials. Tsaldaris claimed that during these meetings, 'the United States recognised Greece's need for immediate economic assistance and was determined to make aid available'.[25] Inverchapel managed to ascertain that the position was not that clear-cut and that the Americans were thinking of a loan. In response to a question from Inverchapel, Byrnes confirmed that a loan would not require the approval of Congress but would come from the Export Import Bank and from funds the bank already had.[26] The new Secretary of State George Marshall, in a press conference given shortly before the embassy presented the notes to the Department of State, indicated that Greece was entitled to the sympathy and respect of the world and that 'it is to the interest of the United States . . . that Greece be assisted to maintain her independence and territorial integrity'.[27]

It seems, then, that whilst there may have been some ambiguity as to where the money would come from, there were clear signs that America was prepared to provide assistance to Greece and Turkey. Based on reports from the embassy, ministers and others, the Foreign Office was in a good position to anticipate the American response to the notes presented by the embassy on 21 February 1947. Bevin, in making his concession to Dalton by agreeing to withdraw financial and military aid to both Greece and Turkey, would have had a pretty clear idea that America would pick up the mantle in South Eastern Europe.

Unsurprisingly, then, on 26 February, the US Administration determined that it had little choice but to offer assistance. Acheson summoned Inverchapel on 1 March and informed him of the Administration's decision. He gave Inverchapel two aide-memoires. The first emphasised the importance of Britain continuing aid in the interim to avoid a collapse of Greece. The second indicated that the Administration saw the issue as being part of a larger problem and that there were issues of common concern in other countries throughout Europe and Asia. It suggested that the two governments enter into informal conversations regarding these problems.[28] Such was the perceived importance of this second point that Inverchapel telephoned Acheson that afternoon for clarification. It was an opportunity for Britain to influence America's foreign policy decisions, something it had wanted to do for some time. It was these proposed conversations which predated the Pentagon talks (see below) and the discussions regarding the Marshall Plan.

The continuation of aid in the interim was a more tricky matter for Inverchapel to handle. The Treasury was insisting upon only providing £2 million per month and even that amount was to be provided as a loan and to be repaid by the Americans or by the Greeks out of money provided by the Americans. Acheson made it clear that any insistence by Britain on such a measure would seriously affect the current negotiations that the Administration was conducting with senior Congressmen. A somewhat embarrassed Inverchapel informed Acheson that he had already sent a cable to London expressing exactly that view. Even allowing for the dollar shortage, it is hard to understand why the British were behaving in such a petty manner. This is particularly so when they were being offered talks on a much wider number of issues – talks which would move them towards the very objective they sought, i.e. to secure their own foreign policy objectives by influencing America's. Inverchapel, who was close to the situation, understood this perfectly well.[29]

What happened next, and the events that led to Truman promulgating the Truman Doctrine in his now famous speech to Congress on 12 March 1947, are well documented elsewhere.[30] Once Truman had made his speech, it was part of the embassy's job to do what it could to use its contact base to ensure that Congress passed the appropriate legislation. As with the Loan Agreement, the embassy needed to tread carefully so as not to be seen to be interfering in American politics. Inverchapel wrote to Bevin informing him that he had launched a 'discreet talking campaign' aimed not only at Congressmen but also at the press and the financial community. The object of such a campaign was to educate the audience to the fact that 'political stability in Europe and elsewhere cannot be achieved without economic stability, and that economic stability in turn depends upon the increased cooperation of the United States though financial assistance'.[31] The embassy also helped the Administration in its submission of evidence to the Congressional committees. Inverchapel liaised closely with Acheson and was instrumental in helping Acheson deal with some of the Congressional questions.[32]

As mentioned in chapter 1, one of the embassy's important roles was the production of regular political reports. Those issued at the time of the Truman Doctrine are good examples of such reports and make interesting reading; they would have been invaluable to individuals sitting in the Foreign Office several thousand miles distant from the action. It is perhaps worth quoting just one, which reported Truman's speech to Congress, in order to give a sense of the impressive nature of these reports:

> The speech was delivered in a flat tone of voice and in a manner completely devoid of any attempt at eloquence. The packed floor and galleries received it soberly and without enthusiasm. On only three occasions was the President interrupted by brief

bursts of applause almost exclusively from members of his own party. Nevertheless, the speech made a deep impression and is regarded as one of the most momentous in American history.[33]

It is interesting to note that even at the time the embassy grasped the importance of the occasion and of the speech. The reports moved beyond mere description and into analysis:

> Excepting in extremist quarters, there is general agreement that something must be done and that the course set by the President is in the right direction. Almost nowhere is the problem regarded as a Greek affair. Greece has merely become the scene of the battle... As matters stand Congressional opinion falls into the following five groups: (a) those who readily accept the President's recommendations, (b) those who accept them reluctantly as the lesser of two evils, (c) those who acknowledge that something must be done but who are reserving judgement on the form which action should take. These three groups constitute the majority. In addition there are (d) those who believe that the United Nations rather than the United States should take responsibility and (e) the die hard isolationists.[34]

The above quote contains a fragment of what was contained in the Weekly Political Report issued after Truman's speech. The report is packed with observation and analysis which would have been of tremendous benefit to anyone in the Foreign Office attempting to follow and understand American policy. It is just a small part of one of many hundreds of reports which the embassy sent to London on a range of issues. It is doubtful whether this level of analysis and insight could ever be achieved without the presence of an embassy on the ground. Clearly the role of representation, that is representation of American events and views to Britain, was an important role and one that the embassy carried out effectively. It is, perhaps, not an exaggeration to suggest that these reports, taken as a whole, would have been indispensable to the conduct of British foreign policy in the period under review.

The embassy did not restrict itself to recording its understanding of political events in regular reports. Such was the reach of the embassy that Inverchapel was able to write to the Prime Minister directly. One such letter, written shortly after Britain announced its withdrawal from Greece, provides an instructive insight into the sensitivity of senior Labour ministers to American behaviour.

Inverchapel pointed out that there were still elements within the Administration which asked whether 'pressure from left wing elements in the Labour Party and trade unions might not ultimately constrain His Majesty's Government to appease rather than resist Soviet encroachment'. Inverchapel cited this as one of the reasons for Eisenhower's refusal to approve the siting of an atomic pile in England. Inverchapel suggested that the Labour backbench rebellion led by Crossman the previous November had done little to improve the situation, nor did the fact that the British government did nothing to discourage the Trade Union Congress from playing an active role in the World Federation of Trade Unions. The Department of State and the American Federation of Labour believed this latter organisation to be Communist-inspired. Inverchapel warned that 'a breach between the TUC and the WFTU would greatly contribute to Anglo-American Relations by dispelling the fear of many responsible Americans who see danger in this association'. Inverchapel suggested that 'our interests in America can be advanced only if the Labour Party and Trade Union Congress are at constant pains to condemn domestic Communists and all their works'.[35]

A second theme, in part connected to the first, was concerned with Britain's strength and her ability to resist Soviet advances. Inverchapel presented the possibility that, at least in American minds, there might be a link between the withdrawal of assistance to Greece and a 'sustained yielding of ground to Russia'. The answer in Inverchapel's eyes was that British spokesmen, both at home and abroad, should 'maintain an even balance between an honest appraisal of our economic and other difficulties (such as might dispose our American friends to assume a larger share of the burdens of world leadership), and a refutation of the notion that we have become too weak to play any effective part ourselves'.[36]

Attlee's response was almost dismissive; he had clearly had enough of the Americans. Attlee lamented the fact that the British were expected to keep troops 'in all kinds of places' whilst the Americans 'contributed very little in that way'. Attlee's exasperation over Palestine also surfaced: 'There is a good deal of annoyance at the light-hearted manner in which the Americans exacerbate our difficulties in Palestine without taking any real responsibility.' Attlee concluded that 'all this leads to a feeling that there is a danger of our being placed in a position of a mere breakwater between the United States and Russia – hence a good deal of Left Wing criticism'.[37] Bevin also wrote to Inverchapel commenting on his letter to the Prime Minister.[38] He too showed little empathy for Inverchapel's remarks and this somewhat supports the assertion that Bevin felt that the embassy was too supportive of the Americans' position.[39] We saw in the previous chapter that Inverchapel was rebuked by Orme Sargent. Although the replies from Attlee and Bevin were not rebukes as such, it seems clear from the above correspondence that Inverchapel was falling out of favour with the Prime Minister and the Foreign Secretary. One cannot help feeling, however, that there was an element of blaming the messenger – perhaps one of the perils of being a diplomat.

It was Britain's request for American aid to Greece which prompted Acheson to write that the Greek and Turkish problem was only one 'part of a much larger problem growing out of the change in Britain's strength'. He continued that it is 'important and urgent that study be given to . . . situations elsewhere in the world which may require analogous, financial, technical and military aid on our part'.[40] Accordingly, Acheson proposed that the Special Ad Hoc Committee of State-War-Navy Coordinating Committee (SWNCC) be instructed to consider the problem and report to Marshall.

The Ad Hoc Committee reported on 21 April 1947. It concluded that 'a planned program of assistance to foreign countries should enable the US to take positive, forehanded, and preventative action [and] promote US security and other national interests'. The report formed the direct link between the Truman Doctrine and the Marshall Plan. The report discussed the dual objectives of American Foreign policy: 'to support economic stability and orderly political processes throughout the world'. The report suggested that substantial overseas aid would be required to fund the dollar gap (i.e. in 1947 America was projected to export $7.5 billion more goods and services than it was projected to import). It concluded that 'under present programs...the world will not be able to continue to buy United States exports at the 1946/47 rate beyond another 12–18 months'. The implications of this would be serious for both the world recovery and employment and business activity in America. The report also suggested that economic weaknesses in some countries could give rise to 'political shifts which adversely affect the security of the United States'.[41]

The Ad Hoc Committee report led to Acheson making a speech to the Delta Council in Cleveland, Mississippi on 8 May 1947, a speech which Truman called 'the prologue to the Marshall Plan'.[42] Whilst Marshall's Harvard speech is now more famous, it was Acheson's speech, made with the full authority of the President, which first set out in public the policy which was later to become the Marshall Plan. The speech, which picked up on the themes in the Ad Hoc Committee report, spelt out the problems in Europe and indicated that it was in America's interest to use its own 'economic and financial resources' to alleviate those problems in order to 'preserve our own freedoms and our own democratic institutions'.[43]

In America, at the time there were widespread press reports on the plight of Europe and the need for reconstruction, and American newsmen were put on notice that the Delta speech was an important one. Acheson also made a point of briefing members of the British press off the record prior to the speech, emphasising the importance of the speech in terms of American policy.[44] 'The word spread quietly among editors in Great Britain, with the result that the Delta speech was treated as a sensation, widely published and commented upon.'[45]

At the same time as the Administration's views were evolving, the Fourth Conference of Foreign Ministers was taking place in Moscow. There was to be another attempt to resolve the differences between the big four powers over the future of Germany and Austria. It is not necessary here to debate the negotiations; the lesson that Marshall learnt, however, was that the Soviets would never accept a settlement in Germany or Austria that did not effectively result in the Soviets controlling those two countries. Since the war, Germany, formerly Europe's greatest industrial nation, had been unable to rebuild its industry and the population was operating at the subsistence level. Marshall, aware of the difficulties being faced in the rest of Europe during the early part of 1947, made the connection between the stagnation in Germany and the failure of the European recovery. Marshall further understood that the Soviets had little interest in a revival of Germany and Western Europe; indeed it was believed that economic weakness in Europe would lead to more Communist gains in countries such as France and Italy. Marshall and his advisers 'all agreed that the Soviet Union was stalling for time while Europe disintegrated and that the United States must initiate action to bring about European recovery'.[46]

On his return to Washington, Marshall, in a radio broadcast on 28 April, said, 'The recovery of Europe has been far slower than expected. Disintegrating forces are becoming evident. The patient is sinking while the doctors deliberate.'[47] The next day Marshall summoned George Kennan, who had returned from the Moscow embassy, to Washington. He told Kennan that the problems of Europe were urgent and instructed him to set up the Policy Planning Department and produce a report on the European situation and a proposal for America's response to it within two weeks. The only advice he gave Kennan was 'avoid trivia'.[48]

Kennan produced his report on 22 May and sent it to Acheson. The report was, in part, based upon the work of the Ad Hoc Committee and the ideas advanced by Acheson in his Delta speech. The report recognised 'that the Communists are exploiting the European crisis and that further communist successes would create serious danger to American security'. The report went on to say that 'aid to Europe should be directed not to the combating of communism as such but to the restoration of the health and economic vigour of European society'. Any plan was to be a European-wide one and not a piecemeal country-by-country one and Kennan insisted that 'for the sake of clarity, for the sake of soundness of concept and for the sake of the self respect of European peoples any initiative must be taken in Europe by the Europeans'. If the initiative did not come from Europe then Kennan warned that it would mean 'that rigor mortis has already set in on the body politic of Europe'.

The report also contained an interesting instruction which indicates the strength of Anglo-American relations at the time: 'That this overall approach be informally and secretly discussed with British leaders at an early date and their assurances of support solicited.'[49]

Whilst Kennan had been working on his report, William Clayton had been in Geneva attending the International Conference on Trade and Employment as the US delegate. He had also had the opportunity to engage in 'frequent consultation with leaders of many governments of Western Europe regarding the deterioration of their economies'.[50] During the flight home towards the end of May, Clayton drafted a memorandum which had a 'powerful effect . . . upon General Marshall's thinking and the framing of his proposal'.[51]

The memorandum contained dramatic phrases, such as 'Europe is steadily deteriorating . . . millions of people in the cities are slowly starving'. Clayton, who was uncompromising in his demands when negotiating the Financial Agreement with the British, now acknowledged that he had 'grossly underestimated the destruction to the European economy by the war'.[52] He added some flesh to the proposal that had been circulating in Washington: 'Europe must have from us a grant of 6 or 7 billion dollars worth of goods a year for three years.'[53] At a meeting on 28 May attended by Marshall, Acheson, Kennan, Clayton and others, the memorandum and Kennan's report were discussed. Marshall sought the views of those in the room but characteristically said little himself. The meeting ended inconclusively.

On 5 June 1947, however, Marshall delivered a speech at Harvard University, during which he said:

> Europe's requirements for the next three or four years of foreign food and other essential products – principally from America – are so much greater than her present ability to pay that she must have substantial additional help or face economic, social, and political deterioration of a very grave character.

America was to provide this help. As Marshall stated: 'It is logical that the United States should do whatever it is able to do to assist in the return of normal economic health in the world.' Marshall indicated that

American policy was 'directed not against any country or doctrine but against hunger, poverty, desperation, and chaos'.[54] The speech, which was drafted by Charles Bohlen (Special Assistant to the Secretary of State), used 'primarily the Kennan and Clayton memorandum'.[55] In echoing these reports Marshall indicated that aid was to be open to all of Europe but would not be offered on a piecemeal basis. Towards the end of the speech Marshall said:

> there must be some agreement among the countries of Europe as to the requirements of the situation and the part those countries themselves will take in order to give proper effect to whatever action might be undertaken by this Government... The initiative, I think, must come from Europe.[56]

According to Acheson, the speech was 'short, simple and altogether brilliant in its statement of purpose'.[57]

What part, then, did the embassy play in forewarning London of the above events? The standard interpretation of how the Harvard speech was converted into action is given by Bullock in his biography of Bevin:

> it was on a small wireless set by his bedside that Bevin first heard the report of Marshall's speech... It is arguable that Bevin's action in the next few days was his most decisive personal contribution as Foreign Secretary to the history of his times. Without any advice from the British Embassy in Washington, and to the surprise of his officials, he came into the Foreign Office next morning and seized upon what was no more than a single sentence in Marshall's speech − 'the initiative, I think, must come from Europe'. Relying solely on his own intuitive judgement, he threw all his energy into conjuring up a European response of sufficient weight and urgency to give substance to Marshall's implied offer of American support.[58]

The implication is that Bevin's 'eureka moment' was based solely on the radio broadcast and was not preceded by any forewarning or analysis by the Washington embassy or the Foreign Office of what might be on offer from America. There is some evidence to counter this suggestion, however.

John Balfour in his memoirs describes a lunch he attended with Gerald Barry, editor of the *News Chronicle*, and Dean Acheson on 22 May 1947. At the lunch, Acheson told Balfour that Marshall was about to make a speech on the issue of world recovery and Acheson, 'using language which proved a fortnight later to be almost identical to the text of the Harvard speech',[59] offered an analysis of Europe's economic plight. Balfour states: 'I reported what Acheson had said to my chief, Archie Inverchapel, who promptly called a meeting of embassy experts to examine the implications of this novel and most encouraging development in American policy'.[60] The views of these experts were set out in a letter from Balfour to Neville Butler, the head of the North American Department at the Foreign Office.[61] The letter did not arrive, however, until the day of the Harvard speech. The Americans were surprised at the speed of Bevin's response; Balfour commented that 'I like to think that Bevin's magnificent initiative was greatly facilitated by the detailed background information made available by Dean Acheson's calculated disclosures to myself.'[62] The above interpretation of events is supported by the Foreign Office records.

A further piece of evidence is the transcript of an oral history interview (given in August 1970) with William P.N. Edwards (the Counsellor at the embassy in charge of the BIS). In the interview, Edwards says that prior to a scheduled return visit to London (a few weeks before the Harvard speech), in line with his usual practice, he met with the leading commentators and columnists in Washington to gather their views. There was a strong and consistent view that American aid for Europe was inevitable, that: 'We (America) will help you (Europe) if you will help yourselves', and that this was 'already being talked of in the highest circles of the Administration'. Believing that this was important, Edwards says that when he arrived in London he went straight to Edmund Hall Patch (Deputy Under-Secretary, Foreign Office) and informed him of these ideas. 'He thought this was so important that he went that very evening to Ernie Bevin... to tell him what was being discussed and what it might become.'[63]

Makins, who worked closely with Bevin in the Foreign Office, has also confirmed that he [Bevin] was 'waiting for, was anticipating, the kind of move, which General Marshall made in his Harvard speech, and therefore he was ready to pick up the ball and run with it'.[64] Makins, in an earlier interview, indicated that the Foreign Office had an intimation of what was coming, i.e. Marshall's speech, and when asked where these intimations came from Makins replied 'I think from informal communications from the embassy'.[65] Hall Patch is also supportive of this view: 'Bevin was encouraged by the Acheson speech [i.e. the speech to the Delta Council in Cleveland which had been reported on by the embassy and the press] and from then on really expected some action such as the Marshall speech'.[66]

These statements, which provide reasonable evidence that the embassy did furnish some warning and background information, also need to be examined in the context of the press coverage at the time and the reports which were being sent to London by the embassy. The press, which is of course hugely influential in American policy making, began discussing the need for large amounts of aid to the whole of Western Europe the day after Truman delivered his speech to Congress on 12 March 1947. All the major commentators, including Walter Lippmann, James Reston and Marquis Childs, wrote pieces indicating the desire to look at the larger picture and suggesting the need for billions of dollars of aid to Europe. The momentum for the call for European aid grew. On 5 April, Walter Lippmann wrote: 'To prevent the crisis that will otherwise engulf Europe... the measures will have to be very large... no less than the equivalent to a revival of lend lease.'[67] The Foreign Office was well aware of this commentary, and the BIS reported such press comment on a daily basis.

The radio addresses of both Marshall and John Foster Dulles (the Republican Foreign affairs spokesmen) on their return from Moscow were also reported to the Foreign Office by the embassy. The embassy suggested that there was 'widespread support for the Secretary of State's declaration that action in Europe cannot await eventual compromise agreements'.[68] The embassy further indicated that such sentiment was supported by both Dulles and Senator Vandenberg.

Acheson's Delta speech[69] fuelled press speculation and towards the end of May, James Reston, in a piece for the *New York Times*, was virtually describing the Marshall Plan: 'What is under urgent and thoughtful consideration is a proposal to call on the nations of Europe to suggest a more coordinated continental economy as a preliminary to the United States meeting them with a large-scale program of continental aid.'[70] In April and May 1947, there were hundreds of articles calling for American aid to Europe. As Joseph Jones (Special Assistant to the Assistant Secretary of State for Public Affairs) pointed out: 'That the administration would propose a pro-gram of aid to Europe had by early May become a virtual certainty.'[71] The embassy reported that 'it is known that State Department offi-cials are deeply concerned over the economic situation particularly in Western Europe' and added 'the widespread interest of the press has all the [earmarks] of a stimulated campaign'.[72] The Foreign Office via the BIS and the embassy's political reports was clearly aware that a discussion was taking place in America on the need for aid to Europe and that, at least within the political establishment, there was support for such action.

At the same time as reporting the commentary in the press, the embassy was also reporting on the political and other developments which were likely to affect European aid. In a paper sent to Bevin enti-tled *United States: The Problem of European Unity*, Inverchapel indicated that European unity was becoming an important issue to Americans. The same paper also suggested that the 'restoration of European order and prosperity is a direct American interest' and further that 'there is a growing belief that a piecemeal approach to the economic and political reconstruction of Europe...is both wasteful and unconstruc-tive'. The report also concluded that 'the atmosphere in this country is in fact more receptive now to proposals for assistance to Western Europe...than it was four months ago'.[73]

The embassy also reported on the formation of the Policy Planning Department – the department which, as noted above, was in part responsible for Marshall's Harvard speech. The embassy was able to comment, in some detail, on the department and its head George Kennan.[74] Both Balfour and Inverchapel had been diplomats in Moscow at the same time as Kennan was attached to the American embassy there. The Foreign Office welcomed the despatch, commenting that the policy Planning Staff's first task would almost certainly be the working out of a new and comprehensive foreign economic policy.[75] In a further political report written on 26 May and received by the Foreign Office on 29 May, the embassy indicated that 'some of the most influential sections of the public no longer doubt that a large-scale programme of foreign aid is indispensable, not merely for the political stability of the world, but also for the domestic prosperity of the United States'. The report also suggested that the method to be used to implement such a policy was being debated but that if the policy planning staff produced a plan which was reasonable then there was a good prospect that it would be accepted by the public and, 'after the inevitable arguments and delays, from Congress as well'.[76]

At the risk of labouring the point, there is one final Political Summary that needs to be mentioned. Written on 1 June and received by the Foreign Office on the day the Harvard speech was delivered, the report offers a detailed analysis of the thoughts circulating in America as to the prospects of foreign aid for Europe and the conditions under which it might be forthcoming. The report, under the subheading 'Need For European Initiative', stated that 'there is wide and increasing recognition that large economic measures will have to be taken by next winter to avert a collapse in Europe . . . The planning in the State Department cannot be carried to its conclusion until Europe, with Britain and France taking the initiative, begins to plan and negotiate for its own recovery.' Under a separate heading, 'The Time Factor', the report indicated that the issue was so important that it was suggested that there might be a special session of Congress in September or October to debate economic questions. The embassy pointed out that time was of the essence not least because the presidential elections loomed in the following year and there was a fear that a breakdown in bipartisan politics might affect the issue. The embassy concluded that 'In these circumstances it is perhaps not fanciful to believe that we are embarking on a fateful "one hundred days" during which we not only have an opportunity but are actually being expected to evolve a pattern for American aid.'[77]

The embassy, then, not only indicated that aid might be forthcoming but also what was expected of Britain and Europe if such aid was to be actually delivered. It does not seem to be the case, then, that Bevin was completely unprepared. Indeed it is perhaps not too far fetched to suggest that due to the embassy reports, Bevin and the Foreign Office were in a good position to take the lead in Europe on the issue. The notion that Bevin was uninstructed has perhaps been given currency by the suggestion that Balfour, purportedly to save money and because he did not believe the speech to be important, sent the speech by diplomatic bag rather than by cable.[78] It is not known if this is true but in a Weekly Political Summary, written two days after the speech, the embassy referred to it as an 'important address'.[79] Also, immediately before the Harvard speech, Acheson collared his favourite three British journalists Leonard Miall, Malcolm Muggeridge and Stewart McColl and 'explained the full import of the Harvard one [speech], asking that they cable or telephone the full text and have their editors send a copy to Ernest Bevin with my estimate of its importance'.[80] This account was confirmed by Miall in an article in the *Listener* written in 1961.[81] It seems odd that Acheson, who was no maverick, would brief the press as to the speech's importance but not embassy officials. Finally it is clear that the Foreign Office, by one means or another, had the speech on 5 June. The Foreign Office files include a Daily Wireless Bulletin containing, amongst other speeches, an advanced copy of Marshall's Harvard speech.[82] The document is date stamped with AN 1973 5 June 1947 and UE 5870 14 July 1947. AN is the Foreign Office designation for the North American Department and UE for the Economic Relations Department.[83] It seems that at least one of the relevant departments in the Foreign Office had a copy of the speech on the day it was delivered.

This analysis is not intended to detract from the fact that Bevin did respond quickly and that such a response was an important act in British post-war history. It is simply to suggest that Bevin was not acting without advice from the British embassy, nor was he 'relying solely on his own intuitive judgement'.[84] Indeed, the embassy was doing exactly what it ought to be doing, i.e. collecting information, analysing it, offering a commentary on it and sending it to London.

On 9 June, Inverchapel informed Marshall that Bevin had been favourably impressed by the Harvard speech and had begun work to put a programme together. Previously Balfour had been able to report that Walter Lippmann had informed him that Lew Douglas, the American ambassador to London, was, in addition to his diplomatic responsibilities, to act as the coordinator of the work of the American representatives in Europe. These representatives were to be responsible for promoting the idea of a plan for continental rehabilitation to the governments to which they were accredited.[85] That the London ambassador was in this position further promoted the idea that Britain was the informal leader of the European response.

Balfour spent the weekend following the Harvard speech on George Kennan's farm; he described Kennan as one of his oldest American friends. Balfour informed Kennan that London was taking urgent steps to follow up Marshall's appeal. Balfour, in a letter to the Foreign Office, was able to confirm that Kennan emphasised 'points already dwelt upon in earlier reports to you'. These included the point that 'the initiative for formulating positive measures for the recovery of Europe must come from the European Governments concerned in the form of an agreement between themselves as to their joint requirements'. Kennan suggested that this was necessary not only because the approach would appeal to Congress but also because such an approach would 'blunt the edge' of accusations by the Communist parties in individual European countries that their governments were becoming 'the tools of American imperialists'. Kennan also warned Balfour that Britain should not expect Clayton on his visit to London to advise the British on what to do; rather it was for the British to make suggestions on their own part.[86] The closeness of British diplomats to important members of the US Administration was to prove a useful tool for Bevin in his formulation of his detailed response.

On the same day that Bevin communicated with Marshall, he also sent a message to Bidault, the French foreign minister, suggesting a joint response to 'the new American approach to Europe'. The French reacted favourably; however, the issue was complicated when

Marshall, at a press conference, made it clear that his proposal was available to all countries in Europe. The Americans did not want the stigma of dividing Europe and apparently decided to take the risk of offering potential aid to the Soviet Union and its satellites. Concerned by this, Bevin decided to go to Paris himself. He met with Bidault on 18 June and the Soviet position preoccupied them both. Bevin was determined not to let the Soviets wreck any proposals. Bidault agreed, but for domestic reasons, i.e. the strength of Communists in the French assembly; he felt the need to issue an invitation to the Soviets. The Soviets accepted and a meeting between the three powers was organised for 27 June.

Prior to the meeting of the three powers, Balfour met with Chip Bohlen and George Kennan. Balfour was informed that, although supportive of the Soviet involvement on the right basis, the Americans had reservations as to the intent behind the Soviet involvement in any European reconstruction plan. Interestingly, Balfour was informed that the 'State Department was not taking the French embassy into its confidence about its attitude towards the Soviet Union's participation in the meeting'.[87] Chip Bohlen was also an old Moscow hand; hence the three attendees at this meeting had served together in Moscow. It is perhaps relevant, then, to quote the remarks by Lord Strang, who had served in the British embassy in Moscow between 1930 and 1933, on working in Russia:

> No one who has served in Moscow can ever be quite the same person again... The pattern of life in the Soviet Union would be incredible if it did not exist. Only those who have watched its processes as they unfold before their eyes can realise how incredible it may appear to be, and yet they can testify that it exists. Those who have had this experience may be pardoned if they think that, among themselves, they can speak a language and carry thoughts which no one who has not shared that experience can fully understand.[88]

Although this is speculation and understanding diplomatic meetings from a distance is not easy, this meeting has the hallmark of an informal suggestion that perhaps Bevin need not try too hard with the Soviets in Paris. It was certainly a message that Bevin would have been pleased to hear.

Inverchapel also informed the Foreign Office of the views of a number of Congressmen gathered for an informal meeting at the embassy. Congress would view the Marshall Plan from a strategic rather than an economic standpoint. It was also felt that because of Soviet intransigence over the previous two years any amount of outward evidence of Soviet willingness to cooperate would be insufficient to persuade Congress to support a plan from which the Soviets gained. As one Congressman put it, 'to most of us the phrase Russian cooperation is a contradiction in terms'.[89] Bevin, courtesy of communications from the embassy, attended the meeting of the three powers in Paris with, as he would have put it, 'the gift of being able to walk away'.

The Soviets went to Paris armed with a large delegation and wrecking tactics. Through several days of talks, Bevin remained determined that the Soviets would not arrest the momentum which he had created. The Soviets attempted several stalling tactics, including demanding that Congress confirm that the money was available before any plan was drawn up and suggesting that each nation simply drew up a list of its requirements rather than integrate them as part of a European plan.[90] The talks ended on 2 July with the Soviets warning the British and French that persisting in their actions would have 'grave consequences' and result in the division of Europe. A European revival was simply not in the Soviets' interest.

Prior to leaving Paris, Bevin agreed with Bidault the terms of a note inviting 22 countries to Paris to discuss a European plan. All the European countries except Spain and the Soviet Union were invited. Of those invited 14 accepted and 8 declined. Stalin intervened to stop the Poles, Czechs and Finns from accepting. Representatives of the affirming nations attended the Conference on European Reconstruction which opened in Paris on 12 July.

The conference formed a Committee of European Economic Cooperation (CEEC) with Bevin in the chair. An Executive Committee was appointed which consisted of Britain, France, the Netherlands, Norway and Italy. Five technical committees were also formed to consider respectively food and agriculture, energy, coal and steel, transport and balance of payment issues. Sir Oliver Franks, who was to become Inverchapel's successor, was brought in by Bevin to chair the executive in his absence. The objective was to 'prepare a report on European availabilities and requirements for the next four years, to be submitted to the United States before 1 September'.[91]

At the same time as Oliver Franks got down to the job of producing a report for the Americans, the Treasury was grappling with the problem of the rapidly increasing drain of Britain's dollar reserves. It was noted above that the monthly dollar drain in the first quarter of 1947 had quadrupled since the end of 1946. This geometric growth was set to continue. One of the provisions of the Financial Agreement was that sterling was to become convertible, at least in regard to current account transactions, one year after the Agreement became effective. Sterling therefore was due to become convertible on 15 July 1947. In early 1947, the government was faced with an escalating drain on its dollar reserves with the knowledge that the date for convertibility was fast approaching.

The Financial Agreement was an inflexible document. There were no provisions for joint consultations to monitor changing circumstances, nor was it possible to alter the loan without reference to the respective legislatures of both countries. The Financial Agreement was entered into on the assumption that there would not be a worldwide shortage of dollars; when it became clear that there was, Britain made no attempt, at least not until it was too late, to discuss the problem with the Americans and therefore to open up the possibility of changing its terms. Dalton considered such an approach in February 1947 but was dissuaded from doing so by both the Treasury and the Bank of England, principally because there was a concern that the new Congress would not agree to any alterations and that the airing of the event in public would be damaging.[92] It was not until June that Dalton raised the issue with Clayton at the talks which took place in London. Even then the requirements of the British must have appeared confusing. At a meeting on 24 June, Bevin said that 'convertibility and non discrimination obligations upon the UK had in his opinion been dated three years too soon'. Clayton then asked why Dalton had not come earlier with these troubles, only to be told by Dalton that 'he was not asking for or suggesting any change in this commitment under the Financial Agreement'.[93] At a further meeting two days later, Eady said he did not contemplate 'any general escape from the convertibility obligation', to be followed shortly by Dalton saying that 'the timetable of the Financial Agreement was "so wrong"' but that 'he did not blame the US –"it is our fault"'.[94]

Britain then moved towards convertibility in a somewhat indecisive mood. In the first month after convertibility was introduced, the drain rose to the rate of $498 million per month. With no apparent respite and with reserves draining rapidly, the Cabinet was forced to take action. On 17 August, the Cabinet agreed that the convertibility of sterling must be suspended.[95] Such a suspension would be a clear breach of the provisions of the agreement and in order to avoid the stigma of the government defaulting on the terms of a loan, Sir Wilfred Eady was despatched to Washington to find a face-saving formula. Eady wanted the Americans to waive the relevant provision of the Financial Agreement, thereby ensuring that Britain was not in breach of the agreement.[96] The US Administration, however, was not prepared to alter the agreement without reference to Congress – a solution which was totally impractical.

The Americans proposed a compromise to be effected by an exchange of notes between Dalton and John Snyder, Vinson's replacement as Secretary of the Treasury. The British note stated: 'This action [suspension of convertibility] is of an emergency and temporary nature which HM Government consider to be within the intentions and purposes of the Financial Agreement.' The American note responded with an acknowledgement of the temporary nature of the British action and the fact that any proposed action by the British would be 'within the framework of the Financial Agreement'.[97] Eady had mitigated Britain's embarrassment.

Fforde notes that 'On the evening of 20 August 1947 the Chancellor of the Exchequer announced over the radio that external convertibility of sterling had been suspended because of an unacceptable drain on external reserves and the fast approaching exhaustion of available credits'.[98] In the first half of 1947, the balance of the loan had been reduced by $1,630 million and in just under two months from 1 July to 23

August, a further $970 million had disappeared.[99] Out of the original loan amount of $3.75 billion, only $400 million remained. However, because Britain had defaulted, this $400 million was frozen.

The convertibility crisis might be seen as something of a failure, not only in terms of the crisis itself, but also in terms of Anglo-American relations. What was the embassy doing in this period with regard to advising the government? It seems clear that the embassy believed that the British government should, at an early stage, keep the Americans informed of any difficulties which might be encountered in honouring the terms of the Financial Agreement. Makins, on his return from Washington, reported that 'before I left Washington Mr Clayton went out of his way to say to me that if we were likely to run into difficulties over the loan we should be well advised to discuss these difficulties with the Americans as soon as possible and not leave it until a late stage'.[100] The embassy also reported Clayton's testimony in front of the Senate Finance Committee which was considering Britain's commitment to convertibility. When asked by the Committee if he had any doubt that Britain would ask for relief from the commitment to convertibility Clayton replied, 'I do not think that she [Britain] will ask for relief but that she will go through with it [convertibility]'.[101] At the meetings between Dalton and Clayton in June (as noted above), Clayton's irritation at not having been forewarned of any problems became apparent.

In addition to Makins' warning, Inverchapel also sent a warning in reference to the Financial Agreement: 'It has been impressed upon me again that United States Treasury Officials are becoming increasingly embarrassed and restless at lack of any sign of action or information from us.'[102] Convertibility was not the only issue that was governed by the agreement; Britain also had an obligation to complete negotiations regarding sterling balances. The embassy reported that Snyder 'regretted that we had not felt able to let him have some communication...at a much earlier date', adding that he was 'considerably piqued'. The Treasury, no doubt, had its own reasons for being reticent in sharing information with the Americans; what the embassy was doing was warning them that such reticence was having an effect on Anglo-American relations.

Whilst John Balfour and Gordon Munro (Finance minister at the embassy and head of the UK Treasury Delegation) were part of the delegation holding talks with the Americans in Washington in August 1947, there is no evidence that the embassy played a significant role in the talks in the way the embassy did in the original Financial Agreement negotiations.[103] Gordon Munro did, however, contribute to the policy debate and a paper produced by him on 25 July 1947 may have been influential in Britain's decision to suspend convertibility.

Munro's analysis of the rate of the dollar drain indicated that the dollars from the credit would run out sometime between 25 October and 16 November; he concluded that in any event the dollar credit would certainly be exhausted by December 1947. Munro also knew, from papers which were being sent to him from London, that the Treasury believed that the dollars to be received from the Marshall Plan would replace those lost by the exhaustion of the credit extended under the Financial Agreement. Munro pointed out, however, that to expect any 'plums from the Marshall tree before the end of May 1948 is, in my opinion [likely] to be optimistic'.[104]

Munro, by reference to the Congressional timetable and an analysis of the American political factors influencing events at the time, provided a detailed explanation as to why Marshall Aid would not be forthcoming until the spring of 1948 at the earliest. In doing so, Munro cited personal conversations with Jesse Wolcott (Republican, Michigan), Chairman of the House Banking and Currency Committee, and other influential Congressmen. Munro concluded that there would be at least a six-month gap between the exhaustion of the credit and the receipt of any proceeds under the Marshall Plan.

After a review of the reserves available to Britain at that time, Munro deduced that they were not sufficient to bridge any gap. Munro's conclusion was that:

A policy to meet the critical post credit days needs formulating as soon as possible. It is exceedingly dangerous and, in my opinion, quite misleading to rely on a speedy implementation of the Marshall scheme and on a 'manageable' period of dollar financing from our own resources. Such a policy will, of course, have to

emanate from London, but I would suggest that as at the date of
exhaustion of the present U.S. credit we suspend all dollar payments to third countries.[105]

Munro also outlined a strategy for informing the Americans of such a
plan and said that the above policy proposal was a 'necessary preliminary move to prevent further deterioration in our financial position
before additional aid is forthcoming from the US Government'.[106]
A review of the Cabinet Conclusions and the Memoranda associated with them make no mention of Munro's paper. It is, therefore,
not possible to say that Munro was responsible for Britain's decision
to suspend convertibility. John Fforde in *The Bank of England and
Public Policy 1941–1958*, however, does record that Munro, on a visit
from Washington, met with Cameron Cobbold (Deputy Governor
Bank of England) on 31 July and advised him, in line with his paper,
that Marshall Aid could not begin until spring 1948. The next day
Cobbold admitted that convertibility could not last and in early
August preparations were set in train for an approach to the American
authorities.[107]
By paying close attention to the Congressional timetable and
the realities of American politics, Munro had understood that the
Treasury and the Bank of England's assumption relating to the anticipated receipt of dollars from Marshall Aid were flawed. Consequently,
he had identified a potential funding gap and had informed the Bank
of England and the Treasury of its consequences. Further, he had even
suggested the remedy, i.e. the suspension of all dollar payments to
third party countries – a remedy which amounted to the suspension
of convertibility.
The final part the embassy played in the Loan Agreement saga was
to assist in securing the release of the final $400 million available
under the credit. As noted above, the $400 million had been frozen
after Britain announced that she was suspending convertibility. It was,
however, $400 million which Britain badly needed. Initially Munro
reported that he was hopeful that the American Treasury Department
could release the $400 million to Britain without 'getting involved
with Congress'.[108] Unfortunately, however, Britain's dollar shortage

became embroiled in certain hearings before the Senate Appropriations Committee. It became apparent that Britain would not be providing the dollars required for joint military operations as was expected and, as a result of this, the American military were asking for a larger appropriation of dollars to compensate. A consequence of this was that Senator Knowland (Republican, California) said that he expected none of the remaining $400 million to be released without the specific consent of Congress, something neither the Administration nor the British wanted.[109]

Christelow (Assistant to Gordon Munro at the Treasury Delegation) met with Frank Southard, an official in the American Treasury Department, and reported that one of the options discussed to avoid this was an exchange of letters between Britain and America whereby Britain reported progress since the suspension of convertibility and, in exchange, America permitted further drawings of the loan. Christelow also reported, however, that Snyder would not now commit himself without at least consulting with Congressional leaders. It was hoped, however, to get the question transferred to the Foreign Relations committee where there would be more sympathetic support for Britain's position.[110]

By November, Munro was able to report some progress. In a meeting with Southard, he established that Snyder had met with both Robert Lovett, who had replaced Acheson as Under-Secretary of State, and James Forrestal (Secretary of Defence) and had enlisted the support of their Departments to be used with the Congressional committees if necessary. Southard also showed Munro a copy of a confidential note which the Treasury was sending to Lovett amplifying the subject. Munro reported that 'it could not have been in stronger language or more in favour of quick release had we been given carte blanche to write it ourselves'.[111] It took until December for Snyder to clear the issue with the Congressional committee and on 4 and 5 December, Sir Stafford Cripps, who had replaced Dalton as Chancellor of the Exchequer, and John Snyder exchanged letters clearing the way for the British to draw down the remaining $400 million available under the Financial Agreement.[112] The embassy, through its connections with the American Treasury Department, had eased the release of the funds which Britain so desperately needed. By keeping London informed, Munro and Christelow had enabled London to monitor the position more precisely and thus assess the risk to their reserve position more accurately.[113]

As the convertibility crisis unfolded the executive committee of the CEEC, under the Chairmanship of Sir Oliver Franks, continued its work. There were, however, a number of difficulties involved in producing the report. The Americans felt that there was not enough integration and that the numbers were too high; even worse there was still a projected dollar deficit in 1951. Kennan was sent to Paris to present the American point of view. His conclusion, however, was that 'we must not look to people in Paris to accomplish the impossible'. Kennan concluded that the long-term problem was a 'more complex one than any of us have realised.'[114]

Nevertheless a report, albeit a provisional one, was produced. It was signed by European foreign ministers in Paris on 22 September 1947. Forrest Pogue notes:

> The report outlined a four year program to promote economic recovery in the sixteen participating countries and Germany by restoring agricultural and industrial production to pre war levels, creating stable internal economic conditions, establishing an organisation to promote economic cooperation among the participating countries and to seek to solve the dollar deficit problem in each country through the expansion of exports.[115]

A Command Paper issued at the time contains the following sentence: 'In September, at the invitation of the United States Government, Sir Oliver Franks and other representatives of the CEEC went to Washington to elucidate and explain the report of the Paris Conference.'[116] But there was a little more to it than this. The Americans were still unhappy with certain aspects of the report. They hoped to reinforce the integration aspects of the report and, as Franks put it, 'chip away' at the proposed level of funding. The real objective, of course, was to make 'the Paris report as attractive as possible for presentation to Congress'.[117]

The method used in Washington to consider Marshall Aid affords a very interesting insight into the workings of the American political system. The executive branch actively sought to build a coalition in support of its proposals, not only through the discussions with members of the legislature on both sides, but also through the involvement of business, academia and the public. The US Administration set up several committees to consider the Marshall Plan, each of which was to address a certain interest group. The most important committee was the President's Committee on Foreign Aid, which was chaired by Averell Harriman (Secretary of Commerce) and consisted of 19 'distinguished citizens representing major sectors of American life'.[118] The committee was based on a suggestion by Senator Vandenberg and it was hoped that it would provide a basis for bipartisan support.

This method of framing legislation alters the methods which an embassy must use to influence the process. Lobbying State Department officials is not enough; a much wider system of influence needs to be in place. The British embassy in Washington sought to exert influence both through the BIS and directly through its diplomats and its consular network. Balfour spoke of the need to 'inspire American public opinion with a sense of urgency and the prospect of great success in connection with the Marshall initiative'.[119] Edwards was a little more modest in his approach, believing that it was really only possible to influence the people who make opinion rather than the public at large. Edwards was conscious of the budget required to influence 150 million Americans directly, a budget which the BIS did not have. Indeed, because of the dollar shortage, the BIS was having its budget cut rather than expanded.

The method used by the BIS was to keep in 'continuous contact, in Washington and New York . . . with all the leading commentators, columnists and editorial writers'. The method used was interesting. Edwards suggests that after a journalist had a meeting in the State Department they would come to the embassy and ask for the British point of view. They would be told, of course, and in the case of those that the BIS knew well 'we would show them our own telegrams from the Foreign Office'.[120] There was clearly, then, a significant degree of trust between certain journalists and the embassy. This would have paid considerable dividends in terms of getting the British point of view across.

In addition to working with American journalists, the BIS also worked closely with the US Administration. The Administration obviously wanted the Marshall proposals to be approved by Congress and was aware of the various lobbies and pressure groups that would put pressure on the Legislature. The Administration, with the BIS, tried to involve those sectors which had a selfish interest in seeing the Marshall plan passed: the farm community, for example, keen to sell produce to Europe and the new technology industries keen to export and, indeed, protect their existing investments in Europe. Companies such as General Electric had a big stake in Britain. Where possible the BIS 'supplied them with information which would help them put their case over'. In general terms, the emphasis was not to 'put much stress on the plight of Europe; rather we emphasized their own self interest'.[121]

The BIS was not simply reactive; it also sought to suggest various tactics which might improve Britain's position in America. Philip Jordan, the embassy Press Officer, made two interesting such proposals. He suggested that the Foreign Office attempted to persuade the Vatican to come out in favour of the Marshall proposals, indicating that it would have a 'great effect in American Catholic circles, which included many of those who most needed convincing as to their value'. The Foreign Office prepared a paper on Jordan's suggestion. Jordan's second proposal was that it would be of tremendous benefit if Robert Brand could return to Washington for a time as 'American respect for him was very high and his influence immense'. Hall Patch spoke to Brand, who indicated that he was going to America to visit his daughters and in any event would be keeping in touch with Balfour. Whilst Brand would undoubtedly have met with influential people in America there is no evidence that he played a significant public role in pushing the Marshall proposals.[122]

Edwards, too, when in London, was able to suggest methods of improving the presentation of Britain in America. Edwards suggested that texts of ministers' speeches should be cabled to the embassy rather than being sent by slower methods. He cited as an example

Cripps' speech to the House of Commons on 25 October 1947, which set out Britain's new economic plans. The full text of the speech had not reached America until six days after it was delivered. Edwards said, 'When I telegraphed London asking for the text of the speech, the reply I received was that their instructions were that the texts of speeches should not be cabled for economy reasons.'[123] This is consistent with a message sent to Makins when he was at the embassy: 'I hope...that you will do what you can to ensure that in the Washington office the telegram is restricted to really urgent matters...our total provision for telegrams in 1946 estimates comes to £1.2 million.'[124] It was noted above that there was a suggestion that for economy reasons Balfour may have been reluctant to telegraph the Harvard speech. Whilst it is impossible to quantify, it is interesting to note that in addition to the staffing issues discussed in chapter 1, the dollar shortage was having a directly adverse effect on diplomacy. The problem was in part corrected, however, in that summaries of speeches by leading ministers and the full text of speeches by Bevin were cabled to Washington. Edwards commented that the change would enable them to make a 'real impact'.

A further point that Edwards addressed which was also having an adverse effect on diplomacy was the 'uncommunicative' nature of the Treasury. Edwards indicated that this had been a problem ever since he had entered government public relations. The particular case in point was the extent of British investments in America. A number of Congressmen had suggested that no further aid should be given to other countries, in particular Britain, until they had sold all of their investments in America. Balfour and Edwards decided that this was a subject on which they should be briefed first, so that the point could be dealt with when raised in Washington and secondly, so that 'Consuls and other British officials in the USA should be enabled to destroy the argument at source if it were raised in the rest of the country'. The Treasury response was that nothing should be said on the subject. Whilst Edwards understood the point that one might not want to disclose the extent of British investments in America, he thought it was 'ridiculous to take the attitude that we must therefore say nothing at all upon the subject'. Edwards commented to the Foreign Office 'you will appreciate the dangers involved in a policy of complete silence upon so controversial a subject'.

The embassy also sought to use its influence in the building of a coalition in support of the Marshall proposals through its diplomats and consular offices. Inverchapel circulated a 23-page briefing note on the Marshall Plan to the consular offices throughout America. In a covering letter, Inverchapel said, 'It would be both improper and impolite for us to indulge in lobbying for the acceptance of the programme which is likely to emerge from the present talks in Paris. But it is the duty of all of us to be fully informed.' Inverchapel implored the recipients to make 'full use of facts and arguments contained in the document' when talking to prominent Americans. He also suggested that the initial reception of the report from the Paris Conference might make all the difference to its effective implementation.[125] The Foreign Office criticised the report's length and starkness but at least conceded that 'Washington was in a much better position to judge what suits the American taste'.[126]

In addition to playing an eclectic and background role in putting together the coalition in support of the Marshall Plan, the embassy was also involved in two sets of talks which took place at the end of 1947. These were the Pentagon talks and the Modus Vivendi talks, both of which were critical to the Marshall Plan discussions, and both of which involved the embassy more directly.

The Pentagon talks have their roots in a document written in September 1946 by an American Foreign Service official called Cornelius Van Engert. The document, entitled *Some Observations on the Strategic Importance of the Middle East to the United States,* was written 'largely as a result of material made available to him by our embassy at Washington'.[127] The document was approved by the Department of State and gained wide circulation including the President and the Foreign Office. The Foreign Office commented that:

> Mr Engert's theme is that in the face of the threat of aggression by Russia, the US and Britain should work for complete harmony on M.E. problems and for agreement on military strategy in that area, and should strive together to win the confidence of the Middle East countries.[128]

Such harmony did not materialise until towards the end of 1947 when Britain and America sat down to discuss a joint approach to the Middle East. The Pentagon talks, as they became known, were triggered by a memo sent by Bevin to Balfour on 30 July 1947 instructing him to inform Marshall of Britain's decision, taken on 'financial and manpower grounds', to withdraw troops from Greece and to reduce the number in Italy.[129] Marshall's response was swift and abrupt: 'I feel that the decision was made at a most harmful time and that such abrupt action makes cooperating unnecessarily difficult.' He added: 'I am still more disturbed at the possible implications of this decision as to the future of British policy.'[130]

At a dinner on the evening of 30 July, Bohlen told Balfour of the US Administration's concern over the manner in which the British informed the State Department of their intention to remove troops from Greece and Italy. Bohlen was concerned with the effect in Greece if the news leaked, and emphasised how dangerous it was 'at this time to have any sudden announcement or information on the subject indicating curtailment in present British positions'. Balfour not only 'thoroughly agreed' but indicated that he intended to send a telegram to London along those lines. Further he intended to emphasise in 'strong terms the bad effect any sudden announcement without adequate consultation with the US Government would have in the US and throughout the world'.[131]

Balfour duly sent a telegram to London along those lines and proffered further advice. Balfour indicated that Britain occupied a special position in American eyes largely because of the belief that she can be 'counted upon to share with the United States the responsibility of defending the democratic position in the world'; Balfour suggested that it would be expedient for Britain to take America into her confidence and even invite comment before taking action. Balfour also suggested that the presence of British troops in various parts of the world was an important bargaining counter in Anglo-American relations.[132] All of these warnings had been made in previous reports from the embassy. Balfour followed up his telegram with a longer letter which dwelt at length on the perception of Britain in America and how this perception was affected by the precipitate action such as the British withdrawal.[133]

Michael Wright, who at that time was Assistant Under-Secretary of State at the Foreign Office and who had been head of Chancery at the embassy, commented that Balfour's letter was a 'strong and reasoned plea' and confirmed his agreement with Balfour's assertion that

> any advantage we might hope to derive from shock tactics is largely, if not wholly, offset by the embarrassment which these cause to the Administration, who find it more difficult to deal with their own public opinion, feel we are not treating them as partners and derive the impression that we are handling matters on a hand to mouth basis.[134]

Bevin, however, was not impressed with Balfour's letter. He indicated that he was troubled by the tone of it and that Balfour had not sought to refute the American allegations. Bevin was most anxious that the 'embassy in Washington should immediately knock down this sort of talk by the Americans'. Bevin was presumably stung by the criticism from his own department and so he even went to the trouble of dictating some notes refuting the allegation of shock tactics and so on.[135]

What this episode demonstrates, if demonstration were needed, is that diplomats (and indeed Foreign Office officials) were not mere messengers. They had a viewpoint as to how their country's interest could best be served. Balfour was prepared to express this viewpoint perhaps knowing that there might be criticism of, or at least commentary on, his actions. It is also another example of the tension that existed between Bevin and the Washington embassy. Bevin clearly felt that the embassy was too soft on the Americans and that the embassy did not put the British point of view, or at least not firmly enough. It was, perhaps, symptomatic of the difference in viewpoint between those at the front line and those further back from the action.

The American response to the withdrawal of troops also provides another example of the US Administration's thoughts on Britain's Labour government. Marshall states in a message to Robert Lovett, who had replaced Acheson as Under-Secretary of State:

> It seems to me that our thorn pulling operations on the British lion continue to be beset by her stubborn insistence on avoiding

the garden path to wander in the thicket of purely local labour party misadventures. They are far too casual... in passing the buck of international dilemma to [the] US.[136]

Bevin protested that there had been no change in British policy and it was subsequently suggested that the problem was the lack of understanding between the two countries on their respective policies in the Middle East. It was proposed that the two countries discuss a joint approach to the subject. Initially the Americans suggested that the military aspects of the Middle East be discussed first, to be followed by a discussion of economic and political policy in the region. Bevin saw little merit, however, in having discussions on 'a purely military footing since our object is to coordinate policy over the whole area, taking into consideration political and economic implications as well as military'. Inverchapel delivered these sentiments to Lovett on 16 September and it was proposed and agreed that the first stage of the talks should take place between military and political experts on each side and for recommendations to be made to Marshall and Bevin in time for the next conference meeting, which was to take place in London at the end of November. Bevin proposed that Inverchapel lead the talks on the British side.[137] In exchange for the Pentagon talks, Bevin was prepared, for the time being, to allow the majority of the British troops to remain in Greece. The withdrawal of troops from Italy became irrelevant due to the decision of the Soviets to ratify the Italian Peace Treaty, which provided for the withdrawal of all British and American troops.

Even though Bevin was under pressure from the Cabinet, it seems curious that he sought to withdraw troops from Greece at such a moment, particularly given that he had identified himself so closely with the Marshall Plan. The risk he took is made clear in a State Department memorandum where it was pointed out that if American troops were asked to replace British troops in Greece serious questions would be raised in Congress and 'the breaking of a common front in Greece through withdrawal of British forces would undoubtedly cause a wave of resentment in this country against the British... and could prejudice US support for continued aid under the Marshall Plan'.[138]

There does not seem to be any evidence that Bevin consulted the embassy in Washington before deciding to withdraw troops. This was perhaps a mistake. Clearly it was not for the embassy to decide where troops were stationed but if a withdrawal was to be made then one of the benefits of an embassy is that they can prepare the ground for any unpalatable decisions and offer advice as to how they might best be delivered. It so happens that the use of shock tactics in this particular case was not too serious but, as the Washington embassy knew, each time Britain behaved like this she diminished herself a little more in the eyes of the US Administration and others.

The Pentagon talks began on 16 October 1947. In addition to Inverchapel, the British group consisted of other representatives of the embassy, i.e. Balfour, W.D. Allen (Counsellor) and T.E. Bromley (First Secretary), Michael Wright of the Foreign Office and various members of the military. The American side was led by Lovett who, in addition to military personnel, was joined by Kennan and Loy Henderson.[139] The British objectives were, inter alia, to 'enlighten the Americans on the importance of the Middle East to the United States of America as well as to the United Kingdom and on British achievements and present policy in the area' and 'to establish broad agreement on the aims of British and American policy'.[140]

Bevin, in a letter to Attlee, said that the British delegation was aware that no financial commitments could be made and that there was no intention that they become involved in detailed economic discussions.[141] These talks, then, would have suited Inverchapel well; he knew a great deal more about the Middle East than he did about economics. In an eloquent opening statement, Inverchapel described a crescent of countries whose orientation is either to western or communist ideas. The crescent stretched from Scandinavia through Europe and the Middle East to the Far East and lay between the western countries and the communist-controlled countries. Referring to the Middle Eastern segment Inverchapel stated that

It is in our view essential that the approach of our two countries towards these peoples, on whom the preservation of peace so largely depends, should be coordinated and that we should work together on a constructive basis.[142]

Inverchapel then went on to outline the strategic issues involved and the ground he hoped to cover in the talks.

Lovett responded positively to Inverchapel's opening remarks. The talks, which were wide ranging (although the Palestinian issue was treated as a 'thing apart') and resulted in some 25 memoranda relating to countries of the Eastern Mediterranean and the Middle East, continued until 7 November. They were a success. 'The British role was to maintain the necessary bases; the Americans to provide economic and political backing.'[143] It was an almost perfect solution from Bevin's point of view and helped to avoid any further misunderstandings that may have affected the progress of the Marshall Plan.[144]

A further set of talks taking place in Washington at the end of 1947 were those which led to the Modus Vivendi 'agreement'. The Modus Vivendi talks led to a resurgence of atomic energy collaboration between America and Britain. It was noted in chapter 3 that atomic energy collaboration, at least in the form it took during the war, broke down in the spring of 1946. One of the reasons given at the time was that collaboration was no longer possible because of the passage of the Atomic Energy Act (McMahon Act). Attlee wrote to Truman in June 1946 setting out Britain's concerns; it was a letter that went unanswered until December 1946 and even then the reply was unsatisfactory.

In early February 1947, Makins, who at the time was a minister at the embassy, 'made his own personal attempt to break the deadlock by setting forth his ideas and proposals for a solution'.[145] Makins, at his own request, called on Acheson at his house in Georgetown. He indicated that he had wanted to outline what he termed a personal solution to the Attlee–Truman correspondence on atomic energy. Whilst he had discussed the matter with Inverchapel and Field Marshal Wilson (British member of the Combined Policy Committee 'CPC') and was making the suggestion with their approval, he had no clearance from London. Makins indicated that in London the issue was both a practical one and a psychological one. In practical terms, the government was keen to proceed with its own programme but felt hampered by various obstacles which arose that could easily be resolved by the Americans. The psychological point was that Britain was unhappy with continuing to cooperate in the supply of raw material which had considerable benefits for the Americans whilst, at the same time, being denied access to technical collaboration. Makins suggested that a particular tone of reply from Truman to Attlee and the making of certain points would go a long way towards assuaging Britain's feelings on the matter.[146]

Makins then outlined a number of points which could be made in a letter from Truman. These included an expression of desire on the part of the Americans to 'cooperate fully and effectively with the British, subject to the limitations of the existing legislation', confirmation that the existing arrangements with regard to the CPC and Combined Development Trust (CDT) remain in place and a statement to the effect that America raised no objection to the development by Britain of her own atomic energy programme. Makins also made the ingenious suggestion that exchange of information should be allowed on all developments which had taken place prior to the passage of the Atomic Energy Act. The implication was that the Act only applied to subsequent discoveries. Acheson found problems with each of Makins' suggestions but said he would discuss the matter inside the Administration and then take it up with the ambassador. Acheson acknowledged that he would not have time to report back to Makins, who was leaving Washington the following week.[147]

Whilst this initiative led nowhere, it is a good example of diplomats on the ground seeking ways to solve problems without necessarily obtaining instructions before doing so. Makins returned to London to take up the position of Assistant Under-Secretary of State at the Foreign Office. He also replaced Neville Butler as the Foreign Office representative attending the Cabinet's Advisory Committee on Atomic Energy.[148] Makins remained closely involved with atomic energy matters and, as will be discussed below, returned to Washington later in the year to participate in the Modus Vivendi talks.

During various discussions between the US Administration and the embassy, it became apparent that the Administration's reticence to cooperate on atomic energy matters was not solely related to the

restrictions put in place by the Atomic Energy Act. The American
Chiefs of Staff had submitted a paper to the Department of State
concluding that it would be unwise to have a store of uranium ore,
indeed, an atomic plant on the periphery of the 'the Anglo-American
Zone of Defence', i.e. in Britain.[149] A reading of the papers on the
issue offers an interesting insight into the extent to which Britain's
reputation had fallen by early 1947, at least in the eyes of the military. Eisenhower informed Field Marshal Wilson that the decision
not to support an atomic programme in Britain was based on a study
of the 'difficulties and conditions that GB and the Western European
States are facing today, and what those conditions might be ten years
hence. It was envisaged that conditions might arise wherein GB
might be subject to pressure from a major power offering conditions
which she might be unable to resist.' Rubbing salt in the wound,
Eisenhower emphasised that this opinion was very strong and was
combined with the apprehension that 'the risk was considered more
political than military'.[172]

Inverchapel wrote to Attlee:

> The military arguments against a pile in the United Kingdom
> might indeed have been expected. On the other hand, the ques-
> tioning of our reliability in future years will be as unpalatable
> to you as it is to us... recent events in the Domestic and Foreign
> Affairs of the United Kingdom have caused a wave of doubt
> about our ability to survive as a first class power.[151]

It must have been as difficult for the diplomats as it was for others to
witness Britain's decline. The diplomats were, to a certain extent, in
the front line. To be attached to an embassy in Washington which was
once thought of as representing a great power and then, within the
space of only a few years, to be representing a nation in rapid decline
cannot but have affected the diplomats personally. It is impossible to
quantify the effect of this change of status on a diplomat's work, particularly since it would probably have affected everyone differently; it
is hard to conceive, though, that such a change in status did not have
some effect.

Ironically it was, in part, Britain's weakness and her need for the aid which led to a partial unlocking of the freeze on Anglo-American atomic energy collaboration and the Modus Vivendi talks. In a statement by Acheson to an Executive Session of the Joint Congressional Committee on Atomic Energy (JCAE) in May 1947, Acheson appraised the committee of the wartime and post-wartime UK–Canadian–American atomic energy agreements. This included the Quebec Agreements, which contained the clause requiring, in effect, British approval before America could use the atomic bomb. Acheson also informed the committee that under the provisions of the CDT supplies of raw material required for atomic bombs were held on a 50:50 basis with the UK.[152] At the time, it was reported that the committee's reaction to Acheson's statement was fairly benign.[153] Subsequently, however, a link was made between Acheson's statement and Marshall Aid.

On 29 August 1947, Senator Bourke Hickenlooper (Republican, Iowa), Chairman of the JCAE, wrote to Marshall informing him that the Quebec Agreement was 'ill advised' and 'must be mutually rescinded'. He also bemoaned the arrangements for uranium allocation and insisted that 'the uranium now in Britain and her future acquisitions must be brought to America'. The Senator then linked his demands to aid for Britain. 'I shall oppose as vigorously as I can, and publicly if necessary, any further aid or assistance to Britain unless these two matters are satisfactorily resolved, because they strike at the heart of our present national security.'[154] In mid-November, Vandenberg also raised the issue of uranium supplies. The suggestion was made, during the course of the Senate Foreign Relations Committee Hearings on the issue of strategic raw materials generally, that Congo uranium might be used as part payment for Marshall Aid.[155] Lovett was now clear that unless the Quebec Agreement was annulled and the uranium supply issue was resolved then the whole matter would become embroiled in the Marshall Aid debate and possibly jeopardise its chances of getting through Congress.

Lovett sought to open discussions with the British. The American tactic at the time was to offer Britain the bait of renewed cooperation and play down the issue of uranium supplies. Margaret Gowing tells us that 'the British did not realise that the main reason for the American anxiety for talks was their determination to get their hands on the uranium which Britain could claim under present arrangements'.[156] This does not appear to be the case, however. Gordon Munro, who had taken over Makins' work on atomic energy issues, wrote to London in early September. He indicated that the embassy had received one or two 'unmistakeable hints from the State Department and the Atomic Energy Commission that the US side are seriously concerned about the present divide-up of Congo Ore'. Adding that 'it looks as though the Americans are running short of ore, are anxious to keep up production of bombs, and are in consequence developing dishonourable intentions towards our reserves... We expect the question of future shipments, and indeed quite possibly the disposal of UK stocks to be raised with us.'[157]

Gowing also says 'in the raw material negotiations the Americans had made no attempt to use Marshall Aid as a bargaining counter'.[158] As noted above, they clearly had made such an attempt. Munro wrote to London explaining this possibility in early October. Munro had been told by Gullion (Special Assistant to the Under-Secretary of State) that 'the question of Britain's [uranium] reserves will be raised in the course of Congressional inquiries and debate on further financial aid to the United Kingdom'. Munro valiantly suggested that any attempt to 'put the squeeze on us over our uranium reserve in the context of the Marshall plan would make the worst possible impression at home and stood no chance at all of success'.[159] That the Administration (as well as Senators) would use Marshall Aid as a lever if necessary can be discerned from a record of a meeting Lovett had with Vandenberg and Hickenlooper. Lovett suggested that the Americans could achieve their objectives 'through normal diplomatic negotiation' rather than using the 'financial lever'; he did add, however, that 'there was no harm... in keeping the "big stick" in plain sight in the corner'.[160]

By 2 December, Inverchapel was able to report that Lovett had been gathering the support necessary from the various American agencies to hold talks with Britain and Canada and that the provisional plan was that the talks would be held within the framework of the CPC. Inverchapel stated that the objective of the talks was to 'establish a new basis for cooperation in future and thereby remove the US–UK and US–Canadian misunderstandings in this field'.[161] The need for talks took on something of an urgent character due to the fact that Lovett needed to provide a solution acceptable to certain vociferous Senators and certainly needed a solution prior to the Congressional hearings into Marshall Aid, which were due to start early in the New Year. Inverchapel cabled Bevin informing him that the talks were of sufficient importance to justify sending people of the calibre of Roger Makins.[162] The American team included George Kennan and again the closeness of the embassy to Kennan proved useful. Inverchapel reported that 'Kennan called specially on Balfour... to emphasise the informal character of the talks' and to stress his belief that it was possible to work back towards the close collaboration that existed during the war.[163]

The formal talks took place on 10 and 15 December in the forum of the CPC. Both Makins and Chadwick were despatched from London to assist in the negotiations. The talks centred upon three topics: technical collaboration, allocation of raw material and the form and substance of a new general agreement to replace the Quebec Agreement. The talks reached a stage where a list of areas suitable for technical collaboration was agreed in exchange for the British accepting the annulment of the Quebec Agreement and surrendering the entire Congo production of uranium ore for the next two years. A sticking point for the British, however, was surrendering the stockpile of uranium which was held in the UK, a point which the Senators had insisted upon.

Makins flew back to London to seek Cabinet instructions. Donald Maclean wrote to Makins whilst he was in London. Gullion had informed Maclean that the present status of the negotiations had been reported to Hickenlooper by the American side and that 'the Senator had emphasised the need to get the matter squared away by the time Congress reassembles'.[164] The Americans were working on a number of levels. The American ambassador in London told Frank Roberts, Bevin's private secretary, that Marshall had asked him to inform Bevin that Marshall thought it most important that Britain hand over some of her raw material stocks to America, adding that 'he [Marshall] had sure information that there would be serious trouble in Congress and more particularly in the Senate if we were not cooperative on this point'.[165]

The inner circle of the Cabinet reluctantly agreed, no doubt mindful of the 'big stick' sitting in the corner. On 7 January, the CPC reconvened and a representative of each country declared its intention to proceed on the basis of documents tabled at the meeting, thereby avoiding the necessity of registering a formal agreement with the UN or having a treaty ratified in public by Congress. Britain had (i) given up her right to veto America's use of atomic weapons (ii) agreed that all supplies of uranium produced in the Congo in 1948 and 1949 were to be allocated to the US and (iii) accepted that if US production plans demanded it then uranium would be provided from the British stockpile.[166] In return, the British had obtained the right to participate in an exchange of information on a number of agreed topics. It transpired that these exchanges provided little of use to the British.

Not surprisingly, Vandenberg told Lovett that 'the State Department negotiations represented a considerable accomplishment, and that more had been obtained than he thought possible'.[167] During Halifax's negotiations on atomic energy issues in early 1946 (see chapter 3), the following remark was made: 'Securing the raw material allocation was one of the few successes the embassy had in negotiations on the atomic energy issue. The British realised that their access to raw material gave them leverage and, perhaps for the first time, played their hand in this regard to something like its full strength.' The stockpile of uranium and access to future supplies was indeed an extremely powerful card in British hands. But the legislator's threat to disrupt Marshall Aid was enough to render it ineffective. The 'big stick' was a potent weapon. The words of John Balfour highlighted in chapter 2 and written in August 1945, echo throughout this discussion: 'The dollar sign is back in the Anglo-American equation.'

The British embassy in Washington appears to have played an effective part in warning London of the major issues of uranium supplies and their linkage to the Marshall Plan. It seems, however, that such warnings made little difference. Britain's position was so weak, and so obviously weak, that Inverchapel, Munro and Makins were powerless to hang on to their trump card. There was perhaps some consolation. After the meeting where the Modus

Vivendi Agreement was ratified Lovett informed the British officials present that he had met with Vandenberg and Hickenlooper who both 'undertook to support the State Department to the limit in keeping atomic energy matters out of the debate on the European Recovery Programme'.[168]

With all major hurdles now cleared, Truman presented the European Recovery Plan to Congress. Hearings of both the Foreign Relations Committee of the Senate and the Foreign Affairs Committee of the House opened on 8 January 1948. 'The published hearings present a... voluminous record. The Foreign Relations Committee heard 9 governmental and 86 other witnesses... The Foreign Affairs Committee heard 25 spokesmen for the Administration and received testimony from about 150 nongovernmental persons.'[169] The published record of the committees amounts to some 3,500 pages. The Chairman of these committees, Vandenberg for the Senate and Representative Charles Eaton for the House, were both keen supporters of the Marshall Plan, and this fact proved to be decisive.[170] There were, of course, opponents to the plan but the advocates were more organised and on 12 March the Senate voted by 69 to 17 to pass the bill, with the Republicans voting 31 to 13 in favour and the Democrats 38 to 4. The bill then moved to the House and on 31 March by a vote of 329 to 74 the bill was approved. In the House, the Republicans voted 171 to 63 in favour and the Democrats 158 to 11. Although the House had largely accepted the Senate's version of the bill, it had made certain amendments; consequently two different versions emerged. These versions were quickly reconciled and on 2 April the House approved the compromise bill by 318 to 75 and the Senate by general acclamation. Truman signed the bill the following day thus turning it into the Economic Cooperation Act of 1948.

The embassy, of course, reported on the events surrounding the passage of the bill through Congress and on the various hearings in the Congressional committees. It did not, however, play any decisive part in the bill's passage; rather it was, as the embassy suggested, 'the Communist coup in Czechoslovakia [which] did more to catapult the ERP bill over its final legislative hurdle'.[171] It was during the bill's passage through Congress, however, that Inverchapel in February 1948 wrote to Marshall informing him that he would be giving up his post in Washington. Although, as noted in chapter 1, the suggestion that he retire was made by Bevin there is a sense that Inverchapel knew he had reached the end of the road:

> I have come to feel a deep respect and affection for this country and its people and I shall be most loath to say goodbye to them.

> At the same time I have taken keen pleasure in my work, although it has, I confess, brought me very near to cracking point.

> But through this sadness of mine there runs a strong thread of something like joy, which it would be disingenuous in me to conceal. In the thought of getting home – home for good, I mean – after practically a life of exile there lies the promise of much happiness.[172]

The role Britain's Washington embassy played during the evolution and consummation of the Marshall Plan demonstrates the eclectic nature and, indeed, importance of the embassy's activities. Perhaps the most decisive part played was in forewarning London of the build-up of the American desire to help Europe. In general terms, the cumulative effect of regular reporting of press commentary, political speeches and current thinking amongst the various parts of the political establishment, which over time builds into a pattern, was of enormous benefit to the Foreign Office. In the particular instance of the Marshall Plan, it afforded Britain an important advantage in formulating a response.

The part the embassy played in the evolution of the Marshall Plan, in all its facets, underlines the competence of the embassy officials. For all his reservations about Inverchapel, Bevin still trusted him to lead the Pentagon talks. Balfour, despite being chastened by Bevin, was regularly commended for his incisive political reports. Makins was prepared to pursue initiatives off his own back, Munro was able to warn London of the American intentions regarding Britain's uranium stocks and Edwards knew that the issue of American aid to Europe was of sufficient importance to alert Hall Patch directly. These are all important interventions by the embassy. In the context of financial and other assistance given to Britain, they were not decisive but one is led to ask the question what would have happened if there was no embassy at all.

CONCLUSION

This book has sought to assess the role of the British embassy in Washington in bilateral Anglo-American relations between 1945 and 1948. It was a varied role which met with varying degrees of success. Each chapter has drawn its own conclusion on the embassy's performance and the importance of the part the embassy played in each of the events discussed. But what can be said about the embassy in general terms? What is it that underpinned the embassy's effectiveness and therefore its importance? The standard models of diplomacy usually distil an embassy's functions into representation and negotiation.[1] Both of these are crucial to an embassy's importance and they certainly were in the Washington embassy between 1945 and 1948. A third factor which was important, although it is difficult to describe it as a function, is decisive influence. It is a time when a diplomat can have a special effect on policy or some other important outcome by virtue of his position or proximity to a particular person or situation at a particular point in time. Decisive influence is exceptional and almost by definition non-systematic. These three issues, representation, negotiation and decisive influence, and how they point to the importance of the embassy's role, are discussed below.

Representation is one of the standard functions of a diplomat. In the Washington embassy, it consisted of the reporting of events, moods and themes taking shape in America and conversely the reporting of the British situation and British aspirations to the American government and people. History, of course, is not only about the decisions made but what those decisions are based upon. The reporting side of the embassy, whether that be the production of Weekly Political Reports, the regular economic reports or those which addressed atomic energy issues, were an important and regular feature of the embassy's work. They provided both officials in the Foreign Office and ministers with essential information on America – information which, in turn, was used to assist in making policy.

The real value of the reports was that they were based not only upon publicly available information but also on information derived directly from members of the Administration, Congressmen, journalists and other influential Americans. This non-public information was obtained by virtue of the embassy's closeness to members of the American establishment. It was this that determined the quality of the information obtained. This intimacy between the diplomats and the key individuals has been demonstrated in this book whether one considers, for example, Halifax and Truman, Balfour and Kennan or Clayton and Brand. There are, of course, many other combinations. A further factor which needs to be stressed in connection with the reporting side of the embassy was the cumulative nature of the activity. The embassy had the virtue of being a permanent institution, and, notwithstanding the fact that individuals come and go, the Chancery Department had access to a backlog of information and comment accumulated over a considerable period of time and hence it was in a position to offer perspective on new information coming into the embassy.

One of the points which emerges from the above is that it was this closeness and indeed depth of knowledge which distinguished the professional diplomat on the ground from the amateur. This distinction was referred to in the context of Keynes and the development of a strategy for the Financial Agreement. Foreign Office officials sometimes attempted to second guess the embassy and often got it wrong. An example of this is Hall Patch's misjudgement of the American mood during the Financial Agreement negotiations. He was not as alive to the sensitivity of the Americans to the relative contributions of Britain and America to the war effort as, for example, Frank Lee of the Treasury Delegation was. This distinction between the amateur and the professional emphasises the embassy's importance. Anyone, in theory, can access information by reading newspapers, by meetings with officials and with legislators and so on but it is the quality that matters and this only comes from an immersion in a culture and from being trusted. There is clear evidence that the embassy was trusted and had a considerable understanding of America.

In addition to the regular reports, the embassy was also responsible for numerous ad hoc reports, which were more directly connected with policy formation. Halifax's letters to the Foreign Office in connection with the Jewish question in America were both informative and prescient. He demonstrated a considerable grasp of the issues connected with Zionism in America and was an early advocate in suggesting the beneficial effects on American opinion of allowing significant immigration into Palestine. It was also Halifax's report and analysis which led to Bevin's suggestion for an Anglo-American Committee to examine the Palestinian question. A further example of ad hoc reporting came with a number of special reports produced around May 1947, which foreshadowed Marshall's proposals for aid to Europe. The reports contained information which was invaluable to Bevin in formulating his response. This included comment on the need for a coordinated European response, analysis on the question of timing and advice on the need to conduct a coordinated campaign in America to galvanise public opinion to support aid for Europe.

Representation was not only about the reporting of American events to Britain, it was also necessary for the embassy to explain Britain to the Americans. This was important in a country where the political system was so open and where diplomats were expected to present their point of view both to the public and to politicians. The process of presenting the British viewpoint took many forms. The most obvious was the BIS, which focused on presenting Britain to the American press. Such was the strength of the relationship between the British officials and the press that the journalists were even allowed sight of Foreign Office telegrams. A second form was when the ambassadors and other diplomats from the embassy were called upon to make speeches to the American public and to certain pressure groups. A further form was when the embassy sought to present the British viewpoint to Congress. Alan Judson, the embassy's Congressional liaison officer, was in direct contact with the

Democratic whip's office, as well as hundreds of Congressmen, and he organised regular meetings at the embassy between Congressmen and the ambassador and other diplomats. The embassy played a significant role in persuading Congressmen to support positions beneficial to the British during both the Financial Agreement and the Marshall Plan debates.

An important ingredient of this representation of Britain, and one which had an impact upon the diplomatic work at the time, was explaining why the British had elected a Labour government and what the consequences of such a government were. Some Americans had something of a phobia of what they perceived to be a socialist government. The embassy, for example, found it necessary to bring in Churchill in an attempt to alleviate Congressional fears regarding a Labour government during the Financial Agreement debate. The embassy was hampered in its discussions regarding atomic energy by the American military's insistence that an atomic pile and associated raw materials should not be situated in Britain. This argument was not only about proximity to the Soviets but also connected to the political complexion of the British government and the influences upon it. Further, Inverchapel's speeches came to be dominated by explanations of the Labour government and why it was elected and what it meant for Britain's future. It is difficult to assess the impact that the election of a Labour government had upon the Washington embassy but, as a minimum, the embassy needed to spend energy and time addressing the issue when it might otherwise have used that time to more productive effect.

Representation was a key part of the Washington embassy's activities. It was a crucial role and formed an important part of Britain's foreign policy making process particularly with regard to its Anglo-American policy. The embassy was effective because it identified and developed relationships with key people, something which was only really possible by having a permanent presence on the ground. The effectiveness of the embassy's representational role was enhanced by the cumulative effect of the knowledge which the embassy had built up over many years. This ability to read America gave the embassy considerable 'soft power' and through this it was able to influence the policy debate in both London and America.

There were impediments to the embassy's role, however. The very closeness that made it so effective upon sometimes caused concerns within the Foreign Office. Bevin did complain that the embassy was perhaps too accommodating of American arguments and was suspicious of the embassy's relationship with members of the US Administration. On occasions, this led Bevin to discount some of the advice which came from the embassy. A further factor which restricted the embassy's impact was the use to which the information it provided was put. Whilst an embassy can be efficient in providing the British government with pertinent and relevant information, the effectiveness of the embassy and the information it provided was constrained by the extent to which the politicians and officials in London were able to respond to and use the information it received. This was particularly apposite in the period under review when ministers and officials were at risk of being overwhelmed by events and, on some occasions, simply could not respond to information coming from the embassy.

The second factor which underlined the importance of the embassy was its ability to conduct negotiations on behalf of the British government. Negotiation, which in essence had the objective of persuading America to adopt policies that Britain wanted, had many aspects to it. These included presenting a case with a view to influencing American policy makers, reporting back differences of opinion and making a judgement as to how far one could go and how far one could trust the person with whom you were negotiating. It can be argued that diplomats were mere messengers and only acted under instructions but this analysis does not correspond with the part the embassy played in, for example, the Financial Agreement negotiations. Whilst there were myriad telegrams going to and from London, each containing instructions and requests for clarification, this does not tell the whole story. The fact that Vinson asked for a 'private talk behind the scenes', the floating of ideas by Halifax without instruction, the dissuading of members of the team from resigning, sending back members of the delegation to London, Attlee deferring to Halifax when deciding whether or not to call in Truman, all point to something more than a diplomat acting under instruction. It is hard to imagine that if the negotiations had been conducted solely by a team of officials sent from

London, without input from the embassy, the negotiations would have been as successful or even concluded at all. This again points to the importance of the embassy.

But why was the Washington embassy likely to be so much more effective than a team sent from London? In part it was for the same reason that the embassy was so effective at representation; that is, because it was close to members of the US Administration. This was not accidental, however, and a part of the embassy's importance resided in its ability to identify and then target influential people. Hence Brand and Halifax were able to enter the Financial Agreement negotiations, for example, already knowing Vinson and Clayton well. This, in turn, led to a more effective dialogue between the two sides. Connected to this is the question of understanding. Knowing what was acceptable to the other side was not only about understanding the person the embassy was negotiating with, but also about having a sound knowledge of the events and attitudes of those outside the negotiations as well. Without this knowledge, it was difficult to assess tactics to be employed and to develop a strategy to follow. The embassy had a good understanding of the needs of Congress and the pressures which the legislators were under; this in turn enabled it to counter arguments and develop tactics to minimise opposition. In short, the embassy was able, because of its unique position, to develop a fuller picture of the negotiating environment. As with representation, negotiation was a continuous and systematic part of the embassy's work. The process was not restricted to large-scale set-piece negotiations such as those for the Financial Agreement but extended to a range of issues including, for example, negotiating the terms of reference for the Anglo-American committee on Palestine, conducting the various atomic energy discussions and leading the Pentagon talks.

Negotiation was not limited to trying to get the Americans to shift ground; sometimes, for example during the Financial Agreement negotiations, the embassy attempted to get London to shift its position. In doing this, the embassy was exercising the diplomat's essential skill – that is, judgement. Assessing the situation on the ground to discern what is and what is not acceptable is something only the diplomat could do. Diplomacy is something of a dark art. A word in a corridor, the strength of a handshake, a raised eyebrow can all communicate information – information which the diplomat must interpret. This is one of the reasons why the embassy was important. This sort of information was only available to the diplomat on the ground and therefore he was the only person who could form a judgement based upon such intangible signals. The divergences of opinion which sometimes existed between those close to a situation and those who were far removed from it was perhaps explained by these intangible signals.

One of the issues which warrants consideration in connection with the embassy's various negotiations is whether or not the embassy was too trusting of the Americans. As mentioned above, Bevin believed that the embassy could be too accommodating. When Halifax was negotiating the Financial Agreement, there is little evidence that his trust and confidence in Vinson and Clayton was misplaced; on the contrary he had a good reading of the pressures they were under. On the other hand in his dealing with Byrnes, particularly in relation to the atomic energy discussions, perhaps his trust was misplaced. It was certainly the case with Makins and Groves. Makins was completely outmanoeuvred by General Groves during the 1945–1946 atomic energy discussions. Placing trust in someone can be a by-product of being close to them. If so, perhaps the close contact the embassy had with the American officials carried an element of risk.

A final factor to consider when assessing the importance of the embassy was its ability to directly and, on occasions, significantly influence certain events. An example of such influence was when Halifax was able to persuade Truman to include John Anderson in the atomic energy talks aboard the presidential yacht. Halifax achieved this even though Attlee had failed. Without the embassy and the regular meetings which had taken place between the President and the British ambassador, it is unlikely that this level of influence could have been developed. Munro's paper highlighting the dollar funding gap at the end of 1947 and how reliance on Marshall Aid was a mistake given the vagaries of the Congressional timetable was a further example. It was Munro's unique position that enabled him to produce a paper which pointed to the inevitability of the suspension of convertibility. The combination of economic insight with knowledge of, and contacts with, the legislature in America placed Munro in a position where he could offer such advice. Again, it is unlikely that this would have been possible without the presence of the embassy and diplomats on the ground.

There are other, perhaps less obvious, examples such as the note sent by Balfour to London in August 1945 urging that Clayton should return immediately and indicating that there was a 'contraction of view' with regard to the Anglo-American relationship and that the Stage III talks should start immediately. Senior ministers met two days later and instructed Halifax and Keynes accordingly. Further to a meeting between Bohlen, Kennan and Balfour, Bevin was able to go to Paris in June 1947 armed with the knowledge that the Americans had reservations as to the intent behind the Soviet involvement in any European aid. It inevitably strengthened Bevin's hand during negotiations and thus maintained the momentum behind Marshall's proposals.

Whilst it is clear that the embassy played an important role in bilateral relations during the period, whether through representation, negotiation or decisive influence, its performance was not faultless. The embassy failed to persuade ministers that Keynes' strategy for the Financial Agreement talks was flawed. Neither Halifax nor Makins was able to counter General Groves' undermining of continued atomic energy collaboration. Nor did the embassy immediately identify Niles as an important component in the Palestinian discussions in Washington. It does not appear that there was anything systematic in these failures, but they do point to issues which became barriers to effective diplomacy.

It was difficult for the embassy to get its point of view across when emotive issues were prevalent. With regard to Stage III talks, for example, there was a strong feeling inside the British establishment that Britain was somehow owed favourable treatment by the Americans. The embassy was unable to counter this point of view even though it understood the realities on the ground, especially when the establishment view was supported by one such as Keynes. As suggested above, there were occasions when the embassy perhaps became too trusting of the Americans. This in turn could have led to the embassy being outmanoeuvred. A breakdown in the normal channels of communication also had detrimental effects on diplomacy. The embassy had over many years established a network of connections at every level between its staff and corresponding staff at the Department of State. The purpose was to exchange information, brief each other and so on. However when normal channels broke down, as they did during the deliberations on the Palestinian issue, then the effectiveness of the embassy was diminished.

Various works on the subject of diplomacy often seek to demonstrate the influence that a diplomat has had on the outcome of a particular event. This ambassador was able to exert influence over that Secretary of State or that ambassador had the ear of that President and so on – the objective being to demonstrate that the embassy, through the individual, was able to have some special effect on policy. This book is no exception to that and has provided examples where an individual can make a difference. This book has also sought, however, to look beyond the individual and look to the embassy as a whole. The British embassy in Washington during the period 1945 to 1948 employed hundreds of people across a number of different functions. It has been demonstrated that during the period the embassy engaged in a range of activities in connection with a number of significant events. The book has also demonstrated the considerable reach which the embassy had across the American political establishment. The conclusion drawn is that whilst individuals were, of course, important it was also the enduring nature of the institution itself which was significant. The embassy's real value was in the cumulative nature of both its knowledge base and its contact base, a value which could only be built up effectively by having a permanent presence on the ground. It was this 'soft power' which enabled the embassy to have influence, whether that was through representation or negotiation, and it was this 'soft power' which gave the embassy its importance.

NOTES

Introduction

1. The categorisation of Anglo-American relations is based upon a similar analysis used in Dennett, Raymond and Turner, Robert (eds), *Documents on American Foreign Relations*. Princeton, New Jersey: Princeton University Press, 1946.
2. Edmonds, Robin, *Setting the Mould: The United States and Britain, 1945–1950*. New York: Oxford University Press, 1986, p. 16.
3. Gillies Donald, *Radical Diplomat: The Life of Archibald Clark Kerr Lord Inverchapel, 1882–1951*. London: Tauris, 1999, p. 211.
4. An exception perhaps is Alan Bullock's *Ernest Bevin: Foreign Secretary, 1945–1951* (1983). Bullock makes a number of references to the ambassadors during the period. Whilst he talks more about Oliver Franks than Halifax or Inverchapel, he does offer some detail on the part Halifax played in the Palestinian issue (pp. 174–177). There is, however, no sustained or systematic review of the embassy or its activities.
5. Three notable works in this field are Terry Anderson's *The United States, Great Britain and the Cold War 1944–1947* (1981), Robin Edmonds' *Setting the Mould: The United States and Britain 1945–1950* (1986) and Robert Hathaway's *Ambiguous Partnership: Britain and America 1944–1947* (1988). Whilst they all offer quotes from embassy officials none of them offers any detailed commentary or analysis on what the embassy was doing or the contribution it was making.
6. Hopkins, Michael, Kelly, Saul, and Young John (eds), *The Washington Embassy, British Ambassadors to the United States, 1939–1977*. Basingstoke: Palgrave, 2009, p. 1.
7. Strang, Lord, *The Foreign Office*. London: George Allen and Unwin, 1955, p. 104.

Chapter 1 The Embassy, the Ambassador and the Political Environment

1. Salter, Arthur, *Slave of the Lamp.* London: Weidenfeld & Nicolson, 1967, pp. 185–186. This passage, written in 1942, is also quoted in Hopkins, Michael Francis, 'Focus of a Changing Relationship: The Washington embassy and Britain's World Role Since 1945', *Contemporary British History* (1998) 12:3, 103–14 and Danchev, Alex, *Oliver Franks: Founding Father.* Oxford: Clarendon Press, 1993, p. 116.

2. Bodleian Library, Oxford, Lord Sherfield papers (formerly Roger Makins) E.4.1 Correspondence and papers Relating to Diplomatic Appointments, 1930–1952 (henceforth Sherfield papers) MS Sherfield 523, *Foreign Service Handbook* January 1948, p. 2. A detailed explanation of the 1943 changes and reasons for them can be found in the Command Paper 6420 *Proposals for the Reform of the Foreign Office 1943* and in Steiner, Zara (ed.), *The Times Survey of Foreign Ministries of the World.* London: Times Books, 1982, pp. 541–574. The changes, in fact, took several years to implement fully.

3. *Foreign Service Handbook*, January 1948, p. 2.

4. *The Foreign Office List and Diplomatic and Consular Year Book.* London: Harrison and Sons, Years 1945–1949 (henceforth known as Foreign Office List).

5. The National Archives, Kew (henceforth TNA) FO 366/2314, Foreign Office Organisation at April 1946.

6. *Foreign Office List* 1945–1948.

7. *Foreign Service Handbook*, January 1948, pp. 4–5.

8. It is important to note that in the post-war period the embassy was not the only source of information for the Foreign Office departments. The growth in international institutions, e.g. the UN, the International Monetary Fund and the International Bank for Reconstruction and Development, led to an increase in the sources of information. For an interesting discussion on the impact of this phenomenon see Beloff, M., *New Dimensions in Foreign Policy.* London: Allen & Unwin, 1961. This book is, however, concerned with bilateral Anglo-American relations and the embassy was the primary source of this information.

9. Dimbleby, David & Reynolds, David, *An Ocean Apart.* London: Hodder & Stoughton, 1988, p. 139.

10. The CPRB was designed to combine the production programmes of Britain and America into a single integrated programme. The CRMB was designed to develop and plan the use of raw material sources.

11. Harry S. Truman Library (henceforth HSTL) President's Secretary's Files (henceforth PSF) Box 193, Folio Combined Boards, Misc Press Releases.

12. TNA, FO 366/1516, Minute *UK Government Machinery in Washington*, by E. Hall Patch, 16 March 1945.

13. TNA, FO 366/1711 Memorandum attached to letter sent to Sir David Scott (Foreign Office) from Inverchapel dated 7 August 1946.

14. The chart has been constructed from the following principal sources: (a) Steiner, Zara (ed.), *The Times Survey of Foreign Ministries of the World*. London: Times Books, 1982, United Kingdom Appendix B A Typical embassy Structure, p. 572; (b) National Archives Washington (henceforth NAW), Record Group 59, Decimal File 45–49, Box 2957, Memorandum entitled *Duties of Individual Members of His Majesty's Embassy for the United Kingdom at Washington 31 July 1945*; (c) TNA, FO 366/1710, Inverchapel to Bevin, 19 June 1946, Memorandum entitled *Organisation of British Representation in Washington*; (d) TNA, FO 366/2336, Inverchapel to Bevin, 1 January 1947, updated Memorandum entitled *Organisation of British Representation in Washington*; e) TNA, FO 366/2078C D. Maclean to R. Barclay, 13 June 1946; f) *Foreign Office Lists* 1945–1948.

15. TNA, FO 366/1572, Michael Wright to Chief Clerks Department, Foreign Office (attached to which is a list of selected embassy staff and salaries), dated 4 February 1946 and TNA, FO 366/1572, Chancery to Finance Department, 18 May 1946 and Diplomatic List 1945–1948.

16. 'Chargé d'Affaires' can have two meanings. There is 'Chargé d'Affaires en titre' and 'Chargé d'Affaires ad interim'. Balfour was the second type which, as the name implies, is a position taken temporarily and only when the ambassador is on leave or out of the country. During these periods, he assumes the full responsibilities of representation and takes charge of the embassy. Chargé d' Affaires en titre is the title given to the head of a Foreign Mission or embassy when for whatever reason there is no intention of appointing an ambassador. Such positions are rare (source: Lord Strang, *Foreign Office* p. 60.)

17. Perhaps surprisingly there is no entry for Balfour in the *Oxford Dictionary of National Biography*. The paragraph was compiled from Balfour, John, *Not too Correct an Aureole: The Recollections of a Diplomat*. Salisbury: Michael Russell, 1983; the *Foreign Office List*, various years and Hopkins, Michael Francis, 'The ambassadorship of Sir Oliver Franks at Washington, 1948–1952' (Leeds PhD 1992).

18. TNA, Bevin Private Office papers (henceforth Bevin papers), FO 800/513, Bevin to Halifax, 11 January 1946.

19. TNA, FO 366/1708, Balfour to Inverchapel, 3 March 1946 enclosing Notes on Private Office prepared by Jack Lockhart.

20. Strang, *The Foreign Office*, p. 104.

21. Donald Maclean served in the Washington embassy from 1944 to 1948. In addition to being a First Secretary in Chancery he was also, towards the end of his tenure, the Secretary of the Combined Policy Committee, the body which oversaw Anglo-American collaboration in the field of atomic energy. Maclean's activities as a spy are now well known. In this book, however, Maclean is treated as a normal functioning member of the embassy, which is how he was regarded as at the time. No attempt has been made to assess the extent of the damage he may have caused or to specifically relate his espionage activities to the role of the embassy.

22. NAW, Record Group 59, Decimal File 45–49, Box 2957, Memorandum entitled *Duties of Individual Members of His Majesty's Embassy for the United Kingdom at Washington 31 July 1945*.

23. Gore-Booth, Paul, *With Truth and Respect*. London: Constable, 1974, p. 144.

24. For a more detailed account of this work see Isaiah Berlin's introduction to Nicholas, H.G. (ed.), *Washington Dispatches, 1941–45*. London: 1981, pp. vii–xiv.

25. TNA, FO 371/52596, D. MacLean to P. Mason, North American Department, 11 March 1946.

26. TNA, FO 371/61002, A. Judson to M. Wright, 29 July 1947.

27. Borthwick Institute, York, Earl of Halifax diary (henceforth Halifax Diaries) 7 March 1945.

28. TNA, FO 366/2336, Inverchapel to Ernest Bevin, 1 January 1947, Memorandum entitled *Organisation of British Representation in Washington*, p. 3.

29. NAW, Record Group 59, Decimal File 45–49, Box 2957, Memorandum entitled *Duties of Individual Members of His Majesty's embassy for the United Kingdom at Washington 31 July 1945*, p. 9 Commercial Department.

30. Zametica, J. (ed.), *British Officials and British Foreign Policy, 1945–1950*. Leicester: Leicester University Press, 1990, p. 10.

31. HSTL Oral History Interview with Sir Roger Makins, conducted by Phillip Brooks in London, 15 June 1964.

32. TNA, FO 366/1516, Minute, *UK Government Machinery in Washington*, p. 3 para. 17.

33. TNA, FO 366/1707, Halifax to Bevin, 29 January 1946.

34. TNA, FO 366/1707, David Scott to Inverchapel, 29 May 1946.

35. TNA, FO 366/1707, Inverechapel to David Scott, 6 June 1946.

36. TNA, FO 366/2078C, D. Maclean to R. Barclay, 13 June 1946.

37. TNA, FO 371/52594, J. Balfour to Bevin attaching memorandum, 29 June 1946.

38. TNA, FO 371/51629, Report on the work of the Attaché for Women's Affairs in Washington, July 1946.

39. Compiled from Burk, Kathleen, Brand, Robert Henry, 'Baron Brand (1878–1963)', *Oxford Dictionary of National Biography*, Oxford University Press. Sept 2004; online edn, May 2006, and Fforde, John, *The Bank of England and Public Policy 1941–1958*. Cambridge: Cambridge University Press, 1992, p. 67.

40. Skidelsky, Robert, *John Maynard Keynes Fighting for Britain 1937–1946*. London: Macmillan, 2000, p. 544.

41. Bodleian Library, Oxford, Brand papers (henceforth Brand papers) Shelf Mark, Brand 196, British Food Mission 1941–1944 and Treasury Delegation Correspondence, Halifax File 1944–1946, Brand to Halifax, 21 November 1944.

42. Brand papers, Shelf Mark Brand 195, Treasury Delegation papers 1944–1946, Brand to Sir Edward Bridges, 13 May 1946.

43. Sherfield papers, MS 522, Inverchapel to Sir O. Sargent, 23 November 1946.

44. TNA, FO 366/1689, Halifax to Bevin, 19 February 1946.

45. HSTL, Oral History Interview with William Edwards, conducted in London on 12 August 1970 by Theodore Wilson.

46. TNA, FO 366/1689, Halifax to Bevin, 19 February 1946.

47. TNA, FO 366/1689, Bevin to Halifax, 18 March 1946.

48. HSTL, Oral History Interview with William Edwards, conducted in London on 12 August 1970 by Theodore Wilson.

49. Bodleian Library, Oxford, Attlee papers (henceforth Attlee papers), Dep. 30, Folio 279–290, letter Grant Mackenzie to Attlee attaching memorandum on *Overseas Publicity in its Wider Aspects*.

50. TNA, FO 371/60998, Report entitled *Visit to the BIS in America* prepared by I.A. Kirkpatrick (Superintending Under-Secretary, North American Information Department at the Foreign Office) 10 January 1947.

51. Ibid.

52. Bodleian, Library, Oxford, Donald Gillies papers re his Biography of Inverchapel (henceforth Gillies papers) Notes of Telephone Conversation with William Edwards, 13 February 1990.

53. See for example note 49 and the numerous footnotes in Anstey, Caroline. 'The Projection of British Socialism: Foreign Office Publicity and American Opinion, 1945–1950', *Journal of Contemporary History*, 19 (April 1984), 417–51.

54. TNA, FO 366/1711 Memorandum attached to letter sent to Sir David Scott (Foreign Office) from Inverchapel dated 7 August 1946.

55. TNA, FO 366/1781, J. Balfour to W.I. Mallet (Establishment and Organisation Department Foreign Office), 11 July 1946.

56. Ibid.

57. More evidence of the public relations benefits of a consulate can be gained from TNA, FO 366/1491, *Report on Cincinnati: A Public Relations Consulate*, prepared by A.H. Tandy 25 October 1945.

58. TNA, Sir R. Campbell Private Office papers (Henceforth Campbell papers), FO 800/524,Halifax to Secretary of State, No. 1625, 13 March 1945.

59. TNA, FO 366/1707, Inverchapel to Sir David Scott, 6 June 1946.

60. Ibid.

61. TNA, C.P. (46) 215, *Notes on Some Overseas Economic and Publicity Problems*, 24 June 1946, Office of the Lord President of the Council.

62. TNA, FO 366/1707, Halifax to Bevin, 29 January 1946.

63. TNA, FO 366/1707, Inverchapel to Sir David Scott, 6 June 1946.

64. First Viscount Grey of Fallodon.

65. Max Beloff, *Imperial Sunset: I, Britain's Liberal Empire*, pp.116–117. As quoted in Reynolds, David, 'Lord Lothian and Anglo American Relations, 1939–1940', *The American Philosophical Society*, 73:2 (1983), 1. James Bryce was a historian and politician who served from 1907 to 1913.

66. D.J. Dutton, 'Wood, Edward Frederick Lindley, first Earl of Halifax (1881–1959)', *Oxford Dictionary of National Biography*, Oxford University Press, Sept. 2004; online edn, May 2006, p. 7.

67. These two paragraphs are based upon readings taken from: (a) Birkenhead, Halifax, *The Life of Lord Halifax*. London: Hamish Hamilton, 1965; (b) Roberts, Andrew, *'The Holy Fox': The Life of Lord Halifax*. London: Phoenix, 1997; (c) D.J. Dutton, 'Wood, Edward Frederick Lindley, first Earl of Halifax (1881–1959)'; and (d) Neal, Lesley, 'The Washington ambassadorship of Lord Halifax 1941–1946'. Oxford M. Litt, 1985.

68. Letter Churchill to Halifax, 20 December 1940, as printed in Halifax, Lord, *Fullness of Days*. New York: Dodd, Mead & Company, 1957.

69. Halifax, Lord, *Fullness of Days*, p. 242.

70. Roberts, Andrew, *'The Holy Fox'*, p. 274.

71. Reynolds, *Lord Lothian*, p. 6.

72. Roberts, *'Holy Fox'*, pp. 282–289.

73. Halifax Diaries, 6 March 1941.

74. Hardy, Henry, *Isaiah Berlin Letters 1928–1946*. Cambridge: Cambridge University Press, 2004, letter Isaiah Berlin to Marie and Mendel Berlin (Parents), 26 October 1941.

75. Hardy, *Isaiah Berlin*, letter Berlin to parents, 21 February 1943.

76. Birkenhead, *Halifax*, p. 502.

77. Ibid., p. 500.
78. Hull, Cordell, *The Memoirs of Cordell Hull Volume II*. London: Hodder & Stoughton, 1948, p. 929.
79. Marshall C. Foundation, Lexington VA, Marshall papers, subgroup VIII Secretary of State, (henceforth Marshall papers) Box 132 Folder 8, Marshall to Halifax, 5 February 1947.
80. Acheson, Dean, *Present at the Creation: My Years at the State Department.* New York: Norton, 1969, p. 68.
81. Birkenhead, *Halifax*, p. 535.
82. Halifax, Lord, *The American Speeches of the Earl of Halifax.* London: OUP, 1947.
83. Churchill College Cambridge, Churchill Archives, papers Relating to Halifax's Time as HM ambassador in Washington 1941–1946 (henceforth Halifax papers), Correspondence with Bevin, Bevin to Halifax, 27 December 1940.
84. *Halifax American Speeches*, The Position of Britain: A Survey of the War Situation, Address to National Republican Club, New York, 6 October 1941, p. 74.
85. *Halifax, American Speeches*, Broadcast address, A Plea for Anglo American Cooperation, 22 September 1945.
86. Roberts, *'Holy Fox'*, p. 288.
87. Halifax Diaries, 12 April 1945.
88. Hathaway, Robert M., *Ambiguous Partnership: Britain and America, 1944–1947.* New York: Columbia University Press, 1988, p. 151.
89. Birkenhead, *Halifax*, p. 545.
90. Halifax papers, Correspondence with Eden, Halifax to Eden, 14 March 1945.
91. Ibid.
92. Halifax papers, Correspondence with Eden, Eden to Halifax, 23 March 1945.
93. Halifax papers, Correspondence with Churchill, Halifax to Churchill, 30 April 1945.
94. NAW, Record Group 59, Decimal File 45–49, Box 2957, Note of conversation between Halifax and Bevin at the Foreign Office reported by a British Official to a US Foreign Service Officer, 18 August 1945.
95. Halifax Diaries, 24 April 1943.
96. Attlee papers Dep. 38, Harold Ickes to Attlee, 4 June 1946.
97. Dalton, Hugh, *High Tide and After: Memoirs 1945–1960.* London: Muller, 1962, p. 148n.
98. Kings College, Cambridge, papers of John Maynard Keynes (henceforth Keynes papers) L/46/65, Halifax to Keynes, 25 January 1946.

99. TNA Inverchapel papers, FO 800/303, Clark Kerr to Ernest Bevin.

100. Gillies papers, Walter Bell to Gillies, 25 July 1991.

101. Bullock, Allen Louis Charles, *Ernest Bevin: Foreign Secretary, 1945–1951*. New York: Oxford University Press, 1983, p.100.

102. Lord Inverchapel was born Archibald John Kerr Clark. In 1911 he took the additional surname of Kerr and hence became Archibald John Kerr Clark Kerr. In 1946 upon his ascent to the House of Lords he became Lord Inverchapel. In this chapter, he is referred to as Clark Kerr or Inverchapel.

103. Gillies, Donald, *Radical Diplomat: The Life of Archibald Clark Kerr Lord Inverchapel, 1882–1951*. London: IBTauris, 1999, p. 53.

104. Brandon, Henry, *Special Relationships*. London: Macmillan, 1989.

105. TNA, Inverchapel papers FO 800/303, Clark Kerr to Ernest Bevin, December 1945.

106. Gillies, *Radical Diplomat*, p. 133.

107. *The Times*, 12 November 1943, as reported in Gillies, *Radical Diplomat*, p. 150.

108. Gillies papers, Walter Bell to Gillies, 25 July 1991.

109. The paragraphs relating to biographical information are based upon readings taken from (a) Gillies, *Radical Diplomat*; (b) Erik Goldstein, 'Kerr, Archibald John Kerr Clark, Baron Inverchapel (1882–1951)', *Oxford Dictionary of National Biography, Oxford University* Press, 2004; (c) Bodleian Library, Oxford, Inverchapel papers (henceforth Inverchapel papers) Journal and Appointment diaries 1945–1946; and (d) Inverchapel papers, 1947–1948, Bevin to Inverchapel, 27 September 1948.

110. Gillies papers, letter Walter Bell to Gillies, 25 July 1991.

111. Halifax papers, Correspondence with Eden, Halifax to Eden, 14 March 1945.

112. Gillies, *Radical Diplomat*, p. 183.

113. London School of Economics, Dalton papers, Dalton Diaries (henceforth Dalton Diary) 26 September 1946.

114. Gillies, *Radical Diplomat*, p. 188.

115. See chapter 3, note 79.

116. Various correspondence contained in TNA, FO 366/1630 including letter P. Dixon to Inverchapel, 26 November 1946.

117. Halifax papers, Correspondence with Eden, Halifax to Eden, 3 December 1945.

118. Hardy, *Isaiah Berlin*, letter to parents, 5 May 1945.

119. TNA, Bevin papers, FO 800 /513, Bevin to Byrnes, 23 January 1946.

120. Henderson, Nicolas, *The Private Office*. London: Weidenfeld & Nicolson, 1984, pp. 48–49.

121. Gillies papers, Note of Telephone conversation with Sir Nicholas Henderson.

122. Ibid.

123. Inverchapel papers, Outsize Files (FO and Speeches) 1945–1948, speech to Foreign Policy Association and the American Academy of Political Science, Philadelphia, 11 January 1947.

124. TNA, Bevin papers FO 800/514, Bevin to Inverchapel, 30 October 1947.

125. TNA, Bevin papers, FO 800/514, Inverchapel to Bevin, 4 November 1947.

126. Inverchapel papers, 1947–1948 C, Telegram transcribed by Inverchapel, Bevin to Inverchapel.

127. TNA, Bevin papers FO 800/514, Telegram Inverchapel to Bevin, 22 December 1947.

128. Gillies papers, Note of Telephone conversation with William Edwards.

129. Brandon, *Special Relationship*, p. 75.

130. Gillies papers, John Hersey to Gillies, 11 November 1991.

131. Inverchapel papers, Outsize Files (FO and Speeches) 1945–1948, St George's Society of New York, 23 April 1948.

132. Brand papers, 197, Correspondence 1941–1945, Brand to Geoffrey Crowther, 16 January 1946.

133. Henderson, 'The Washington embassy: Navigating the Waters of the Potomac', *Diplomacy and Statecraft*, 1:1 (March 1990) 42.

134. TNA, FO 371/44536, Halifax to Foreign Office, Weekly Political Summary, 14 April 1945. Rather presciently this same telegram suggested that Messrs Vinson and Clayton would be the strongest members of the team and the 'strongest hands at the helm'.

135. Inverchapel papers, Appointment Diaries, 1945–1946.

136. TNA, FO 371/61046, Pamphlet by Blair Bolles entitled *Who Makes Foreign Policy*, 20 March 1947, published by the Foreign Policy Association (henceforth, *Who Makes Foreign Policy*).

137. *Official Register of the United States*. 1 May 1946, Compiled by United States Civil Service Commission, Washington: United States Government Printing Office (henceforth *Official Register of the United States, 1946*).

138. TNA, FO 371/61053, Supplement to Weekly Political Report, 24 December 1946.

139. TNA, FO 371/61112, *Leading Personalities of the United States*, 1947. Sent by Inverchapel to Bevin, 7 November 1947 (henceforth, *Leading Personalities of the United States*).

140. *Congressional Directory*, Washington: Government Printing Office, 1945.

141. Brand papers, Correspondence 1941–1946 Washington, sub file Correspondence with Sir Wilfred Eady 1944–1946, Brand to Eady, 13 January 1945.

142. TNA, FO 371/61050, Pamphlet by Blair Bolles, *Reorganisation of the State Department*, 15 August 1947, published by the Foreign Policy Association (henceforth *Reorganisation of the State Department*).

143. *Leading Personalities of the United States* and TNA, FO 371/51673, report by embassy on James Byrnes, 5 January 1946.

144. David L. Anderson, *Byrnes, James Francis*, American National Biography Online, Feb. 2000.

145. *Leading Personalities of the United States.*

146. TNA, FO 371/44620, Halifax to Eden, 11 July 1945.

147. Byrnes, James F., *All in One Lifetime.* London: Museum Press, 1960, p. 354.

148. Truman, Harry S., *Memoirs: 1945, Year of Decisions.* New York: Signet, 1955, p. 606.

149. In 1944, at the last minute, Roosevelt substituted Truman's name for that of Byrnes for the vice presidential candidate partly because of fear that Byrnes's Roman Catholic origins and subsequent conversion to Protestantism would give rise to opposition on religious grounds, but also because he was regarded as too conservative in labour matters.

150. Mark A. Stoler, *Marshall George Catalett, Jr*, American National Biography Online, Feb. 2000.

151. Library of Congress, Washington DC, papers of Clark M.Clifford (henceforth Clifford papers), Box 1, Folder 8, *Memorandum for the President*, Prepared by Clark Clifford, 1947.

152. TNA, FO 371/61043, Inverchapel to Foreign Office, 8 January 1947.

153. Marshall papers, Engagement Records, Box 159, Folders 3–14, Appointment Calendar and Lists, 1946–1948.

154. This paragraph is based on readings taken from (a) Beisner, Robert, *Dean Acheson: A Life in the Cold War.* Oxford: Oxford University Press, 2006; (b) Smith, Joseph and Davis, Simon, *Historical Dictionary of the Cold War.* Maryland: Scarecrow Press, 2000; and (c) *Leading Personalities of the United States.*

155. *Leading Personalities of the United States.*

156. This paragraph is based on readings taken from (a) J.S. Hill, *Clayton, William Lockhart*, American National Biography online Feb. 2000; (b) Smith and Davis, *Historical Dictionary of the Cold War*; and (c) *Leading Personalities of the United States.*

157. This paragraph is based on readings taken from (a) Mayers, David, *The Ambassadors and America's Soviet Policy.* New York: Oxford University Press, 1995; (b) Kennan, George F., *Memoirs 1925–1950.* New York: Bantam, 1967; and (c) Smith and Davis, *Historical Dictionary of the Cold War.*

158. *Leading Personalities of the United States.*

159. This paragraph is based on readings taken from (a) Gary B. Ostrower, *Lovett, Robert Abercrombie*. American National Biography, Feb. 2000; (b) Smith and Davis, *Historical Dictionary of the Cold War*; and (c) *Leading Personalities of the United States*.

160. Chart II is taken from *Foreign Policy Reports*, 'Reorganization of the State Department' by Blair Bolles, 15 August 1947, TNA, FO 371/61050. In the post-war period, a culture clash developed between the traditional officials in the department who believed that foreign policy decisions were political ones, and the new type of employee who was more focused on economic and strategic issues. In an attempt to resolve this clash, Marshall reorganised the department. He was only partially successful. For a more detailed discussion on this, see Steiner, Zara (ed.), *The Times Survey of Foreign Ministries of the World*. London: Times Books, 1982, pp. 583–589.

161. *Official Register of the United States*.

162. TNA, FO 371/61045, Balfour to Neville Butler, 31 January 1947.

163. Record of a conversation with C. Bohlen, 28 July 1948 as reported in Anstey, Caroline, *Foreign Office Efforts to Influence American Opinion 1945–1949*, PhD thesis, p. 254.

164. TNA, FO 371/68022, Inverchapel to Foreign Office, 24 December 1947.

165. Bolles, *Who Makes Foreign Policy*, p. 67.

166. Brand papers, File 197, Correspondence, 1941–1946 Washington, Brand to Eady, 6 June 1946.

167. Brand papers, File 197, Correspondence 1941–1946 Washington, Brand to Eady, 19 December 1945.

168. Keynes papers, L/E/175, Keynes to Eady, 18 October 1945.

169. TNA, FO 371/68022, 1941–1947 Voting Record of Four Key Committees of Congress, January 1948.

170. In 1945/46 there were 81 committees; after the Monroney–La Follette Reorganisation Bill passed on 10 June 1946 these were reduced to 34 (TNA, FO 371/ 51609). The Senate Foreign Relations Committee formed in 1816 was the first Senate committee to be formed

171. *Congressional Directory*, Washington: Government Printing Office, various sessions (henceforth *Congressional Directory*).

172. The members of these groups and other notables such as journalists, intellectuals, businessmen, etc., were often referred to as the 'Foreign Policy Public'. They amounted to approximately 25% of the adult population and were attentive to foreign policy questions. For a very interesting discussion on this and on the relationship between the President, Congress and public opinion, see Paterson, Thomas G., 'Presidential Foreign Policy, Public Opinion, and Congress: The Truman Years', *Diplomatic History*, 3:1 (1979), 1–18.

173. Bolles, *Who Makes Our Foreign Policy*, p. 72.
174. Ibid., p. 73.
175. Ibid, p. 62.
176. Ibid.
177. Report on Information Work in the USA by William Edwards, 27 June 1949, as reported in Anstey, Caroline, 'Foreign Office Efforts to Influence American Opinion 1945–1949', PhD thesis.
178. Brand papers, File 197 Correspondence 1941–1946 Washington, Brand to Chancellor of the Exchequer, 23 August 1944.
179. Ibid.

Chapter 2 The Financial Agreement

1. TNA, FO 115/4225, Balfour to Foreign Office, 21 August 1945.
2. HSTL Official File (henceforth OF) Box 1037, Folder 356 1945, *Twentieth Report to Congress on Lend Lease Operations for the Period Ended June 30 1945*, 30 August 1945.
3. HSTL, PSF, Box 23, Folder, Lend Lease, *Brief on Lend Lease*, undated.
4. Truman, Harry S., *Memoirs: 1945, Year of Decisions*. New York: Signet, 1955, p. 524.
5. Dell, Edmund, *The Chancellors: A History of the Chancellors of the Exchequer 1945–1990*. London: Harper Collins 1996, p. 21.
6. For more on this see Strang, *The Foreign Office*.
7. The financial arrangements between Britain and America were variously discussed in terms of Stages I, II, and III. I was the period before the war with Germany ended, II was the period after the war with Germany ended but before the end of the war with Japan and III was after the end of the war with Japan.
8. Variously – Gardner, Richard N., *Sterling Dollar Diplomacy: Anglo American Collaboration in the Reconstruction of Multilateral Trade*. London: Clarendon Press, 1956, p. 178; Keynes, Lord, *The Collected Writings of John Maynard Keynes* (ed. D. Moggridge) vol. XXIV. Cambridge: University Press for Royal Economic Society, p. 377; and Leffler, Melvyn P.A., *Preponderance of Power: National Security, the Truman Administration, and the Cold War*. Stanford: Stanford University Press, 1992, p. 62.
9. Cairncross, Alec, *Years of Recovery: British Economic Policy 1945–1951*. London: Methuen, 1985, p. 8.
10. Keynes called this 'austerity' in his first draft.
11. TNA, CAB 66/65/51, Former reference WP (45) 301 Memorandum prepared by Keynes entitled *Overseas Financial Policy in Stage III*, dated 3 April 1945

and circulated by John Anderson on 15 May 1945 (henceforth TNA, *Overseas Financial Policy in Stage III*).

12. TNA, Overseas Financial Policy in Stage III.

13. Clarke, Sir Richard, *Anglo-American Economic Collaboration in War and Peace 1942–1949* (ed. Alec Cairncross). Oxford: Clarendon Press, 1982, p. 54.

14. Sterling balances, perhaps more accurately described as sterling liabilities, were amounts owed by Britain to a number of countries around the world – predominantly those within the sterling area. These balances grew considerably during the war as Britain incurred obligations to fund its war effort. Of these balances two-thirds were attributable to Indian and Egypt alone. These balances, in fact, ended up at £14 billion rather than £12 billion. They also became a source of confusion since the Americans came to regard them as in effect Lend Lease, i.e. a gift, whereas the Bank of England regarded them as a debt and as such Britain as the manager of the international currency sterling had a sacrosanct obligation to honour them.

15. TNA, *Overseas Financial Policy in Stage III*.

16. TNA, *Overseas Financial Policy in Stage III*.

17. Brand papers, File 198, Correspondence with Keynes 1929–1946, letter Brand to Mrs Wooton, 20 November 1946.

18. Keynes papers, L/B/2/ 101–104, Brand to Keynes, 5 April 1945.

19. See for example Brand papers, File 198, Correspondence with Keynes 1929–1946, Brand to Keynes, 5 June 1945.

20. Brand papers, File 198, Correspondence with Keynes 1929–1946, Brand to Keynes, 25 April 1945.

21. Keynes papers, L/B/2/, Keynes to Brand, 15 February 1945.

22. Brand papers, File 198, Correspondence with Keynes 1929–1946, Brand to Keynes, 25 April 1945.

23. TNA, T 236/449, Note of a Conversation in Lord Keynes Room, 7 March 1945.

24. Halifax Diaries, 2 February 1945.

25. TNA, T 236/449, Brand to Eady, 1 February 1945.

26. Clemson University, South Carolina, Clemson University Library, Special Collections, Byrnes papers (henceforth Byrnes papers) Box 1, Folder 10, Memorandum dated 20 April 1945 addressed to the President.

27. Byrnes papers, Box 1, Folder 10, letter Baruch to Byrnes dated 13 March 1946.

28. Quarterly Report for the Months of January February March 1945 as contained in Hachey, T.E., *Confidential Dispatches: Analysis of America by the British Ambassador, 1939–1945*. Evanston, IL: New University Press, 1974, p. 270.

29. Dobney, F. (ed.), *Selected Papers of William Clayton*. Baltimore: Johns Hopkins, 1971, letter Clayton to Hoffman 14 May 1943, p. 71.

30. Brand papers, File 197, Correspondence with Wilfred Eady 1944–1946, Brand to Eady, 13 January 1945.

31. Ibid.

32. HSTL, Office files, Box 1037, Folder 356, 1945, Memorandum for the President, Vinson to Truman, 22 August 1945.

33. Brand papers, File 197, Miscellaneous Correspondence Washington 1941–1946, Brand to Keynes, 5 April 1945.

34. *Foreign Relations of the United States Diplomatic Papers* (henceforth FRUS) 1945 Vol. VI *The British Commonwealth The Far East.* Washington, DC: US Government Printing Office, 1969 (henceforth 1945, Vol. VI) Memorandum Clayton to Vinson, 25 June 1945, p. 54.

35. TNA, FO 371/45698, Memorandum by Hall Patch, 3 August 1945.

36. University of Kentucky, Margaret I. King Library, Vinson Papers (henceforth Vinson Papers) Box 00148, Folder SS/Loan, Paraphrase of Telegram, American embassy, London to Secretary of State Washington, 17 August 1945.

37. Ibid.

38. Keynes Papers, pp/45/187/37, Editor *Herald Tribune* to Keynes, 2 January 1946.

39. Nicholas, H.G. (ed.), 'Introduction' to *Washington Dispatches, 1941–45.* London: 1981, p. x.

40. Edmonds, Robin, *Setting the Mould: The United States and Britain, 1945–1950.* New York: Oxford University Press, 1986, p. 98.

41. TNA, FO 371/44536, Weekly Political Summary, 31 March 1945.

42. TNA, FO 371/44536, Supplementary to Weekly Political Summary, 15 April 1945.

43. Ibid.

44. TNA, FO 371/44557, Balfour to Bevin, 9 August 1945.

45. See for example TNA, FO 371/38523, Memorandum entitled *The Essentials of American Policy*, 21 March 1944.

46. Leo Crowley was a member of Roosevelt's Cabinet 1942–1943, head of Economic Warfare 1943 and Foreign Economic Administrator 1943–1945. Crowley, one of America's leading Catholics, took a harsh attitude towards the British and was not popular amongst British officials in Washington.

47. TNA, FO 115/4225, Balfour to Foreign Office, 21 August 1945.

48. TNA, T 236/437, Record of Meeting of ministers, 23 August 1945.

49. TNA, T 236/437, Record of Meeting of ministers, 23 August 1945.

50. Ibid.

51. The island of Tarawa in the British colony of the Gilbert and Ellice Islands was recaptured by US Marines from the Japanese after a fierce battle on 23–24 November 1943. Halifax had previously suggested to Eden in 1943

that Britain give Tarawa to the American people. Halifax again pressed Eden in July 1945. Gifting Tarawa was 'one of those rare opportunities for a magnanimous action which would cost us little and which would really touch the heart of a friendly and sentimental people. It is with that thought in mind that I plead that the question be once again carefully reviewed' (TNA, FO 371/44623, Halifax to Eden, 2 July 1945). For various reasons the idea did not meet favour in the Foreign Office and was turned down; this, however, did not stop another attempt. Balfour wrote 'The ambassador would like to renew his strong plea for re-examining the earlier refusal...the gift of Tarawa would be just the sort of unsolicited gesture on our part which, assuming a favourable outcome of the financial discussions now about to open here, would make it easier for the US Administration to sell the result to their Congress and public' (TNA, FO 371/44671, Balfour to Neville Butler, 13 September 1945). Tarawa never was gifted to the Americans.

52. TNA, T 236/437, Record of Meeting of ministers, 23 August 1945.
53. Halifax Diaries, 14 July 1943.
54. Skidelsky, *Keynes*, p. 368.
55. Moggridge, *Collected Writings of Keynes*, containing letter Keynes to F.A. Keynes, 4 November 1945.
56. Keynes Papers, W/12/1–4, Halifax to Keynes, 16 August 1945.
57. TNA, T 236/437, Eady to Bridges, 15 August 1945.
58. TNA, T 236/437, Draft letter Chancellor to Foreign Secretary, undated.
59. Halifax Diaries, 23 August 1945.
60. See for example Halifax Diaries, 2 April, 28 June, 10 July and 8 August 1945 and Brand papers, File 196, Brand to Halifax, 28 February 1945.
61. Melvin I. Urofsky, 'Vinson, Fred', *American National Biography* Online, Feb. 2000.
62. *Leading Personalities in the United States*.
63. Halifax Diaries, 27 July 1945.
64. Command Paper, 6708, Financial Agreement.
65. TNA, Bevin papers, FO 800/512, Halifax to Bevin, 10 September 1945.
66. Halifax Diaries, 10 September 1945.
67. FRUS, 1945, vol. VI, Memorandum on Financial and Trade Discussions, Acheson to Certain American Missions, 10 September 1945, p. 121.
68. FRUS, 1945, vol. VI, Minutes of Meeting of the US–UK Combined Top Committee, 11 September 1945, p. 123.
69. *New York Times*, 12 September 1945.
70. TNA, FO 371/45700, Hall Patch to Butler, 15 September 1945.
71. TNA, FO 371/45700, Transcript of Halifax's and Keynes's opening remarks at press conference held on 13 September 1945.
72. Ibid.

73. Halifax Diaries, 12 September 1945.

74. Minutes of Top Committee Meeting 17 September 1945 as reproduced in Moggridge, *Collected Writings of Keynes*, p. 484.

75. *New York Times*, 21 September 1945.

76. TNA, FO 371/45702, Hall Patch to N. Butler, 21 September 1945.

77. TNA, T 236/438, Lee to Keynes, 24 September 1945.

78. Halifax Diaries, 17 September 1945.

79. TNA, FO 371/45700, Keynes to Dalton, 21 September 1945.

80. TNA, FO 371/45716, Minutes US–UK Economic Negotiations Finance Committee, 20 September 1945.

81. TNA, FO 371/45700, Keynes to Dalton, 21 September 1945.

82. TNA, Bevin papers, FO 800/512, Halifax to Bevin, 26 September 1945.

83. TNA, FO 371/45701, Halifax to Bevin, 27 September 1945.

84. TNA, FO 371/45701, Keynes to Bevin, 27 September 1945.

85. TNA, FO 371/45701, Note on file cover UE 4478, 28 September 1945.

86. TNA, T 236/439, Halifax to Bevin, 6 October 1945.

87. On 20 October 1945, the American government announced its acceptance of an invitation of the British government to participate in an Empire Wide Telecommunications Conference to be held in Bermuda. The conference was convened for late November 1945. Prior to the war, Cable and Wireless, because it controlled the network, had an effective monopoly on the routing of certain calls through London and controlled the rates charged. At the conference, America secured its objectives of (a) direct radio telegraphed circuits rather than having them all routed through London and (b) uniformly low rates for all telecommunications companies.

   On 15 January 1946 delegates from the British and American governments inaugurated a conference, again in Bermuda, to settle outstanding issues on Civil Aviation. On 11 February, a joint statement was released covering the areas of agreement and resolving all the outstanding issues.

88. Pressnell, L.S., *External Economic Policy Since the War: the Post-war Financial Settlement*. London: HMSO 1986, p. 274.

89. Diary entry 29 September 1945, Howson, Susan and Moggridge, Donald (eds), *The Wartime Diaries of Lionel Robbins and James Meade, 1943–1945*. London: Macmillan, 1990, p. 224.

90. FRUS 1945 vol. VI, Memorandum on Progress of US–UK Negotiations, Clayton to Truman, 24 September 1945, p. 134.

91. TNA, FO 371/45702, Hall Patch to Butler, 26 September 1945.

92. TNA, FO 115/4226, Keynes to Eady, I October 1945.

93. Halifax Diaries, 27 September 1945.

94. Ibid.

95. Bullen, R. & Pelly M. (eds), *Documents on British Policy Overseas Series 1 Vol. III Britain and America: Negotiation of the United States Loan 3 August–7 December 1945*. London: HMSO 1986, p. 153.

96. Halifax Diaries, 25 September 1945.

97. TNA, T 247/47, Keynes to Dalton, 1 October 1945.

98. Ibid.

99. Halifax Diaries, 29 September 1945.

100. Robbins, Lord, *Autobiography of an Economist*. London: Macmillan 1971, p. 206.

101. TNA, FO 115/4226, Wright to Halifax, 29 September 1945.

102. See for example Halifax Diaries, 23, 25, and 29 September, 3, 6 and 13 October. See also Halifax, *American Speeches*, p. 411.

103. *Terms of Assistance* Memorandum prepared by Keynes and reproduced in Moggridge, *The Collected Writings of Keynes*, p. 504.

104. TNA, FO 371/45702, Dalton to Halifax, 8 October 1945.

105. TNA, Bevin papers, FO 800/512, Keynes to Dalton, 9 October 1945.

106. TNA FO 371/45703, Dalton to Halifax *et al*, 13 October 1945.

107. Brand papers, File 197, Eady to Brand, 13 October 1945.

108. TNA, FO 371/45708, Record of a Meeting of ministers, 5 November 1945.

109. TNA, FO 371/45704, Keynes to Dalton, 18 October 1945.

110. Halifax Diaries, 17 October 1945.

111. TNA, FO 371/45704, Keynes to Dalton, 18 October 1945.

112. Keynes papers, L/E/175, Keynes to Eady, 12 October 1945.

113. Ibid.

114. Halifax Diaries, 9 October 1945.

115. Halifax Diaries, 17 October 1945.

116. See for example HSTL, Clayton papers, Department of State papers, Record Group 59, Box 8, F. Oct 45, Senator Moore to Clayton, 12 October 1945.

117. Halifax Diaries, 5 October 1945.

118. TNA, FO 371/45699, Financial Discussions – Reports on Press, various dates.

119. TNA, FO 371/44538, Supplementary to Weekly Political Summary, 12 October 1945.

120. See for example, Vinson papers, Box 00148, Folder SS/Loan, Memorandum entitled Financial Assistance to Britain, Luxford to Vinson, 12 October 1945.

121. TNA, Bevin papers, FO 800/512, Halifax to Bevin, 15 October 1945.

122. Halifax Diaries, 29 October 1945.

123. Halifax Diaries, 18 October 1945.

124. TNA, Butler papers, FO 800/537, Halifax to Prime Minister, 18 October 1945.
125. TNA, FO 115/4227, Keynes to Bridges, 19 October 1945.
126. TNA, FO 115/4227, Halifax to Bevin, 28 October 1945.
127. Information from Sir Frederick Harmer, Keynes's personal assistant at the talks, as contained in Pressnell, *External Economic Policy*, p. 295.
128. TNA, FO 371/45706, Halifax and Keynes to Dalton, 28 October 1945.
129. TNA, FO 371/45706, Dalton to Halifax and Keynes, 29 October 1945.
130. Halifax Diaries, 28 October 1945.
131. London School of Economics, Dalton papers, Dalton Diaries (henceforth Dalton Diaries), 6 November 1945.
132. TNA, T 236/466, Dalton to Halifax and Keynes, 6 November 1945.
133. TNA, T 236/456, Brand to Eady, 30 October 1945.
134. TNA FO 371/45708, Record of a Meeting of ministers, 5 November 1945.
135. TNA, FO 371/45706, Hall Patch to Coulson, 9 November 1945.
136. Account by Sir Frederick Harmer as given in Skidelsky, *Keynes*, p. 432
137. Ibid.
138. TNA, FO 371/45716, Minutes of a meeting of the Finance Committee held on 15 November 1945.
139. Skidelsky, *Keynes*, p. 434.
140. TNA, FO 371/45710, Keynes to Eady and Bridges, 21 November 1945.
141. TNA, FO 115/4227, Halifax to Bevin, 20 November 1945.
142. TNA, Bevin papers, FO 800/512, Attlee to Halifax, 24 November 1945.
143. TNA, T 236/441, Record of a Meeting of ministers held on 23 November 1945.
144. Ibid.
145. That is, the proposals contained in TNA, Bevin papers, FO 800/512, Attlee to Halifax, 24 November 1945.
146. Bullen, *Negotiation of US Loan*, p. 358 note 5.
147. Ibid.
148. Halifax Diaries, 5 February 1946.
149. TNA, FO 371/45710, Dalton to Keynes, 26 November 1945.
150. TNA, FO 371/45711, Dalton to Halifax, Keynes and Brand, 29 November 1945.
151. TNA, FO 371/45711, British Mission to Cabinet Offices, 30 November 1945.
152. TNA, FO 371/45711, Attlee and Dalton to Halifax, 30 November 1945.
153. Moggridge, *Collected Writings of Keynes*, p. 604.
154. TNA, FO 371/45713, Bridges to Eady, 4 December 1945
155. TNA, FO 371/45713, Attlee to Bridges, 5 December 1945.
156. TNA, FO 371/45713, Halifax to Attlee and Bevin, 5 December 1945.

157. Brand papers, File 197, Brand to Lord Altringham, 28 January 1946.

158. Brand papers, File 197, Brand to Eady, 19 December 1945.

159. Vinson papers, Box 00149, File UK Loan December, Statement made in Washington by the President and in London by the Prime Minister on 6 December 1945.

160. Vinson papers, Box 00149, File January – March 1946, Vinson to Keynes, 1 January 1946.

161. TNA, FO 115/ 4206, Record of Conversation with Wilcox, 13 December 1945.

162. Ibid.

163. TNA, FO 371/52993, Economic Summary for Week Ending 5 January 1946.

164. Brand papers, File 197, Brand to Dalton, 1 February 1946.

165. Keynes papers, Halifax to Keynes, 25 January 1946.

166. Brand papers, File 197, Brand to Dalton, 1 February 1946.

167. TNA, FO 371/51606, Weekly Political Summary from Washington to Foreign Office, 2 February 1946.

168. Halifax Diaries, 30 January 1946.

169. TNA, FO 371/52590, Brand to Keynes, 2 February 1946.

170. TNA, FO 371/51606, Weekly Political Summary Washington to Foreign Office, 19 January 1946.

171. Public papers of the Presidents of the United States, Harry S. Truman. 1946. Washington DC GPO 1961–1964, p. 98.

172. Brand papers, File 197, Brand to Dalton, 1 February 1946.

173. TNA, FO 371/45714, Maclean to Coulson, 8 December 1945. It is interesting to note that the position was reversed when only people in positions of responsibility and leaders were polled. In this case the majority were in favour of a loan. As Donald Maclean pointed out when reporting these results, this difference may be the crux of the battle in Congress.

174. Edmonds, Robin, Setting the Mould: The United States and Britain, 1945–1950. New York: Oxford University Press, 1986, p. 96.

175. TNA, FO 115/4227, Halifax to Attlee, 21 December 1945.

176. TNA, Bevin papers, FO 800/513, Attlee to Halifax, 10 January 1946.

177. TNA, FO 115/4227, Halifax to Attlee, 21 December 1945.

178. Brand papers, File 197, Brand to Eady, 21 March 1946.

179. Ibid.

180. Ibid.

181. TNA, FO 371/52593, Brand to Eady, 22 March 1946.

182. TNA, FO 371/52593, Eady to Brand, 26 March 1946.

183. TNA, FO 371/52593, Halifax to Dalton, 26 March 1946.

184. TNA, FO 371/52953, Eady to Brand, Extract from Chancellor's speech, 11 April 1946.

185. TNA, FO 371/52590, Halifax to Bevin, 31 January 1945.

186. Dalton Diaries, 29 March 1946.

187. TNA, FO 371/51632, Report on Churchill's Visit to America, Halifax to Bevin, 15 April 1946.

188. Halifax Diaries, 3 March 1946.

189. Bullen, R. & Pelly, M. (eds), Documents on British Policy Overseas, Series 1 Volume IV: Britain and America Atomic Energy, Bases and Food 12 December1945–31 July 1946. London: HMSO 1987, p. 157 note 23.

190. For a fuller explanation of this see Toye, Richard, 'Churchill and Britain's Financial Dunkirk', Twentieth Century British History, 15:4 (2004), 329–360.

191. TNA, FO 371/52953, Mr Churchill and the Loan, Note by J.A. Judson of a Private Discussion between Churchill and a group of Congressmen, 14 March 1946.

192. Ibid.

193. These were Vandenberg (Republican, Michigan) and Connally (Democrat, Texas) who [both] went to the foreign ministers Conference in Paris and therefore missed the vote. Source: Congressional Record, Vol. 92, Part 3, 79th Congress 2nd Session, p. 4082, 22 April 1946.

194. TNA, FO 371/68022, Chart Giving 1941–1947 Voting Record of Members of Four Key Committees of Congress on Foreign and Economic Policy Issues, Prepared by C. Child, 14 January 1948.

195. See for example Churchill's Off the Record Talk on 12 March 1946, TNA, FO 371/51632, Maclean to Dixon, 12 March 1945.

196. For a fuller account of Churchill's activities in this regard see Toye, Richard, 'Churchill and Britain's Financial Dunkirk'.

197. TNA, FO 371/51606, Weekly Political Report, 10 March 1946.

198. TNA, T 236/461, Washington to Cabinet Office, 12 February 1946.

199. Truman Library, Official Files, Box 170, Folder 1946, Statement by Fred M. Vinson, Secretary of the Treasury, before the Senate Committee on Banking and currency 5 March 1946.

200. TNA, FO 371/51606, Weekly Political Report, 10 March 1946.

201. TNA, FO 115/4253, The Consideration by Congress of the Anglo American Financial Agreement, Prepared by the embassy, 15 August 1946.

202. TNA, FO 371/51642, Judson to Randall, 12 August 1946. Also, for a more detailed account of the passage of the bill through Congress and an interesting analysis of the influence of the 'Communist menace' upon the debates see Hedland, Richard P., ' Congress and the British Loan, 1945–1946: A Congressional Study', PhD dissertation, University of Kentucky, 1976.

203. Halifax Diaries, 10 May 1946.

204. TNA, FO 371/52955, Washington to Cabinet Office, 10 May 1946.

205. TNA, FO 371/52937, Inverchapel to Foreign Office, 27 June 1946.

206. TNA, FO 371/51642, Judson to Randall, 12 August 1946.

207. See for example various reports contained in TNA, FO 371/52955, FO 371/52956 and FO 371/52957

208. See for example Vinson papers, Box 00169, Memorandum: World War I Debt of the United Kingdom to the United States, undated.

209. TNA, FO 371/52957, Note on Loan prepared by Judson, 23 May 1946.

210. TNA, FO 371/52957, Note on World War I Debt and the Loan Debate prepared by Judson, 25 June 1946.

211. TNA, FO 371/ 52957, Note on Loan Debate, prepared by Judson, 6 June 1946.

212. Brand papers, File 197, Brand to Eady, 6 June 1946.

213. TNA, FO 371/52957, Inverchapel to Foreign Office, 3 July 1946.

214. TNA, FO 371/68022, Chart Giving 1941–1947 Voting Record of Members of Four Key Committees of Congress on Foreign and Economic Policy Issues, Prepared by C. Child, 14 January 1948.

215. TNA,T 236/443, Inverchapel to Bevin, 15 July 1946.

216. Ibid.

217. Brand papers, File 197, Eady to Brand, 13 October 1945.

218. See for example TNA, T 247/ 47 Dalton to Keynes, 2 October 1945 or FO 371/45701 Eady to Keynes, 3 October 1945.

Chapter 3   Atomic Energy Collaboration, 1945–1946

1. Telegram from Halifax to Bevin dated 12 December 1945 as reproduced in Bullen & Pelly, *DBPO* Series 1 Vol. IV, p. 1.

2. TNA, Sir Ronald Campbell Private Office papers (henceforth Campbell papers), FO 800/524, Minute by the Prime Minister, 13 January 1945.

3. TNA, Neville Butler Private Office papers (henceforth Butler papers), FO 800/538, Minute North American Department by Neville Butler, 17 April 1946.

4. This paragraph is based upon thoughts presented on p. 67 of 'A Report to the President by Special Committee of National Security Council On Atomic Energy Policy With Respect to the United Kingdom and Canada March 2 1949', Truman papers, PSF, Box 174, Folder AE Declaration US/UK.

5. TNA, Campbell papers, FO 800/533, P.L. Rowan to Sir Alexander Cadogan, 17 August 1945.

6. Sir John Anderson was Home Secretary and minister of Home Security, 1939–1940; Lord President of the Council, 1940–1943; Chancellor of

the Exchequer, 1943–1945 and the chief representative of Churchill's Government on atomic energy matters. Anderson was appointed Chairman of the Advisory Committee on Atomic Energy notwithstanding the fact that he sat on the opposition benches.

7. Gowing, M., 'Britain America and the Bomb', reproduced in Dilks, D. (ed.), *Retreat from Power Volume Two: After 1939*. London: Macmillan Press, 1981, p. 124.

8. Hewlett, Richard G., and Anderson, Oscar E., *A History of the United States Atomic Energy Commission, Vol I: The New World, 1939/1946*. Pennsylvania: Pennsylvania University Press, 1962, p. 259.

9. Manhattan Engineering District, often referred to simply as the Manhattan Project, was the code name the Americans used for the atomic project.

10. Hewlett, *New World*, p. 265.

11. Tube Alloys was the code name the British used for the atomic project.

12. Quebec Agreement as reproduced in Baylis, John, *Anglo-American Defence Relations, 1939–1984: the Special Relationship*, 2nd edn. London: Macmillan, 1984, p. 23.

13. See for example Sherfield papers, MS Memoirs, Washington 1944–1947: Atomic energy, p. 17 as quoted in Kelly, S., 'No Ordinary Foreign Office Official: Sir Roger Makins and Anglo-American Atomic Relations, 1945–1955', *Contemporary British History*, 14:4 (Winter 2000), 109.

14. All phrases in quotes in this paragraph are taken from The Declaration of Trust, dated 13 June 1944, as reproduced in Baylis, *Anglo American Defence Relations*, p. 25.

15. Niels Bohr and other scientist were beginning to suggest that Britain and the United States should 'tell the world about the bomb in an effort to achieve international control and head off a fateful arms race' (Hewlett, *New World*, p. 326).

16. Hyde Park Aide Memoire, dated 19 September 1944, as reproduced in Baylis, *Anglo American Defence Relations*, p. 28.

17. TNA, Campbell papers, FO 800/524, Minute Produced by Ronald Campbell, 21 February 1945. Further evidence of this is contained in a letter from John Chadwick to John Anderson, 22 February 1945 enclosing a note of a conversation with General Groves held on 1 February 1945.Both documents can be found in TNA, FO 800/524.

18. TNA, Campbell papers, FO 800/524, Minute Produced by Ronald Campbell, 21 February 1945.

19. TNA, Campbell papers, FO 800/524, J. Anderson to Churchill, 16 January 1945

20. Stimson was Secretary of War until September 1945 when he was replaced by his Under-Secretary Robert Patterson.

21. TNA, Campbell papers, FO 800/524, WL Webster to Ronald Campbell, 8 February 1945. Webster was a British Official in the Office of Scientific Research and Development and the British Joint Secretary of the CPC.

22. TNA, Campbell papers, FO 800/524, J. Anderson to Churchill, 16 January 1945.

23. Initially Halifax attended the CPC meetings by invitation; he does not appear in the minutes as a formal member until the meeting held on 13 October 1945.

24. TNA, Campbell papers, FO 800/524, J. Anderson to Halifax, 21 March 1945.

25. TNA, Campbell papers, FO 800/524, Minute Produced by Ronald Campbell, 21 February 1945.

26. TNA, Campbell papers, FO 800/526, J. Anderson to Field Marshal Wilson, 1 June 1945.

27. HSTL, Oral History Interview with Sir Roger Makins by Phillip Brooks, 15 June 1964.

28. Truman, Harry S., Memoirs: 1945, Year of Decisions. New York: Signet, 1955, p. 574.

29. FRUS, 1945, Volume II, Attlee to Truman, 8 August 1945, p. 36.

30. TNA, Bevin papers, FO 800/512, Attlee to Truman, 16 August 1945.

31. Truman, Memoirs: 1945, Year of Decisions, p. 576.

32. TNA, CAB 134/7, Cabinet Advisory Committee on Atomic Energy, Relations with the United States, Note by Makins, 24 September 1945.

33. FRUS, 1945, Volume II, Minutes of a Meeting of the Secretaries of State, War and Navy, 10 October 1945, p. 55.

34. TNA, CAB 130/7, Cabinet Advisory Committee on Atomic Energy, Relations with the United States, Note by Makins, 24 September 1945.

35. FRUS 1945, Volume II, Minutes of the Combined Policy Committee, 13 October 1945, p. 57.

36. TNA, CAB 134/6, List of Advisory Committee on Atomic Energy Minutes (ACAE) 1945 Series and CAB 134/7, List of Advisory Committee on Atomic Energy Memoranda (ACAE) 1945 Series.

37. TNA, CAB 130/2, Minutes of Meetings of Gen 75 Committee (Gen 75) Series and CAB 130/3, List of Memoranda, GEN 75 Meetings (Gen 75) Series.

38. Halifax Diaries, 25 September 1945.

39. TNA, Butler papers, FO800/535, Halifax to Attlee and Bevin, 25 September 1945. Note that in addition to being Superintending Under-Secretary of the North American Department in the Foreign Office Neville Butler was also a member of the Cabinet Advisory Committee on Atomic Energy.

40. TNA, GEN 75/3, The Atomic Bomb: Letter From the Prime Minister to President Truman, 25 September 1945.

41. *Public Papers of the Presidents of the United States: Harry S. Truman*, 1945, pp. 362–366.

42. TNA, Butler papers, FO 800/537, Halifax to Foreign Office, 20 October 1945.

43. TNA, Butler papers, FO 800/537, Halifax to Foreign Office, 25 October 1945.

44. TNA, GEN 75/13, Discussion in Washington on Atomic Energy, Note by Secretary of the Cabinet, 6 December 1945.

45. Attlee papers, Deposit 25, Halifax to Attlee, 2 November 1945.

46. TNA, Butler papers, FO 800/537, Halifax to Attlee, 3 November 1945.

47. TNA, FO 115/4228, Makins to Halifax 6 November 1945.

48. Paul, Septimus, *Nuclear Rivals: Anglo-American Atomic Relations 1941–1952.* Columbus: Ohio State University Press, 2000, p. 80.

49. Halifax Diaries, 7 and 10 November 1945.

50. TNA, Butler papers, FO 800/538, Butler to Campbell, 15 November 1945.

51. TNA, Bevin papers, FO 800/438, Text of Communiqué on Atomic Energy, 15 November 1945.

52. Bush, Vannevar, *Pieces of the Action.* New York: William Morrow, 1970, p. 296.

53. Gormley, James, 'The Washington Declaration and the Poor Relation: Anglo American Atomic Diplomacy 1945–1946', *Diplomatic History* 8 (Spring 1984), 135.

54. Hewlett, *New World*, p. 466; see also HSTL, Oral History Interview with Sir Roger Makins by Phillip Brooks, 15 June 1964.

55. Memorandum, dated 4 November 1945 by N.M. Butler sent to Sir Alexander Cadogan as reproduced in Bullen & Pelly, *DBPO* Series 1 Vol. II, p. 580.

56. Truman, *Memoirs*, p. 576.

57. Footnote No. 4 in Bullen & Pelly, *DBPO* Series 1 Vol. II, p 586.

58. Sherfield papers, MS Memoirs, 'Washington 1944–1947, Atomic energy, p. 16 as quoted in Kelly, S., 'No Ordinary Foreign Office Official: Sir Roger Makins and Anglo-American Atomic Relations, 1945–1955', *Contemporary British History* 14:4 (Winter 2000), 109.

59. FRUS, 1945, Vol. II, *Negotiations with the British and Canadians, 1–16 November*, Memorandum by Captain R. Gordon Arneson to the Secretary of War (Patterson), 17 April 1946, p. 63.

60. FRUS, 1945, Vol. II, *Memorandum by President Truman, the British Prime Minister (Attlee), and the Canadian Prime Minister (King)*, 16 November 1945, p. 75.

61. The Anderson Groves Memorandum recommended six points to be considered by the CPC when preparing a new document to replace the Quebec

Agreement. The first point prohibited the use of atomic weapons without consultation; the second barred the disclosure of information to other countries without consultation, the third and fourth points dealt with the sourcing and allocation of raw materials. The fifth point provided for full cooperation in the field of basic research and allowed for cooperation on development and design of plants on an ad hoc basis if approved by the Combined Policy Committee. The final point referred to the constitution of the Combined Development Committee and its activities.

62. FRUS, 1945, Vol. II, Memorandum by the Commanding General, Manhattan Engineer District (Groves), and the Chairman, British Advisory Committee on Atomic Energy (Anderson), to the Chairman of the Combined Policy Committee (Patterson), 16 November 1945, p. 75.

63. Sherfield papers, Memoirs '1944–1947: Atomic Energy' p. 3 as quoted in Kelly, *No Ordinary Foreign Office Official*, p. 109.

64. FRUS,1945, Vol. II, *Negotiations with the British and Canadians, 1–16 November*, Memorandum by Captain R. Gordon Arneson to the Secretary of War (Patterson), 17 April 1946, p. 63.

65. TNA, GEN 106/2, Record of the Anglo American Discussions on Atomic Energy, 12 December 1945. For more background information on this see HSTL Oral History Interview with R. Gordon Arneson by Niel Johnson 21 June 1989.

66. Paul, *Nuclear Rivals*, p. 82.

67. The membership of the committee at this date included Secretary of State Byrnes, Secretary for War Patterson, Halifax, Field Marshal Sir Henry Maitland Wilson and Dr Vannevar Bush. The joint Secretaries to the committee were Major General Groves and Roger Makins. Others often attended by invitation.

68. FRUS, 1945, Vol. II, Minutes of the Combined Policy Committee held on 4 December 1945, p. 86.

69. TNA, Butler papers, FO 800/541, Makins to Ricket, 15 December 1945.

70. Churchill Archives, Chadwick papers, Makins to Butler, 22 January 1946.

71. TNA, FO 115/4305, Makins to Rickett, I February 1946.

72. FRUS, 1946 Vol. I, Draft Report to the Combined Policy committee by subcommittee dated 15 February 1946, p. 1207.

73. TNA, Campbell papers, FO 800/527, Minute to Prime Ministers from Sir John Anderson, 9 February 1946.

74. FRUS 1946 Vol. I, Memorandum by the Commanding General, Manhattan Engineering District (Groves), to the Secretary of State, 13 February 1946, p. 1205.

75. FRUS, 1946 Vol. I, Minutes of CPC Meeting, 15 February 1946, p. 1213.

76. Gowing, *Independence and Deterrence*, Vol. I, p. 98.

77. TNA, FO 115/4306, Halifax and Field Marshal Wilson to Anderson, 17 February 1946.

78. TNA, FO 115/4305, Makins to Ricket, 1 February 1946.

79. Igor Gouzenkou was a lieutenant in the Soviet Army posted as a cipher clerk to the Soviet embassy in Ottawa. He defected in the autumn of 1945 and disclosed that the Soviets had penetrated the Manhattan project. He revealed, amongst other things, that Alan Nunn, a British atomic scientist working on the project, was a spy. This information became public on 19 February 1946.

80. Churchill Archives, Chadwick papers, *Embassy Report on Congressional and Public Opinion in the USA on the Use and Control of Atomic Energy*, No. 13, Period February 1 to 18 February 1945.

81. TNA, FO 115/4305, Makins to Ricket, 4 February 1946.

82. TNA, Campbell papers, FO 800 /527, Makins to Butler, 22 January 1946.

83. Churchill Archives, Chadwick papers, Makins to Butler, 22 January 1946.

84. TNA, FO115/ 4306, Halifax and Filed Marshall Wilson to Anderson, 17 February 1946.

85. TNA, FO 115 /4306, Attlee to Halifax and Field Marshal Wilson, 6 March 1946.

86. FRUS 1946 Vol. I, Minutes of CPC, 15 April, p. 1230.

87. Ibid.

88. Halifax Diaries, 15 April 1946.

89. FRUS, 1946, Vol. I, Attlee to Truman, 16 April 1946, p. 1232.

90. TNA, Bevin papers, FO 800/438, Truman to Attlee, 20 April 1946.

91. Baylis, *Anglo American Defence Relations*, p. 32.

92. Acheson, Dean, *Present at the Creation: My Years at the State Department*, New York: Norton, 1969, p. 164.

93. TNA, FO 115/4306, Makins to Rickett, 6 March 1946.

94. TNA, FO 115/4306, Halifax and Field Marshal Wilson to Anderson, 19 February 1946.

95. TNA, Butler papers, Halifax to Anderson, 2 May 1946.

96. TNA, AB 16/286, Memorandum detailing raw material allocation for 1946, 13 May 1946.

97. TNA, Butler papers, FO 800/580, *Future Cooperation Between the US, the UK and the Canadian Governments*, Draft Memorandum by the Prime Minister, May 1946. Attlee had been advised that the withholding of all technical information by the Americans would delay the British plans for large-scale production by between six months and a year. On the other hand he was advised that without raw material the project could not proceed at all.

98. Footnote of a Foreign Office Minute, dated 23 May 1946, by N.M. Butler as reproduced in Bullen & Pelly, DBPO Series 1 Vol. IV, p. 297.

99. Gowing, *Independence and Deterrence*, Vol. I, p. 106.

100. Ibid., p. 108.

101. Churchill Archives, Chadwick papers, Chadwick to Anderson, 17 April 1946.

102. Footnote to the above letter as reproduced in Bullen & Pelly, *DBPO* Series 1 Vol IV, p. 252.

103. Gowing, *Independence and Deterrence*, Vol. I, p. 109.

104. Edmonds, *Setting the Mould*, p. 86.

105. Gowing, *Independence and Deterrence*, Vol. I, p. 14. Statement by the Prime Minister and Mr Churchill on the Atomic Bomb, 6 August 1945.

106. Sherfield, Lord (previously Sir Roger Makins), 'Britain's Nuclear Story 1948–52: politics and technology', *Round Table*, 65, p. 194 as quoted in Kelly, *No Ordinary Foreign Office Official*.

107. Halifax Diaries, 4 February, 18 October and 21 December 1945.

108. *Leading Personalities in the United States*.

109. TNA, Butler papers, FO 800/580, Makins to Rickett, 6 June 1946.

110. HSTL, PSF, Box 174, Folder, Atomic Energy Declaration UK/US, Attlee to Truman, 6 June 1946.

111. Kelly, *No Ordinary Foreign Office Official*, p. 122.

112. Paul, *Nuclear Rivals*, p. 83.

113. See for example Nicholson, Harold, 'Diplomacy Then and Now', *Foreign Affairs* 40 (Oct. 1961), 39–49.

114. TNA, Butler papers, FO 800/580, *Future Cooperation Between the US, The UK, and the Canadian Government*, draft Memorandum by the Prime Minister, May 1946.

115. Telegram from Halifax to Bevin dated 12 December 1945 as reproduced in Bullen & Pelly, *DBPO* Series 1 Vol. IV, p. 1.

Chapter 4   Palestine

1. TNA, FO 115/4219, Memorandum Halifax to Byrnes, 19 October 1945.

2. Memorandum by Mr J. Balfour, minister at the Washington embassy as contained in Bullen, R. & Pelly, M., *Documents on British Policy Overseas Series 1 Volume IV: Britain and America: Negotiations and the United States Loan*. London: HMSO 1985, p. 5.

3. Palestine, Statement of Policy, Command Paper 6019, May 1939, p. 1.
4. Morgan, Kenneth O., *Labour in Power 1945–1951*. Oxford: Clarendon Press, 1984, p. 206.
5. TNA, FO 371/68014, 'The Political History of Palestine under British Administration', Memorandum by His Britannic Majesty's Government presented in July 1947 to the United Nations Special Committee on Palestine. See also TNA, FO 371/52526, Balfour to Congressman Weiss, 3 January 1946.
6. Palestine, Statement of Policy, Command Paper 6019, May 1939.
7. Cohen, M.J., *Palestine and the Great Powers 1945–1948*. Princeton, New Jersey: Princeton University Press, 1982, p. 8.
8. Bullock, Allen Louis Charles, *Ernest Bevin: Foreign Secretary, 1945–1951*. New York: Oxford University Press, 1983, p. 164.
9. Harris, Kenneth, *Attlee*. London: Weidenfeld & Nicolson, 1982, p. 390.
10. FRUS, 1945 Vol. VIII, *Memorandum by the Director of the Office of Near Eastern and African Affairs to the Acting Secretary of State*, 20 March 1945, p. 695. It is interesting to note Harry Hopkins' version of this meeting as recounted by Halifax in his diaries. 'The President had been much more interested in their offerings than their problems, on which he had made every sort of loose promise' Halifax Diaries 15 April 1945.
11. TNA, FO 371/44605, Halifax to Foreign Office, *Note on United States Jewish Population, 1937–1943*, 21 December 1944.
12. Library of Congress, Clark Clifford papers, Box 1, Folder 8, Memorandum for the President, p. 13.
13. Cohen, M.J., *Truman and Israel*. Berkeley, California: University of California Press, 1990, p. 63.
14. *Official Register of the United States*, Various, 1945–1948.
15. Pika, Joseph, A., 'Interests Groups and the White House under Roosevelt and Truman', *Political Science Quarterly*, 102:4 (Winter 1987–1988), 656.
16. Cohen, *Truman and Israel*, p. 77. See also Library of Congress, Loy Henderson papers, Box 11, Henderson to Rosenberg, 24 October, 1975 and Barbara Blumberg, Niles David K, *American National Biography Online 2000*.
17. HSTL, Truman papers, PSF, Subject File Foreign Affairs, Box 160, Folder Palestine 1945–1946, Stettinius to Truman, 18 April 1945.
18. See for example HSTL, Truman papers, PSF, Subject File Foreign Affairs, Box 160, Folder Palestine 1945–1946, Memoranda for the President dated 1 May and 26 May 1945 from J. Grew (Acting Secretary of State).
19. It should be noted, however, that this sympathy did not extend to mass immigration. A poll taken in 1945 revealed that 5% of Americans were in favour of more immigration but 51% were against any further immigration.

20. TNA, FO 115/4218, Campbell to Halifax, 14 June 1945.

21. TNA, FO 115/4218, Halifax to Eden, 1 July 1945.

22. TNA, FO 800 /484, Bevin papers, Truman to Churchill, 24 July 1945.

23. FRUS, 1945, Vol. VIII, Attlee to Truman, 31 July 1945, p. 719.

24. Earl Harrison was the US government representative on the Intergovern-mental Committee on Refugees. He was also a former Commissioner of Immigration and Naturalisation.

25. FRUS, 1945, Vol. VIII, Truman to Attlee, 31 August 1945, p. 738.

26. Truman, Harry, S., *Memoirs: Years of Trial and Hope, 1946–1952*. New York: Signet, 1956, p. 138.

27. HSTL, Rosenman papers, Box 1 Folder Earl Harrison, Summary of the First and Partial Report of Earl G Harrison, undated.

28. FRUS, 1945, Vol. VIII, Truman to Attlee, 31 August 1945, p. 739.

29. FRUS, 1945, Vol. VIII, Attlee to Truman, 14 September, p. 739.

30. TNA, FO 115/4218, Tandy to Halifax, Balfour and Wright, 15 September 1945.

31. TNA, Bevin papers, FO 800 /484, Attlee to Truman, 16 September 1945.

32. Clemson University, Walter Brown papers, Diary Entry 17 September 1945.

33. Bullock, *Ernest Bevin*, p. 175.

34. FRUS, 1945, Vol. VIII, Memorandum by the Chief of the Division of Near Eastern Affairs (Merriam) to the Director of the Office of Near Eastern and African Affairs (Henderson), 26 September 1945, p. 745.

35. Hardy, Henry, *Isaiah Berlin Letters 1928–1946*. Cambridge: Cambridge University Press, 2004, Appendix Entitled *Zionist Politics in Wartime Washington*, the text of which formed the basis of the first Jacob Herzog Memorial Lecture, 1972.

36. HSTL, Rosenman papers, Box 4, Folder Palestine, Rosenman to Truman, 7 September 1945.

37. Foreign Office List 1945–1948.

38. TNA, FO 371/68650, Wright to Hadow, 6 May 1948.

39. Ibid.

40. TNA, FO 371/68650, Hadow to Wright, 9 May 1948.

41. TNA, FO 371/68650, Gore-Booth to Foreign Office, 1 August 1945.

42. See Nicholas, H.G. (ed.), *Washington Dispatches, 1941–45*. London: 1981 and Hachey, T.E., *Confidential Dispatches: Analysis of America by the British ambas-sador, 1939–1945*. Evanston, IL: New University Press, 1974.

43. Bullock, *Ernest Bevin*, p. 174.

44. TNA, FO 115/4218, Halifax to Eden, 1 July 1945.

45. TNA, Bevin papers, FO 800/ 484, Halifax to Bevin and Attlee, 3 October 1945.

46. TNA, FO 371/44538, Political Report, Halifax to Foreign Office, 7 October 1945.

47. TNA, Bevin papers, FO 800/484, Halifax to Bevin and Attlee, 8 October 1945.

48. When Halifax visited Britain in August 1945 he met with Ronald Campbell and Michael Wright at the Foreign Office. They informed him that the Foreign Office had been favourably impressed with Halifax's despatch dated 1 July and were all for 'getting ourselves under some jointly American umbrella if we are going to have trouble' (Halifax Diaries 3 August 1945).

49. TNA, Bevin papers, FO 800/484, Halifax to Bevin and Attlee, 3 October 1945.

50. TNA, Bevin papers, FO 800/484, Bevin to Attlee, 30 July 1945.

51. Bullock, *Ernest Bevin*, p. 176.

52. TNA, Bevin papers, FO 800/ 484, Foreign Office to Washington, 13 October 1945.

53. TNA, Bevin papers, FO 800/484, Halifax to Bevin, 14 October 1945.

54. TNA, FO 115/4219, Halifax to Byrnes, 19 October 1945.

55. TNA, FO 115/4219, Informal Record of Conversation between Halifax and Byrnes, prepared by British embassy, 19 October 1945.

56. FRUS, 1945, Vol. VIII, Record of Conversation between Halifax and Byrnes, prepared by Department of State, 19 October 1945, p. 777. See also Record of Conversation between Halifax and Byrnes prepared by Department of State, 22 October 1945, p. 780.

57. TNA, FO 115/4219, Halifax to Byrnes, 19 October 1945.

58. HSTL, David Niles papers, Box 28, *Report of Anglo American Committee of Enquiry*, 20 April 1945.

59. FRUS 1945, Vol. VIII, Record of Conversation between Halifax and Byrnes prepared by the Department of State, 19 November 1945, p. 827.

60. Halifax Diaries, 7 November 1945.

61. HSTL, Rosenman papers, Box 4, Folder Palestine, Rosenman to Truman, 23 October 1945.

62. Halifax Diaries, 6 November 1945.

63. Aldrich, Richard J., *The Hidden Hand: Britain, America and Cold War Intelligence*. London: John Murray, 2001, chapter 12. See also FRUS 1945, Vol. VIII, Aide Memoire British Embassy to Department of State, 6 November 1945, p. 813.

64. Aldrich, *The Hidden Hand*, chapter 12 and Bullock, *Ernest Bevin*, p. 178.

65. The committee consisted of the following members: (American) Judge Joseph Hutcheson, Chairman, Frank Aydelotte, Frank Buxton, Bartley Crum, James McDonald William Phillips (British) Sir John Singleton, Chairman,

Wilfred Crick, Richard Crossman, Sir Frederick Leggett, Major Reginald, Manningham-Buller, Lord Morrison.

66. Morgan, *Labour in Power*, p. 210.
67. TNA, FO 371/45388, Halifax to Foreign Office, 7 December 1945.
68. HSTL, Niles papers, Rosenman to Crum, 13 December 1945.
69. TNA, FO 371/45389, Handwritten note on file cover, E9828, by H. Beeley (Eastern Department), 17 December 1945.
70. TNA, FO 371/45389, Halifax to Foreign Office, 18 December 1945.
71. TNA, FO 371/52508, Tandy to Baxter (head of Eastern Department), 23 January 1945.
72. TNA, FO 371/52505, Halifax to Foreign Office, 13 January 1945.
73. TNA, FO 371/51606, Halifax to Foreign Office Supplementary to Weekly Political Summary, 31 December 1945.
74. Halifax Diaries, 18 December 1945.
75. HSTL Niles papers, Box 29, Folder Israel January–June 1946, Memorandum of conversation Dr Edward Acheson, 24 February 1946.
76. TNA, FO 371/44539, Halifax to Foreign Office, Supplementary to Weekly Political Summary, 29 November 1945.
77. TNA, FO 371/52555, J. Robey (Vice Consul, New York Consulate) to T. Bromley (First Secretary embassy), 19 August 1946.
78. TNA, FO 115/4250, Memorandum entitled *Jewish Affairs in the United States*, prepared by T. Bromley (First Secretary at the embassy), 22 November 1946.
79. This subject has been comprehensively covered in Anstey, Caroline, *Foreign Office Efforts to Influence American Opinion 1945–1949*. London School of Economics and Political Science, PhD thesis 1984. Chapter 7 *Publicity on Palestine*.
80. For an account of this meeting see TNA FO 371/52506, Summary of a Report of Dr Chaim Weizmann on his recent trip to America, 21 January 1946.
81. HSTL, David Niles papers, Box 28, *Report of Anglo American Committee of Enquiry*, 20 April 1945.
82. Northedge, F.S., 'Britain and the Middle East' in Ovendale, Ritchie (ed.), *The Foreign Policy of the British Labour Governments, 1945–1951*. Leicester: Leicester University Press, 1984, p. 154.
83. FRUS, 1946, Vol. VII, Byrnes to Truman, 19 April 1946, p. 584.
84. Acheson, Dean, *Present at the Creation: My Years at the State Department*. New York: Norton, 1969, p. 173.
85. FRUS, 1946, Vol. VII, Harriman to Byrnes, 1 May 1946, p. 589.
86. Acheson, *Present at the Creation*, p. 173.
87. Bullock, *Ernest Bevin*, p. 258.

88. TNA, FO 371/52519, Halifax to Foreign Office, 27 April 1946.
89. TNA, FO 371/52521, Halifax to Foreign Office, 4 May 1946.
90. TNA, FO 371/52521, Minute by J.G. Ward, 8 May 1946.
91. Hardy, Henry, *Isaiah Berlin Letters*, Appendix Entitled *Zionist Politics in Wartime Washington*, p. 668.
92. Gillies, *Radical Diplomat*, p. 197.
93. TNA, FO 115/4250, Inverchapel to Bevin, 20 June 1946.
94. TNA, FO 371/52560, Chancery to Eastern Department, 27 September 1946.
95. TNA, FO 371/52560, Sargent to Inverchapel, 4 November 1946.
96. See FO 115/4250 and FO 371/52566.
97. Acheson, *Present at the Creation*, p. 178.
98. FRUS, 1946, Vol. VII, Pinkerton (American Consul General at Jerusalem) to Byrnes, 27 May 1946, p. 615.
99. FRUS, 1946, Vol. VII, Pinkerton (American Consul General at Jerusalem) to Byrnes, 2 May 1946, p. 590.
100. TNA, FO 371/52528, Inverchapel to Foreign Office, 12 June 1946.
101. TNA, FO 371/52542, Bevin Speech on 12 June 1946, Labour Party Conference, Bournemouth, as contained in *Foreign Affairs*, Labour Publications Department.
102. TNA, FO 371/52529, Inverchapel to Foreign Office, 13 June 1946.
103. TNA, FO 371/52529, Foreign Office to Washington, 14 June 1946.
104. See for example TNA, FO 115/4250, Balfour to Senator Wagner, 23 June 1946.
105. TNA, FO 371/52529, Inverchapel to Bevin, 14 June 1946.
106. Ibid.
107. TNA, Bevin papers, FO 800/513, Inverchapel to Bevin, 15 July 1946.
108. TNA, Bevin Papers, FO 800/513, Bevin to Inverchapel, 25 July 1946.
109. Donovan, Robert J., *Conflict and Crisis: the Presidency of Harry S. Truman, 1945–1948*. New York: Norton, 1977, p. 319.
110. TNA, FO 371/52546, Inverchapel to Foreign Office, 30 July 1946.
111. TNA, FO 371/52546, Inverchapel to Foreign Office, 31 July 1946.
112. TNA, FO 371/52558, Cane to Balfour, 7 September 1946.
113. TNA, FO 371/52558, Balfour to R. Howe (Foreign Office), 12 September 1946.
114. See for example Bullock, *Ernest Bevin*, p. 298, and Donovan, *Conflict and Crisis*, p. 319.
115. TNA, FO 371/52555, Balfour to Baxter, 30 August 1946.
116. TNA, FO 115/4250, Minute by Donald Maclean, 11 September 1946.
117. FRUS, 1946, Vol. VII, Truman to Attlee, 12 August 1946, p. 682.
118. Bullock, *Ernest Bevin*, p. 304.

119. Cohen, Michael J., 'Truman and Palestine, 1945–1948: Revisionism, Politics and Diplomacy', *Modern Judaism*, 2:1 (February 1982), 7.

120. FRUS, 1946, Vol. VII, Truman to Attlee, 3 October 1945, p. 703.

121. FRUS, 1946, Vol. VII, Attlee to Truman, undated, p. 704.

122. TNA, FO 371/52560, Inverchapel to Foreign Office, 3 October 1946.

123. HSTL, Hannegan papers, Box 6, Bartley Crum to Hannegan, 1 October 1946. See also correspondence between Fitzpatrick and Hannegan and Truman and Hannegan.

124. FRUS, 1946, Vol. VII, Attlee to Truman, 4 October 1946, p. 705.

125. TNA, FO 115/4250, Inverchapel to Bevin, 12 October 1946.

126. Dalton Diaries, 5 October 1946.

127. TNA, FO 371/52566, Bevin to Attlee, 26 November 1946.

128. TNA, FO 115/4250, Memorandum of Discussion between Mr Bevin and Lord Inverchapel, 13 November 1946.

129. TNA, FO 115/4250, Silver to Inverchapel, 18 November 1946.

130. Gillies, *Radical Diplomat*, p. 197.

131. HSTL, Acheson papers, Box 117, Folder Palestine, MEMCON November 1946, DA & Inverchapel, Appendix B Notes on Palestine 1945–1947.

132. TNA, FO 371/52566, Memorandum Bevin to Attlee, 26 November 1946.

133. Ibid.

134. Acheson, *Present at Creation*, p. 178.

135. Harris, *Attlee*, p. 396.

136. Northedge, 'Britain and the Middle East', p. 157.

137. TNA, FO 371/61054, Weekly Political Summary, 7 March 1947.

138. Truman, *Years of Trial and Hope*, p. 154.

139. TNA, FO 371/68650, Balfour to Bevin, 24 May 1948.

140. Dalton Diaries, 24 February 1947.

141. Henderson, 'The Washington embassy: Navigating the Waters of the Potomac', *Diplomacy and Statecraft*, 1:1 (March 1990), 42.

Chapter 5   The Marshall Plan

1. Inverchapel papers, Outsize File 1945–1948, Speeches 1947, Speech to the Newcomen Society, 21 March 1947.

2. Economic Survey for 1947, Command Paper 7046, p. 9.

3. Cmd 7046, p. 9.

4. Ibid., p. 11.

5. Ibid., p. 3.

6. Ibid., p. 19.

7. TNA, FO 371/62399, *United Kingdom Foreign Exchange Position and the World Dollar Shortage*, note prepared by Chancellor of the Exchequer for George Marshall, 16 June 1947.

8. Ibid.

9. Gardener, *Sterling Dollar Diplomacy*, p. 309.

10. Donovan, Robert J., *Conflict and Crisis: the Presidency of Harry S. Truman, 1945–1948*. New York: Norton, 1977, p. 231.

11. Donovan, *Conflict and Crisis*, p. 229.

12. For embassy comment on these election results, see TNA, FO 371/51611, Weekly Political Summary, November 1946.

13. HSTL, Truman papers, Truman Diary.

14. Smith, Joseph, and Davis, Simon, *Historical Dictionary of the Cold War.* Scarecrow Press, 2000, p. 262.

15. TNA, FO 371/51606, Weekly Political Report, 3 March 1946.

16. Ambrose, Stephen, and Brinkley, Douglas, *Rise to Globalism.* Penguin, 1997, p. 77.

17. Truman was already dissatisfied with Byrnes and would probably have sacked him any event. Byrnes never settled under Truman and on occasions would undermine Truman's authority; such behaviour was rooted in the fact that Byrnes was passed over in favour of Truman when Roosevelt chose his vice presidential running mate in 1944. Byrnes always felt he should have been President.

18. Great Britain Foreign Office: Weekly Political Intelligence Summaries, January–June 1947, p. 23.

19. Weekly Political Intelligence Summaries, January–June 1947, p. 22.

20. FRUS, 1947, Vol. V, Aide Memoirs British Embassy to State Department, 21 February 1947, pp. 32–37.

21. TNA, FO 115/4335, Bevin to Inverchapel, 17 March 1947.

22. FRUS, 1946, Vol. VII, Memorandum by the British Embassy in Greece to the American embassy in Greece, 5 November 1946.

23. TNA, FO 115/4259, Minute by Donald Maclean entitled *Assistance for Greece and Turkey*, 28 October 1946.

24. FRUS, 1946, Vol. VII, Memorandum by the British Embassy in Greece to the American embassy in Greece, 5 November 1946.

25. HSTL, Oral History Interview with Hon Constantine Tsaldaris with Phillip Brooks 4 May 1964. See also Freeland, Richard M., *The Truman Doctrine and the Origins of McCarthyism: Foreign Policy, Domestic Politics, and Internal Security, 1946–1948*. New York: Schocken Books, 1974, p. 90.

26. FRUS, 1947, Vol. V, Memorandum of Conversation by Byrnes, 4 January 1947, p. 1.

27. Marshall papers, Box 157, Folder 7, Memorandum of the Press and Radio News Conference on 14 February 1947.

28. FRUS, 1947, Vol. V, See Various Memorandum of Conversations by Acheson and attached Aide Memoires, 1 March, 4 March, 8 March 1947, pp. 71, 79, 105 respectively. See also HSTL, Acheson papers, Box117, Folder Truman Doctrine, Notes Truman Doctrine: Section II The Decision, 29 January 1967.

29. Ibid.

30. See for example Bostdorff, Denise, *Proclaiming the Truman Doctrine*. Texas A&M University Press, 2008; Leffler, Melvyn P.A., *Preponderance of Power: National Security, the Truman Administration, and the Cold War*. Stanford: Stanford University Press, 1992; and Jones, M. Joseph, *The Fifteen Weeks*. London: Viking Press, 1955.

31. TNA, FO 371/62420, Inverchapel to Bevin, 18 March 1947.

32. TNA, FO 115/4331, Inverchapel to Foreign Office, 15 March 1947.

33. TNA, FO 371/61054, Weekly Political Summary, 15 March 1947.

34. Ibid.

35. TNA, FO 115/4335, Inverchapel to Attlee, 10 March 1947.

36. Ibid.

37. TNA, FO 115/4335, Attlee to Inverchapel, 23 March 1947.

38. TNA, FO 115/4335, Bevin to Inverchapel, 17 March 1947.

39. See for example Hopkins, Michael, Kelly, Saul, and Young John (eds), *The Washington Embassy, British Ambassadors to the United States, 1939–1977*. Basingstoke: Palgrave, 2009, chapter 3, 'Lord Inverchapel, 1946–1948', by Martin Folly, p. 64.

40. FRUS, 1947, Vol. V, Acheson to Patterson (Secretary of War), 5 March 1947, p. 94.

41. FRUS,1947, Vol. III, Report of the Special Ad Hoc Committee of the State-War-Navy Coordinating Committee, 21 April 1947, p. 205.

42. Truman, Harry, S., *Memoirs: Years of Trial and Hope, 1946–1952*. New York: Signet, 1956, p. 113.

43. Speech delivered by Dean Acheson, on the requirements of reconstruction, in Delta, Mississippi, 8 May 1947 as contained in *Documents on International Affairs 1947–1948* (ed. Margaret Carlyle), London: Oxford University Press for the Royal Institute of International Affairs, p. 17.

44. Leonard Miall of the BBC, Malcolm Muggeridge of the *Daily Express* and Stewart McCall of the *News Chronicle*.

45. Jones, M. Joseph, *The Fifteen Weeks*. London: Viking Press, 1955, p. 212.

46. Ibid., p. 223.

47. FRUS, 1947, Vol. III, Editorial Note on Radio Address, 28 April 1947, p. 219.

48. Kennan, George F., *Memoirs 1925–1950*. New York: Bantam, 1967, p. 326.
49. FRUS, 1947, Vol. III, Policy With Respect to American Aid to Western Europe Views of the Policy Planning Staff, 23 May 1947, p. 225.
50. HSTL, Clayton papers, Box 60, Folder, Marshall Plan Memorandum 1947, *The European Crisis*, May 1947.
51. Acheson, Dean, *Present at the Creation*, p. 230.
52. HSTL, Clayton papers, Box 60, Folder, Marshall Plan Memorandum 1947, *The European Crisis*, May 1947.
53. Ibid.
54. Marshall papers, Box 155, Folder 6, Remarks by the Secretary of State at Harvard University on June 5, 1947.
55. Jones, *Fifteen Weeks*, p. 255.
56. Marshall papers, Box 155, Folder 6, Remarks by the Secretary of State at Harvard University on 5 June, 1947.
57. Acheson, *Present at Creation*, p. 233.
58. Bullock, *Ernest Bevin*, p. 404.
59. Balfour, John, *Not too Correct an Aureole: The Recollections of a Diplomat*. Salisbury: Michael Russell, 1983, p. 118.
60. Ibid.
61. TNA, FO 371/62411, Balfour to Butler, letter headed *United States Financial Assistance to Foreign Countries* enclosing Record of Conversation Between Dean Acheson, Mr Balfour and Gerald Barry of the *News Chronicle*, 23 May 1947, Received by Foreign Office 5 June 1947.
62. Balfour, *Not too Correct an Aureole*, p. 119.
63. HSTL, Oral History Interview with William P. Edwards conducted by Theodore A. Wilson in London on 12 August 1970.
64. HSTL, Oral History Interview with Roger Makins conducted by Theodore A. Wilson in London on 10 August 1970.
65. HSTL, Oral History Interview with Roger Makins conducted by Philip C. Brooks in London on 15 June 1964.
66. HSTL, Oral History Interview with Hall Patch conducted by Philip C. Brooks in London on 8 June 1964.
67. Jones, *Fifteen Weeks*, p. 229. See also HSTL Jones papers, Box 1 and Box 65, Various Press Articles by Walter Lippmann and others.
68. TNA, FO 371/61054, Advanced Weekly Political Summary, 3 May 1947.
69. The embassy reported the Delta Speech in its Political Report, 10 May 1947. TNA, FO 371/61054.
70. Jones, *Fifteen Weeks*, p. 237.
71. Ibid., p. 239.
72. TNA, FO 371/61054, Weekly Political Summary, 19 May 1947.

73. TNA, FO 371/61047, Inverchapel to Bevin, United States: The Problem of European Unity, 7 May 1947.

74. TNA, FO 371/61047, Balfour to Bevin, 15 May 1947.

75. TNA, FO 371/61047, Minute on Foreign Office file cover AN1795 by FBA Randall, 3 June 1947.

76. TNA, FO 371/61054, Weekly Political Summary, 26 May 1947.

77. TNA, FO 371/61055, Weekly Political Summary, Economic Foreign Policy, 1 June 1947.

78. See Bullock, *Bevin*, p. 404 and Jones, *Fifteen Weeks*, p. 256.

79. TNA, FO 371/61055, Weekly Political Summary, 7 June 1947.

80. Acheson, *Present at Creation*, p. 234.

81. Miall, Leonard, 'How the Marshall Plan Started', *The Listener*, 4 May 1961, pp. 779–781.

82. TNA, FO371/ 62411, US Information Service, Daily Wireless Bulletin 409, 5 June 1947.

83. Roper, Michael, *The Records of the Foreign Office 1782–1968*. Kew: Public Records Office Publications, 2002.

84. Note a similar argument in support of the embassy is presented in Folly, Martin, 'Lord Inverchapel, 1946–1948', in Hopkins, Michael, Kelly, Saul, and Young, John (eds), *The Washington Embassy, British Ambassadors to the United States, 1939–1977*. Basingstoke: Palgrave, 2009, p. 59.

85. TNA, FO 371/62411, Balfour to N. Butler, 31 May 1947.

86. TNA, FO 371/62399, Balfour to Butler, 10 June 1947. The extent to which certain British ministers were out of touch and presumably ignorant of embassy soundings can be gleaned from a diary entry by Dalton. 'Mr Clayton-Doctrinaire Willie [has] spent quite a lot of hours with the PM, Foreign Secretary, myself and P.B.T. It is surprising how many hours one can spend with people and yet reach no sharply outlined conclusion. C. has no plan, but we have tried to help him both by giving him large quantities of statistics on our, and other dollar shortages, and by impressing on him that we are something more than just a bit of Europe' (Dalton Diaries, 27 June 1947).

87. TNA, FO 371/62401, Inverchapel to Foreign Office, 24 June 1947.

88. Strang, William, *Home and Abroad*. London: Andre Deutsch, 1956, p. 61.

89. TNA, FO 371/62402, Inverchapel to Foreign Office, 26 June 1947.

90. For a fuller discussion of the Soviet position see Parrish, Scott and Narinsky, Mikhail, 'New Evidence on the Soviet Rejection of the Marshall Plan: Two Reports', *Cold War International History Project*, Working Paper No. 9 (Washington DC, March 1994).

91. FRUS, 1947, Vol. III, Footnote 1, p. 331.

92. TNA, FO 371/62263, Sir David Waley to G. Bolton (Bank of England), 18 February 1947.
93. FRUS, 1947, Vol. III, Summary of First Meeting of Under-Secretary Clayton and ambassador Douglas with British Cabinet Members, 24 June 1947, p. 273.
94. FRUS, 1947, Vol. III, Summary of Third Meeting of Under-Secretary Clayton and ambassador Douglas With Cabinet Members, 26 June 1947, p. 293.
95. TNA, CAB/128/10, Conclusions of a Meeting of the Cabinet, 17 August 1947.
96. TNA, CAB/129/20, Balance of Payments Memorandum by the Chancellor of the Exchequer, 16 August 1947.
97. Exchange of Notes on 20 August 1947 as contained in *Documents on International Affairs 1947–1948* (ed. Margaret Carlyle). London: Oxford University Press for the Royal Institute of International Affairs, p. 70.
98. Fforde, *Bank of England and Public Policy 1941–1958*, p. 31.
99. Newton, C.C.S., 'The Sterling Crisis of 1947 and the British Response to the Marshall Plan', *The Economic History Review*, 37:3 (Aug. 1984), 398.
100. TNA, FO 371/62263, Minute by Roger Makins, 19 February 1947.
101. TNA, FO 371/62264, Inverchapel to Foreign Office, 22 March 1947.
102. TNA, FO 371/62263, Inverchapel to Foreign Office, 13 February 1947.
103. HSTL, Snyder papers, Box 34, Folder UK General 1946–1948, Note: Conference to Discuss British Economic Conditions As Affecting The Anglo-American Financial Agreement, 22 August 1947.
104. TNA, FO 115/4337, Paper entitled *The United States Line of Credit to the United Kingdom: The Gap*, Gordon Munro 25 July 1947.
105. Ibid.
106. Ibid.
107. Fforde, *The Bank of England*, p. 151.
108. TNA, FO 371/62273, Munro to Christelow, 16 September 1947.
109. TNA, FO 371/62274, Christelow to Eady, 23 September1947.
110. TNA, FO 371/62274, Christelow to Eady, 26 September 1947.
111. TNA, FO 371/62276, Munro to Eady, 1 November 1947.
112. HSTL, Snyder papers, Cripps to Snyder, 4 December 1947 and Snyder to Cripps, 5 December 1947.
113. It is interesting to note that as Munro had predicted in his memorandum of 25 July Britain's dollar position became critical in November. The position became so bad that certain senior Cabinet ministers held discussions with Douglas (the American ambassador in London) to consider ways in which Britain's dollar resources might be reinforced. These discussions were so

secret that 'the British Cabinet, as a whole, had no knowledge' of them (FRUS, 1947, Vol. III, Douglas to Marshall, 5 November 1947).

114. FRUS, 1947, Vol. III, Situation With Regard To European Recovery Program, 4 September 1947, p. 397.

115. Pogue, Forrest, *George C. Marshall: Statesman 1945–1949.* New York: Viking, p. 233.

116. Command Paper 7388, Convention for European Economic Cooperation, p. 4.

117. Pogue, *General Marshall*, p. 234.

118. Price, Harry Bayard, *The Marshall Plan and its Meaning.* New York: Cornell University Press, 1955, p. 41.

119. TNA. FO 371/62412, Note of Meeting with Inverchapel and others, 26 June 1947

120. HSTL, Oral History Interview with William P. Edwards conducted by Theodore A. Wilson in London on 12 August 1970.

121. HSTL, Oral History Interview with William P. Edwards conducted by Theodore A. Wilson in London on 12 August 1970.

122. TNA, FO 371/62410, Minute of Conversation between Jordan and F.B.A. Randall, 9 July 1947.

123. TNA, FO 371/61004, Minute Sheet, Edwards to Wright, 7 November 1947.

124. Sherfield papers, MS 522, Folder 1945–1947, Foreign Office to Makins, 24 May 1946.

125. TNA, FO 371/62416, Inverchapel to British Consulates in North America, 13 September 1947.

126. TNA, FO 371/62416, Note by F.B.A. Randall on cover of file UE 8789, 27 September 1947.

127. TNA, FO 371/61074, Foreign Office to Cabinet Office, 25 February 1947.

128. TNA, FO 371/61074, Note on folder of file AN 350 by D.A. Logan (North American Department), 31 January 1947.

129. TNA, FO 115/4318, Bevin to Balfour, 30 July 1947.

130. FRUS, 1947, Vol. V, Marshall to Bevin, 1 August 1947, p. 274.

131. FRUS, 1947, Vol. V, Memorandum of Conversation, Bohlen to Lovett, 1 August 1947, p. 271.

132. TNA, FO 371/61003, Balfour to Foreign Office, 1 August 1947.

133. TNA, FO 371/61003, Balfour to M. Wright, 8 August 1947.

134. TNA, FO 371/61003, Note by Michael Wright, 14 August 1947.

135. TNA, FO 371/61003, Tactics with the United States Administration, Hennicker (Assistant Private Secretary to Bevin) to Orme Sargent, 19 August 1947.

136. FRUS, 1947, Vol. V, Marshall to Lovett, 25 August 1947, p. 313.

137. FRUS, 1947, Vol. V, Chronological Summary of Correspondence and Exchanges of Views Leading up to the Discussions With the British on the Middle East, Memorandum prepared by the Department of State, undated, p. 488.

138. Ibid.

139. TNA, Bevin papers, FO 800/476, General Statement, undated.

140. TNA, Bevin papers, FO 800/476, Draft Steering Brief for Washington Conversations on the Middle East, 2 October 1947.

141. TNA, Bevin papers, FO 800/476, Bevin to Attlee, 9 October 1947.

142. FRUS, 1947, Vol. V, Draft Notes for Remarks by the United Kingdom at the Opening of the United States–United Kingdom talks on the Middle East, 16 October 1947, p. 566.

143. Bullock, *Ernest Bevin*, p. 475.

144. Whilst the Pentagon talks did not result in any formal treaty the National Security Council and the President on the American side and the British Chiefs of Staff Committee with the Prime Minister in the chair approved identical memoranda that were produced as a result of the talks.

145. HSTL, Truman papers, PSF, Box 174, Folder Atomic Energy Declaration US/UK, Appendices to a Report to the President by Special Committee of National Security Council on Atomic Energy Policy with Respect to the United Kingdom and Canada, 2 March 1949, p. 87.

146. FRUS, 1947, Vol. I, Memorandum of Conversation between Acheson and Makins, 1 February 1947, p. 785.

147. Ibid.

148. Churchill Archives, Churchill College Cambridge, Chadwick papers, Note by Joint Secretaries of the Advisory Committee on Atomic Energy (47) 19, 19 March 1947.

149. TNA, Butler papers, FO 800/597, J.S.M. Washington to Cabinet Office, 5 March 1947.

150. Ibid.

151. TNA, Butler papers, FO 800/ 597, Inverchapel and Wilson to Attlee, 5 March 1947.

152. FRUS, 1947, Vol. I, Statement by Acheson to an Executive Session of the Joint Congressional Committee on Atomic Energy, 12 May 1947, p. 806.

153. TNA, AB 16/285, J.S.M. Washington to Cabinet Office, 14 May 1947.

154. FRUS, 1947, Vol. I, Hickenlooper to Marshall, 29 August 1947, p. 833.

155. TNA, AB 16/2017, Munro to Stewart, 15 November 1947.

156. Gowing, *Independence and Deterrence,* Vol. 1, p. 243.

157. TNA, AB 16/2017, Munro to Stewart (Cabinet Office), 5 September 1947.

158. Gowing, *Independence and Deterrence*, p. 248.
159. TNA, AB 16/2017, Munro to Stewart (Cabinet Office), 2 October 1947.
160. FRUS, 1947, Vol. I, Minutes of Meeting of American Members of CPC with Chairman of JCAE and Chairman of Senate Foreign Relations Committee, 26 November 1947, p. 870.
161. TNA, AB 16/2022, Inverchapel to Foreign Office, 2 December 1947.
162. TNA, Bevin papers, FO800/438, Inverchapel to Bevin, 4 December 1947.
163. TNA, AB /2022, Inverchapel to Foreign Office, 6 December 1947.
164. TNA, FO 371/62788, Maclean to Makins, 22 December 1947.
165. TNA, Bevin papers, FO 800/438, Note by Frank Roberts, 18 December 1947.
166. Gowing, *Independence and Deterrence*, Modus Vivendi Agreement, Annex 1, p. 267.
167. FRUS, 1948, Vol. I, Memorandum of conversation by E. Gullion, 7 January 1948, p. 678.
168. TNA, FO 115/4421, Draft Report on Negotiations for Cooperation Between the United Kingdom, the U.S.A. and Canada on Atomic Energy Matters prepared by Makins, 9 January 1948.
169. Price, *Marshall Plan*, p. 61.
170. Pogue, *General Marshall*, p. 238.
171. TNA, FO 371/68014, United States Weekly Political Summary No. 6, 8 May 1948.
172. Marshall papers, Box 130, Folder 56, Inverchapel to Marshall, 5 February 1948.

Conclusion

1. On this see for example Barston, R.P., *Modern Diplomacy*. London: Longman, 1988; Berridge, G.R., *Diplomacy Theory and Practice*. Basingstoke: Palgrave Macmillan, 2005; Watson, Adam, *Diplomacy: The Dialogue Between States*. London: Methuen, 1982.

BIBLIOGRAPHY

Government Papers

The National Archives, Kew, London

AB 16	Ministry of Supply and UK Atomic Energy Authority
CAB 65	Confidential Cabinet Minutes
CAB 78	Ministerial Meetings Minutes
CAB 126	Tube Alloy Committee Minutes
CAB 128	Cabinet Conclusions
CAB 129	Cabinet Memoranda
CAB 130&134	Records of Cabinet Committees
FO 115	Washington Embassy Papers
FO 366	Diplomatic Administration Offices
FO 371	Political Departments general correspondence
FO 800/272–279	Sir Orme Sargent Private Office Papers
FO 800/303	Inverchapel, Baron Private Office Papers
FO 800/434–522	Ernest Bevin Private Office Papers
FO 800/523–532	Sir Ronald Campbell Private Office Papers
FO 800/533–610	Neville Butler Private Office Papers
FO 800/432, & 612–617	Roger Makins Private Office Papers
T230	Cabinet Office, Economic Section and Treasury
T236	Treasury, Overseas Finance Division
T247	Treasury, Papers of Lord Keynes

National Archives, Washington DC

Record Group 59 State Department Decimal Files 1945–1949
Record Group 56 Department of the Treasury Great Britain 1935–1949

Harry S. Truman Library, Independence, Missouri

Record Group 59 State Department Decimal Files: Office Files for Assistant
         Secretary for Economic Affairs and Under-Secretary for
         Economic Affairs 1946–1947

Private Papers

Bodleian Library, Oxford

Attlee papers
Brand papers
Inverchapel papers
Lord Sherfield papers (formerly Roger Makins)

The Borthwick Institute, University of York

Halifax Diary

British Library of Economic and Political Sciences, London

Dalton Diary

Churchill College, Cambridge

Attlee Notes on autobiography
Bevin papers
Cadogan Diary
Chadwick papers
Halifax papers
Noel Baker papers
Roberts papers

Clemson University Library, Clemson South Carolina

Brown Diary
Byrnes papers

Kings College, Cambridge

Keynes papers

Manuscripts Division, Library of Congress, Washington, DC

Bohlen papers
Clifford papers
Harriman papers
Henderson papers

Marshall Foundation, Lexington, Virginia

Marshall papers

Special Collections Library, University of Kentucky, Lexington, Kentucky

Vinson papers

Harry S. Truman Library, Independence, Missouri

Acheson papers
Ayers papers
Clayton papers
Elsey papers
Jones papers
Niles papers
Rosenman papers
Snyder papers
Truman papers
Weizman papers

Transcripts of Oral History Interviews: Acheson, Clifford, Elsey, Gordon Arneson, Harriman, Henderson, Hickerson, Lovett, Miall, Rosenman, Synder, Thorp and Tsaldaris

Printed Primary Sources

Command Papers CMD Series

Butler, R. & Pelly, M. (eds) *Documents on British Policy Overseas Series 1 Vol. I The Conference at Potsdam July–August 1945.* London: HMSO, 1984.
––––––– *Documents on British Policy Overseas Series 1 Vol. II Conferences and Conversations 1945: London, Washington and Moscow.* London: HMSO 1985.
Bullen, R. & Pelly, M. (eds) *Documents on British Policy Overseas Series 1 Vol. III Britain and America: Negotiation of the United States Loan 3 August–7 December 1945.* London: HMSO, 1986.
––––––– *Documents on British Policy Overseas Series 1 Vol. IV Britain and America Atomic Energy, Bases and Food 12 December 1945–31 July 1946.* London: HMSO, 1987.

Carlyle, Margaret. *Documents on International Affairs 1947–1948*. London: Oxford University Press for Royal Institute of International Affairs, 1952.

Congressional Record. Vols. 91–4, 1945–1948.

Congressional Directory. 79th and 80th Congress. Washington DC: GPO, 1945–1948.

Dennet, R. & Turner, R. (eds) *Documents on American Foreign Relations*. Princeton: Princeton University Press for the World Peace Foundation, 1945–1948.

Documents on European Recovery and Defence March 1947–April 1949. London: Oxford University Press for Royal Institute for International Affairs, 1949.

Foreign Office List and Yearbook 1945–1948.

Foreign Relations of the United States 1945–1948, various editors, Washington DC: Government Printing Office, 1969–1974.

Hachey, T.E. *Confidential Dispatches: Analysis of America by the British Ambassador, 1939–1945*. Evanston, IL: New University Press, 1974.

House of Commons Debates 1945–1948.

Nicholas, H.G. (ed.) *Washington Dispatches, 1941–45*. London: 1981.

Official Register of the United States 1945–1948. Compiled by United States Civil Service Commission.

Public Papers of the Presidents of the United States, Harry S. Truman 1945–1948. Washington DC: GPO, 1961–1964.

Yasamee, H. & Hamilton, K. (eds) *Documents on British Policy Overseas Series I Vol. VII The United Nations Iran, Cold War and World Organisation 1946–1947*. London: HMSO 1995.

Newspapers

The New York Times
The Times
The Washington Post

Autobiographies and Memoirs

Acheson, Dean. *Present at the Creation: My Years at the State Department*. New York: Norton, 1969.

Balfour, John. *Not too Correct an Aureole: The Recollections of a Diplomat*. Salisbury: Michael Russell, 1983.

Barclay, Sir Roderick. *Ernest Bevin and the Foreign Office 1932–1969*. London: published by the author, 1975.

Bohlen, Charles E. *Witness to History, 1929–1969*. New York: Norton, 1973.

Brandon, Henry. *Special Relationships*. London: Macmillan, 1989.

Bush, Vannevar. *Pieces of the Action*. New York: William Morrow, 1970.

Byrnes, James. *Speaking Frankly*. London: William Heinemann, 1947.

——— *All in One Lifetime*. London: Museum Press, 1960.

Dalton, Hugh. *High Tide and After: Memoirs 1945–1960*. London: Muller, 1962.

Elsey, George. *An Unplanned Life.* Columbia, MO: University of Missouri Press, 2005.

Gore-Booth, Paul. *With Truth and Respect.* London: Constable, 1974.

Groves, Leslie R. *Now It Can Be Told.* New York: Harper & Row, 1962.

Halifax, Lord , *Fullness of Days.* New York: Dodd, Mead & Company, 1957.

Healey, Denis. *The Time of My Life.* London: Penguin Books, 1990.

Henderson, Nicolas. *The Private Office.* London: Weidenfeld and Nicolson, 1984.

Hull, Cordell. *The Memoirs of Cordell Hull Volume II.* London: Hodder & Stoughton, 1948.

Jones, M. Joseph. *The Fifteen Weeks.* London: Viking Press, 1955.

Kennan, George. *Memoirs 1925–1950.* New York: Bantam, 1967.

Pearson, Lester B., 'Mike'. *Lester Pearson Memoirs 1897–1948 Through Diplomacy to Politics.* London: Victor Gollancz, 1973.

Robbins, Lord. *Autobiography of an Economist.* London: Macmillan, 1971.

Salter, Arthur. *Slave of the Lamp.* London: Weidenfeld & Nicolson, 1967.

Strang, Lord. *Home and Abroad.* London: Andre Deutsch, 1956.

Truman, Harry. *Memoirs: 1945, Year of Decisions.* New York: Signet, 1955.

———— *Memoirs: Years of Trial and Hope, 1946–1952.* New York: Signet, 1956.

Published Diaries, Letters and Papers

Clarke, Sir Richard. *Anglo-American Economic Collaboration in War and Peace 1942–1949* (ed. Alec Cairncross). Oxford: Clarendon Press, 1982.

Dilks, D (ed.) *The Diaries of Sir Alexander Cadogan, 1938–1945.* New York: Putnam, 1971.

Dobney, F. (ed.) *Selected Papers of William Clayton.* Baltimore: Johns Hopkins, 1971.

Halifax, Lord. *The American Speeches of the Earl of Halifax,* London: OUP, 1947.

Hardy, Henry. *Isaiah Berlin Letters 1928–1946.* Cambridge: Cambridge University Press, 2004

Howson, Susan & Moggridge, Donald (eds) *The Wartime Diaries of Lionel Robbins and James Meade, 1943–1945.* London: Macmillan, 1990.

———— *Meade, James. The Collected Papers of James Meade, Volume IV The Cabinet Office Diary 1944–1946.* London: Unwin Hyman, 1990.

Millis, Walter (ed.) *The Forrestal Diaries.* New York: Viking Press, 1951.

Moggridge, Donald (ed.) *The Collected Writings of John Maynard Keynes, Activities 1944–1946, Transitions to Peace* vol. XXIV, Cambridge: Macmillan Cambridge University Press for Royal Economic Society, 1979.

Nicholson, Nigel (ed.) *Harold Nicholson Diaries and Letters 1945–1962.* London: Collins, 1968.

Pimlott, Ben (ed.) *The Political Diary of Hugh Dalton, 1918–1940, 1945–1960.* London: Jonathan Cape, 1986.

Vandenberg, Jr. A.H. (ed.) *The Private Papers of Senator Vandenberg.* Boston: Houghton Mifflin, 1952.

Secondary Sources

Other Books

Addison, Paul & Jones, Harriet. *A Companion to Contemporary Britain 1939–2000*. Oxford: Blackwell Publishing, 2005.

Aldrich, Richard. *The Hidden Hand: Britain, America and Cold War Intelligence*. London: John Murray, 2001.

Aldrich, Richard J. & Hopkins, Michael F. (eds) *Intelligence Defence and Diplomacy*. Ilford: Frank Cass, 1994.

Alexander, G.M. *The Prelude to the Truman Doctrine: British Policy in Greece, 1944–1947*. Oxford: Clarendon, 1982.

Allen, H.C. *Great Britain and the United States: A History of Anglo American Relations (1783–1952)*. London: Oldhams Press, 1954.

Anderson, Terry. *The United States, Great Britain and the Cold War 1944–1947*. Colombia, MO: University of Missouri Press, 1981.

Baldwin, David A. *Economic Development and American Foreign Policy, 1943–1952*. Chicago: University of Chicago Press, 1972.

Barnett, Correlli. *The Audit of War: The Illusion and Reality of Britain as a Great Nation*. London: Papermac, 1991.

——— *The Lost Victory: British Dreams, British Realities, 1945–1951*. London: Macmillan, 1995.

Barston, R.P. *Modern Diplomacy*. London: Longman, 1988.

Bartlett, C.J. *The Special Relationship: A Political History of Anglo-American Relations since 1945*. London: Longman, 1992.

Baylis, John. *Anglo-American Defence Relations, 1939–1984: The Special Relationship*. London: Macmillan, 1984.

——— *Ambiguity and Deterrence: British Nuclear Strategy 1945–64*. Oxford: Clarendon Press, 1995.

Baylis, John. (ed.) *Anglo American Relations since 1939*. Manchester: Manchester University Press, 1997.

Beisner, Robert. *Dean Acheson: A Life in the Cold War*. Oxford: Oxford University Press, 2006.

Beloff, M. *New Dimensions in Foreign Policy*. London: Allen & Unwin, 1961.

Bernstein, Barton. (ed.) *Politics and Policies of the Truman Administration*. Chicago: Quadrangle Books, 1970.

Berridge, G.R. *Diplomacy Theory and Practice*. Basingstoke: Palgrave Macmillan, 2005.

Berridge, G.R. & James, Alan. *A Dictionary of Diplomacy* (2nd edn). Hampshire: Palgrave, 2003.

Best, Richard A., Jr. *'Cooperation With Like Minded Peoples': British Influence on American Security Policy, 1945–1949*. New York: Greenwood, 1986.

Birkenhead, *Earl of   Halifax: The Life of Lord Halifax*. London: Hamish Hamilton, 1965.

Bostdorff, Denise. *Proclaiming the Truman Doctrine*. Texas: A&M University Press, 2008.

Bridges, Lord [Edward]. *The Treasury*. London: George Allen and Unwin, 1966.

Bullock, Allen Louis Charles. *Ernest Bevin: Foreign Secretary, 1945–1951*. New York: Oxford University Press, 1983.

Burridge, Trevor. *Clement Attlee*. London: Jonathan Cape, 1985.

Campbell, J. *The United States in World Affairs 1945–1947*. New York: Harper & Brothers for the Council on Foreign Relations, 1947.

Cairncross, Alec. *Years of Recovery: British Economic Policy 1945–1951*. London: Methuen, 1985.

Calvocoressi, Peter. *Survey of International Affairs, 1947–1948*. London: Oxford University Press, 1952.

Charmley, J. *Churchill's Grand Alliance: The Anglo American Special Relationship, 1940–1957*. London: Hodder & Stoughton, 1995.

Cohen, Michael. *Palestine and the Great Powers 1945–1948*. Princeton, NJ: Princeton University Press, 1982.

——— *Truman and Israel*. Berkeley: University of California Press, 1990.

Dallek, Robert. *Franklin D. Roosevelt and American Foreign Policy 1932–1945*. New York: Oxford University Press, 1995.

Danchev, Alex. *Oliver Franks: Founding Father*. Oxford: Clarendon Press, 1993.

Dell, Edmund. *The Chancellors: A History of the Chancellors of the Exchequer 1945–1990*. London: Harper Collins, 1996.

Dilks, D. (ed.) *Retreat from Power Volume Two: after 1939*. London: Macmillan Press, 1981.

Dimbleby, David & Reynolds, David. *An Ocean Apart*. London: Hodder & Stoughton, 1988.

Dobson, Alan. *Anglo American Relations in the Twentieth Century*. London: Routledge, 1994.

Dockrill, M.L. & Young, J.W. (eds) *British Foreign Policy 1945–1956*. London: Macmillan, 1989.

Donovan, Robert J. *Conflict and Crisis: the Presidency of Harry S. Truman, 1945–1948*. New York: Norton, 1977.

Dumbrell, John. *A Special Relationship Anglo American Relations in the Cold War and After*. Basingstoke: Palgrave Macmillan, 2001.

Eckes, Alfred, E., Jr. *The Search for Solvency: Bretton Woods and the International Monetary System, 1941–1947*. Austin, TX: University of Texas Press, 1975.

Edmonds, Robin. *Setting the Mould: The United States and Britain, 1945–1950*. New York: Oxford University Press, 1986.

Ellwood, David. *Rebuilding Europe: Western Europe, America and Post war Reconstruction*. New York: Longman, 1992.

Fforde, John. *The Bank of England and Public Policy 1941–1958*. Cambridge: Cambridge University Press, 1992.

Freeland, Richard M. *The Truman Doctrine and the Origins of McCarthyism: Foreign Policy, Domestic Politics, and Internal Security, 1946–1948*. New York: Schocken Books, 1974.

Gaddis, John Lewis. *The United States and the Origins of the Cold War 1941–1947*. New York: Columbia University Press, 1972.

Gardner, Richard N. *Sterling Dollar Diplomacy: Anglo American Collaboration in the Reconstruction of Multilateral Trade*. London: Clarendon Press, 1956.

Gillies, Donald. *Radical Diplomat: the Life of Archibald Clark Kerr Lord Inverchapel, 1882–1951*. London: Tauris, 1999.

Gimbel, John. *The Origins of the Marshall Plan*. Stanford, CA: Stanford University Press, 1976.

Gowing, Margaret. *Britain and Atomic Energy, 1939–1945*. London: Macmillan, 1964.

———*Independence and Deterrence: Britain and Atomic Energy, 1945–1952*, 2 vols. London: Macmillan, 1974.

Hahn, Peter. *Caught in the Middle East: Policy Towards the Arab Israeli Conflict, 1945–1961*. Chapel Hill, NC: University of North Carolina Press, 2004.

Harris, Kenneth. *Attlee*. London: Weidenfeld & Nicolson, 1982.

Hathaway, Robert M. *Ambiguous Partnership: Britain and America, 1944–1947*. New York: Columbia University Press, 1988.

Herken, Gregg. *The Winning Weapon*. New York: Knopf, 1980.

Herman, John. *The Paris Embassy of Sir Eric Phipps*. Brighton: Sussex Academic Press, 1998.

Hershberg, J.G. *James B. Conant: Harvard to Hiroshima and the Making of the Nuclear Age*. Stanford, CA: Stanford University Press, 1993.

Hewlett, Richard & Anderson, Oscar. *A History of the United States Atomic Energy Commission, Vol. I: The New World, 1939/1946*. Pennsylvania: Pennsylvania University Press, 1962.

Hewlett, Richard & Duncan, F. *A History of the United States Atomic energy Commission, Vol. 2: Atomic Shield, 1947–1952*. Pennsylvania: Pennsylvania University Press, 1969.

Hogan, Michael J. *The Marshall Plan: America, Britain, and the Reconstruction of Western Europe, 1947–1952*. New York: Cambridge University Press, 1987.

Hollowell, Jonathan (ed.) *Twentieth Century Anglo American Relations*. Palgrave, 2001.

Hopkins, Michael. *Oliver Franks and the Truman Administration: Anglo American Relations 1948–1952*. London: Frank Cass, 2003.

Hopkins, Michael, Kelly, Saul, & Young, John (eds) *The Washington Embassy, British Ambassadors to the United States, 1939–1977*. Basingstoke: Palgrave, 2009.

Jenkins, Simon & Sloman, Anne. *With Respect Ambassador: An Enquiry into the Foreign Office*. London: BBC, 1985.

Johnson, Gaynor. *The Berlin Embassy of Lord D'Abernon, 1920–1926*. London: Palgrave, 2002.

Kennedy, Paul. *The Realities Behind Diplomacy: Background Influences on British External Policy 1865–1980.* London: Fontana, 1981.

Key, V.O. *Public Opinion and American Democracy.* New York: Knopf, 1961.

Kolko, Joyce & Kolko, Gabriel. *The Limits of Power: The World and United Sates Foreign Policy, 1945–1954.* New York: Harper & Row, 1972.

Kuniholm, Bruce. *The Origins of the Cold War in the Near East: Great Power Conflict and Diplomacy in Iran, Turkey and Greece.* Princeton, NJ: Princeton University Press, 1980.

Leffler, Melvyn P. *A Preponderance of Power: National Security, the Truman Administration, and the Cold War.* Stanford, CA: Stanford University Press, 1992.

Leifer, M. (ed.) *Constraints and Adjustments in British Foreign Policy.* London: Allen & Unwin, 1972. Leventhal, F. & Quinault, R. (eds) *Anglo American Attitudes (From Revelation to Partnership).* Ashgate Publishing, 2000.

Louis, William Roger. *The British Empire in the Middle East, 1945–1951: Arab Nationalism, the United States and Post War Imperialism.* Oxford: Clarendon Press, 1984.

Louis, William Roger & Headley Bull (eds) *The Special Relationship: Anglo American Relations Since 1945.* Oxford: Clarendon Press, 1986.

Macdonald, Ian S. (ed.) *Anglo American Relations since the Second World War.* New York: St Martin's Press, 1974.

Mallalieu, William C. *British Reconstruction and American Policy, 1945–1955.* New York: Scarecrow Press, 1956.

Manderson-Jones, R.B. *The Special Relationship: Anglo American Relations and Western European Unity, 1947–1956.* New York: Crane Russak, 1972.

Mayers, David. *The Ambassadors and America's Soviet Policy.* New York: Oxford University Press, 1995.

McNeill, William Hardy, *America, Britain, & Russia: Their Cooperation and Conflict 1941–1946.* London: Oxford University Press, 1953.

Miscamble, Wilson. *From Roosevelt to Truman: Potsdam, Hiroshima, and the Cold War.* Cambridge: Cambridge University Press, 2007.

Milward, Alan. *The Reconstruction of Western Europe, 1945–1951.* London: Methuen, 1984.

Morgan, Kenneth O. *Labour in Power 1945–1951.* Oxford: Clarendon Press, 1984.

Moser, John. *Twisting the Lion's Tail: Anglophobia in the US 1921–1948.* London: Macmillan Press, 1999.

Nicholas, H.G. *The Nature of American Politics.* Oxford: Oxford University Press, 1980.

Nicholson, Harold. *Diplomacy.* London: Oxford University Press, 1950.

Northedge, Frederick. *British Foreign Policy: The Process of Readjustment, 1945–1961.* London: Allen & Unwin, 1962.

———— *Descent from Power: British Foreign Policy 1945–1973.* London: Allen & Unwin, 1974.

Ovendale, Ritchie. (ed.) *The Foreign Policy of the British Labour Governments, 1945–1951*. Leicester: Leicester University Press, 1984.

Ovendale, Ritchie. *The English-Speaking Alliance: Britain, the United States, the Dominions and the Cold War, 1945–1951*. London: Allen & Unwin, 1985.

————*Anglo-American Relations in the Twentieth Century*. Basingstoke: Macmillan, 1998.

Paul, Septimus. *Nuclear Rivals: Anglo–American Atomic Relations 1941–1952*. Columbus: Ohio State University Press, 2000.

Pedan, G.C. *The Treasury and British Public Policy 1906–1959*. Oxford: Oxford University Press, 2000.

Pelling, Henry. *The Labour Governments 1945–1951*. London: Macmillan, 1984.

———— *Britain and the Marshall Plan*. London: Macmillan, 1988.

Penrose, E.F. *Economic Planning for Peace*. Princeton, NJ: Princeton University Press, 1953.

Pogue, Forrest. *George C. Marshall: Statesman 1945–1949*. New York: Viking, 1987.

Pollard, Robert. *Economic Security and the Origins of the Cold War, 1945–1950*. New York: Columbia University Press, 1985.

Pressnell, L.S. *External Economic Policy since the War. Vol. I: The Post War Financial Settlement*. London: HMSO, 1986.

Price, Harry Bayard. *The Marshall Plan and its Meaning*. New York: Cornell University Press, 1955.

Reynolds, David. *Britannia Overruled: British Policy and World Power in the Twentieth Century*. New York: Longman, 1991.

———— *The Creation of the Anglo American Alliance, 1937–1941: A Study in Competitive Cooperation*. Chapel Hill: North Carolina Press, 1981.

Roberts, Andrew. *'The Holy Fox': The Life of Lord Halifax*. London: Phoenix, 1997.

Roper, Michael. *The Records of the Foreign Office 1782–1968*, Kew: Public Records Office Publications, 2002.

Rothwell, Victor. *Britain and the Cold War, 1941–1947*. London: Jonathan Cape, 1982.

Ryan, Henry Butterfield. *The Vision of Anglo America: The US–UK Alliance and the Emerging Cold War, 1943–1946*. Cambridge: Cambridge University Press, 1987.

Sayers, R.S. *Financial Policy 1939–1945*. London: HMSO, 1956.

Skidelsky, Robert. *John Maynard Keynes Fighting for Britain 1937–1946*. London: Macmillan, 2000.

Smith, Joseph & Davis, Simon. *Historical Dictionary of the Cold War*. Maryland: Scarecrow Press, 2000.

Snetsinger, John. *Truman, the Jewish Vote, and the Creation of Israel*. Stanford: Hoover Institution Press, 1974.

Steiner, Zara. (ed.) *The Times Survey of Foreign Ministries of the World*. London: Times Books, 1982.

Storey, William. *US Government and Politics*. Edinburgh: Edinburgh University Press, 2007.

Strang, Lord. *The Foreign Office*. London: George Allen and Unwin, 1955.

—— *The Diplomatic Career*. London: Andre Deutsch, 1962.

Temperley, Howard. *Britain and America since Independence*. Basingstoke: Palgrave, 2002.

Thorne, C. *Allies of a Kind*. London: Hamish Hamilton, 1978.

Turner, Arthur Campbell. *The Unique Partnership: Britain and the United States*. New York: Pegasus, 1971.

Watson, Adam. *Diplomacy: The Dialogue Between States*. London: Methuen, 1982.

Watt, D.C. *Succeeding John Bull: America in Britain's Place, 1900–1975*. Cambridge: Cambridge University Press, 1984.

Williams, Appleman William. (ed.) *The Shaping of American Diplomacy*. Chicago: Rand McNally, 1956.

Wittner, Lawrence S. *American Intervention in Greece, 1943–1949*. New York: Columbia University Press, 1981.

Woods, Randall. *A Changing of the Guard: Anglo American Relations, 1941– 1946*. Chapel Hill: University of North Carolina Press, 1990.

Yergin, Daniel. *Shattered Peace. The Origins of the Cold War*. New York: Penguin, 1990.

Young, John. *Twentieth Century Diplomacy: A Case Study of British Practice 1963– 1976*. Cambridge: Cambridge University Press, 2008.

Zametica J. (ed.) *British Officials and British Foreign Policy, 1945–1950*. Leicester: Leicester University Press, 1990.

Articles and Theses

Adamthwaite, Anthony. 'Britain and the World, 1945–1949: The View from the Foreign Office', *International Affairs*, 61 (Spring 1985), pp. 223–235.

Anstey, Caroline. 'The Projection of British Socialism: Foreign Office Publicity and American Opinion, 1945–1950', *Journal of Contemporary History*, 19 (April 1984), pp. 417–451.

—— 'Foreign Office Efforts to Influence American Opinion 1945–1949', PhD thesis, London School of Economics and Political Science, 1984.

Bernstein, Barton. 'The Quest for Security: American Foreign Policy and International Control of Atomic Energy, 1942–1946', *Journal of American History*, 60 (March 1974), pp. 1003–1044.

—— 'The Atomic Bomb and American Foreign Policy, 1941–1945: An Historiographical Controversy', *Peace and Change*, 2 (Spring 1974) pp. 1–16.

—— 'The Uneasy Alliance: Roosevelt, Churchill, and the Atomic Bomb, 1940–1945', *The Western Political Quarterly*, 29:2 (June 1976), pp. 202–230.

Bourantonis, Dimitris & Johnson, Edward. 'Anglo American Diplomacy and the Introduction of the Atomic Energy Issue in the United Nations: Discord and Cooperation in 1945', *Contemporary British History*, 18:4 (Winter 2004), pp. 1–21.

Boyle, Peter. 'The British Foreign Office View of Soviet–American Relations, 1945–1946', *Diplomatic History*, 3 (Summer 1979), pp. 307–320.

—— 'The British Foreign Office and American Foreign Policy 1947–1948', *The Journal of American Studies*, 16 (December 1982), pp. 373–389.

Carlton, D. 'Great Britain and Nuclear Weapons: The Academic Inquest', *British Journal of International Studies*, 2:2 (July 1976).

Chace, James. 'Marshall Plan Commemorative Section: An Extraordinary Partnership: Marshall and Acheson', *Foreign Affairs*, May/June 1997.

Clay, Henry. 'Britain's Declining Role in World Trade', *Foreign Affairs*, 24 (April 1946), pp. 411–428.

Cohen, Michael J. 'Truman and Palestine, 1945–1948: Revisionism, Politics and Diplomacy', *Modern Judaism*, 2:1 (February 1982), pp. 1–22.

Cromwell, William C. 'The Marshall Plan: Britain and the Cold War', *Review of International Studies*, 8 (October 1982), pp. 233–249.

Cull, Nicolas. 'The Fall and Rise of a Fox Hunting Man Abroad: Lord Halifax as British Ambassador to the United States in 1941', MA Thesis paper presented to the Institute of Contemporary British History Conference, 15 July 1989.

Dinnerstein, Leonard. 'America, Britain & Palestine: The Anglo American Committee of Enquiry and the Displaced Persons, 1945–1946', *Diplomatic History*, 4 (Summer 1980), pp. 283–301.

Dobson, Alan P. 'Labour or Conservative: Does it Matter in Anglo American Relations?', *Journal of Contemporary History*, 25:4 (October 1990), pp. 387–407.

Feis, Herbert. 'Political Aspects of Foreign Loans', *Foreign Affairs*, 23 (July 1945), pp. 600–619.

—— 'The Future of British Imperial Preferences', *Foreign Affairs*, 24 (April 1946), pp. 661–674.

Fossedale, D. & Mikhail, B. 'Marshall Plan Commemorative Section: A Modest Magician: Will Clayton and the Building of Europe', *Foreign Affairs*, May/June 1997.

Frazier, Robert. 'Did Britain Start the Cold War? Bevin and the Truman Doctrine', *Historical Journal*, 27 (Sept. 1984), pp. 715–27.

Gaddis, John Lewis. 'Was the Truman Doctrine a Real Turning Point?', *Foreign Affairs*, 52 (January 1974), pp. 386–402.

Goldberg, A. 'The Atomic Origins of the British Nuclear Deterrent', *International Affairs*, XL:4 (July 1964), pp. 409–429.

Gormley, James. 'The Washington Declaration and the Poor Relation: Anglo American Atomic Diplomacy 1945–1946', *Diplomatic History*, 8 (Spring 1984).

Haron, Miriam J. 'Anglo-American Relations and the Question of Palestine, 1945–1947', PhD thesis, Fordham University, 1979.

Hedland, Richard P. 'Congress and the British Loan, 1945–1946: A Congressional Study', PhD thesis, University of Kentucky, 1976.

Henderson, Nicolas. 'The Washington Embassy: Navigating the Waters of the Potomac', *Diplomacy and Statecraft*, 1:1 (March 1990).

Hinds, Allister. 'Sterling and Imperial Policy, 1945–1951', *The Journal of Imperial and Commonwealth History*, 15:2 (1987), pp. 148–169.

Hitchens, Harold L. 'Influences on the Congressional Decision to Pass the Marshall Plan', *Western Political Quarterly*, 21 (March 1968), pp. 51–68.

Hopkins, Michael Francis. 'Focus of a Changing Relationship: The Washington Embassy and Britain's World Role since 1945', *Contemporary British History*, 12:3 (1998), pp. 103–14.

———— 'The Ambassadorship of Sir Oliver Franks at Washington, 1948–1952', PhD thesis, University of Leeds, 1992.

Jackson, Scott. 'Prologue to the Marshall Plan', *Journal of American History*, 65 (March 1979), pp. 1043–1068.

Kelly, S. 'No Ordinary Foreign Office Official: Sir Roger Makins and Anglo-American Atomic Relations, 1945–1955', *Contemporary British History*, 14:4 (Winter 2000), pp. 107–124.

Kindleberger, Charles. 'Marshall Plan Commemorative Section: In the Halls of the Capitol: A Memoir', *Foreign Affairs*, May/June 1997.

Knight, Wayne Stone. 'The Nonfraternal Association: Anglo American Relations and the Breakdown of the Grand Alliance, 1945–1947', PhD thesis, The American University, 1979.

Kunz, Diane. 'Marshall Plan Commemorative Section: The Marshall Plan Reconsidered: A Complex of Motives', *Foreign Affairs*, May/ June 1997.

Lawson, Fred H. 'The Iranian Crisis of 1945–1946 and the Spiral Model of International Conflict', *International Journal of Middle East Studies*, 21 (August 1989), pp. 307–326.

Lee, Sabine. '"In no sense vital and actually not even important"? Reality and Perception of Britain's Contribution to the Development of Nuclear Weapons', *Contemporary British History*, 20:2 (June 2006), pp. 159–185.

Leffler, Melvyn P. 'The United States and the Strategic Dimensions of the Marshall Plan', *Diplomatic History*, 12 (Summer 1988), pp. 277–306.

Mayhew, Christopher. 'British Foreign Policy since 1945', *International Affairs*, 26:4 (Oct. 1950), pp. 477–486.

Maddox, Robert J. 'Atomic Diplomacy: A Study in Creative Writing', *Journal of American History*, 59 (March 1973), pp. 925–934.

Maier, Charles. 'The Politics of Productivity: Foundations of American International Economic Policy after World War II', *International Organisation*, 31 (Autumn 1977), pp. 607–633.

———— Comments on Michael J. Hogan, 'The United States European Unity and the Origins of the Marshall Plan', Seminar on 4 November 1981, at Woodrow Wilson International Centre for Scholars, Washington DC. Transcript.

McKenzie, Francine. 'Renegotiating a Special Relationship: The Commonwealth and Anglo-American Economic Discussions, September–December 1945', *The Journal of Imperial and Commonwealth History*, 26:3 (Sept. 1998), pp. 71–93.

Miscamble, Wilson D. 'Rejected Architect and Master builder: George Kennan, Dean Acheson and Postwar Europe', *The Review of Politics*, 58:3 (Summer 1996), pp. 437–468.

Nachmani, Amikam. '"It's a Matter of Getting the Mixture Right": Britain's Post-War Relations with America in the Middle East', *Journal of Contemporary History*, 18:1 (January 1983), pp. 117–140.

Neal, Lesley. 'The Washington Ambassadorship of Lord Halifax 1941–1946', M Litt, Oxford, 1985.

Newton, C.C.S. 'The Sterling Crisis of 1947 and the British Response to the Marshall Plan', *The Economic History Review*, 37:3 (Aug. 1984), pp. 391–408.

Nicolson, Harold. 'Diplomacy Then and Now', *Foreign Affairs*, 40 (Oct. 1961), pp. 39–49.

Ovendale, R. 'The Palestine Policy of the British Labour Government, 1945–1946', *International Affairs*, 55 (July 1979), pp. 409–431.

———— 'The Palestine Policy of the British Labour Government 1947: the decision to withdraw', *International Affairs*, LVI (1980), pp. 73–93.

Parrish, Scott & Narinsky, Mikhail. 'New Evidence on the Soviet Rejection of the Marshall Plan: Two Reports', *Cold War International History Project*, Working Paper No. 9. Washington, DC, March 1994.

Paterson, Thomas G. 'Presidential Foreign Policy Public Opinion, and Congress: The Truman Years', *Diplomatic History*, III:I (1979), pp. 1–18.

Pika, Joseph, A. 'Interests Groups and the White House under Roosevelt and Truman', *Political Science Quarterly*, 102:4 (Winter 1987–1988), pp. 647–668.

Polk, Judd & Gardner Patterson. 'The British Loan', *Foreign Affairs*, 24 (April 1946), pp. 439–440.

Reynolds, David. 'The Origins of the Cold War: The European Dimension, 1944–1951', *Historical Journal*, 28 (June 1985), pp. 497–515.

———— 'A "Special Relationship"? America, Britain and the International Order since the Second World War', *International Affairs*, 62:1 (Winter 1985–1986), pp. 1–20.

———— 'Competitive Cooperation: Anglo American Relations in World War Two', *Historical Journal*, 23 (March 1980).

———— 'From World War to Cold War: The Wartime Alliance and the Post-War Transitions, 1941–1947', *Historical Journal*, 45:1 (Mar. 2002), pp. 211–227.

———— 'Lord Lothian and Anglo American Relations, 1939–1940', *The American Philosophical Society*, 73:2, 1983.

———— 'Marshall Plan Commemorative Section: The European Response: Primacy of Politics', *Foreign Affairs*, May/June 1997.

Schrafstetter, Susanna. 'Loquacious . . . and pointless as ever? Britain, the United States and the United Nations Negotiations on International Control of Nuclear Energy, 1945–1948', *Contemporary British History*, 16:4 (Winter 2002), pp. 87–108.

Sharp, Paul. 'For Diplomacy: Representation and the Study of International Relations', *International Studies Review*, 1:1 (Spring 1999), pp. 33–57.

Sherfield Lord (previously Sir Roger Makins). 'Britain's Nuclear Story 1948–52: Politics and Technology', *Round Table*, 65, p. 194.

Smith, R. & Zametica, J. 'The Cold War Warrior: Clement Attlee Reconsidered, 1945–1947', *International Affairs* (Spring 1985), pp. 237–251.

Staerck, Gillian (ed.) 'The Role of the British Embassy in Washington', *Contemporary British History*, 12:3 (1998), pp. 115–138.

Toye, Richard. 'Churchill and Britain's Financial Dunkirk', *Twentieth Century British History*, 15:4 (2004), pp. 329–360.

——— 'The Attlee Government, the Imperial Preference System and the Creation of the Gatt', *English Historical Review*, cxviii. 478 (Sept. 2003).

——— 'The Labour Party's External Economic Policy in the 1940s', *Historical Journal*, 43:1 (March 2000), pp. 189–215.

Warner, Geoffrey. The Anglo-American Special Relationship, *Diplomatic History*, 13 (Fall 1989), pp. 479–499.

Weiler, Peter. 'British Labour and the Cold War: the Foreign Policy of the Labour Governments 1945–1951', *Journal of British Studies*, 26 (Jan. 1987), pp. 54–82.

Wheeler N.J. 'British Nuclear Weapons and Anglo American Relations, 1945–1954', *International Affairs*, (Winter 1985/1986), pp.72–93.

Wiebes, C. & Zeeman, B. 'The Pentagon Negotiations March 1948: The Launching of the North Atlantic Treaty', *International Affairs*, 59:3 (Summer 1983), pp. 351–363.

Wolfe, Robert. 'Still Lying Abroad? On the Institution of the Resident Ambassador', *Diplomacy and Statecraft*, 9:2 (July 1998), pp. 23–54.

INDEX